GOVERNING
THE INTERNET

iPOLITICS: Global Challenges in the Information Age

RENÉE MARLIN-BENNETT, SERIES EDITOR

GOVERNING THE INTERNET

The Emergence of an International Regime

MARCUS FRANDA

LYNNE
RIENNER
PUBLISHERS

BOULDER
LONDON

Published in the United States of America in 2001 by
Lynne Rienner Publishers, Inc.
1800 30th Street, Boulder, Colorado 80301
www.rienner.com

and in the United Kingdom by
Lynne Rienner Publishers, Inc.
3 Henrietta Street, Covent Garden, London WC2E 8LU

Library of Congress Cataloging-in-Publication Data
Franda, Marcus F.
    Governing the Internet : the emergence of an international regime / by Marcus Franda.
       p. cm.—(iPolitics)
    Includes bibliographical references and index.
    ISBN 1-55587-999-3 (alk. paper)
    1. Internet—Law and legislation. I. Title. II. Series.
K564.C6 F73 2001
341.7'577—dc21

                                             2001019068

British Cataloguing in Publication Data
A Cataloguing in Publication record for this book
is available from the British Library.

Printed and bound in the United States of America

The paper used in this publication meets the requirements
of the American National Standard for Permanence of
Paper for Printed Library Materials Z39.48-1984.

5 4 3 2 1

To Vonnie,
an extraordinary lifetime companion,
who made this and so much else possible

Contents

Acknowledgments

Many of the ideas in this book originated at the University of Chicago in the late 1950s and early 1960s when I was first exposed to the wonders of the computer as a graduate student. They were nurtured during the late 1960s and early 1970s, during a ten-year period when I was a research associate at the Center for International Studies at the Massachusetts Institute of Technology, where some of the earliest experiments with Internet-related matters were already in progress. Interaction with several computer-based social science projects—and especially with Ithiel de Sola Pool, one of the founders of the field of political communication—made me realize the enormous potential of the computer and the possibility of what would eventually become the Internet.

The Asia Foundation somewhat reluctantly provided me with practical experience in computer networking when Poonsook Pantitanonta and I, despite resistance from our San Francisco headquarters, insisted on building the first fully computerized office at the Asia Foundation in Bangkok during my tenure as head of the foundation for Thailand, Burma, Laos, Cambodia, and Vietnam in the 1980s. The foundation also enabled me to work with many Thai leaders to develop a series of grants designed to help the Thai Supreme Court and other courts in Thailand build their first computer networks. In the late 1980s this led to my participation in worldwide projects to computerize judicial records throughout Asia during the three years I headed the Asia Foundation office in Washington, D.C.

Much of the substance of this book reflects my practical involvement with international business. Some of the highlights include a three-year term as the elected vice president of the American Chamber of Commerce in Thailand in the 1980s, participation in the many activities of the Asia Pacific Chambers of American Commerce and the U.S. Chamber of Commerce in Washington, D.C., and a number of consultancies with international business since the early 1970s. I am particularly indebted to the leaderships of the IBM offices in Asia and of Motorola in Schaumburg, Illinois, for encounters with projects that gave me special insights into the challenges of building information technology capabilities worldwide.

My intellectual interest in studying the Internet as an international regime was first piqued in the mid-1990s when Charles H. Miller and I jointly taught a seminar at the University of Maryland—the title of which changed each semester it was taught—on the technical, business, and public policy aspects of international telecommunications. Charlie had just retired after almost forty years at AT&T, where he had concluded his career as a vice president involved in policy development and implementation of the court-ordered divestiture. I learned far more from Charlie than he ever realized and owe considerable gratitude to both the many bright students who enrolled in our seminars and the illustrious list of invited speakers who presented so many imaginative ideas and concepts. Students who have challenged my evolving ideas and exposed me to new thoughts and materials in the seminars and courses I have taught since—on international regime theory, concepts of private authority, international business, international organization, and international law—are too numerous to mention individually, but they know who they are. They have contributed to my education at least as much as I have to theirs.

Finally, I must acknowledge the contributions of key institutions that have provided me with opportunities to pursue academic endeavors that have contributed to this book. These include grants from the Ford Foundation, the Carnegie Endowment, the National Science Foundation, the Fulbright program, the Agency for International Development, a number of Rockefeller family enterprises, my twelve-year association with Colgate University, and my ten-year appointment as director of international affairs at the University of Maryland. Support from these and other sources has made it possible for me to travel to and do research in almost a hundred countries, during which time, particularly in recent years, I have collected materials for this book and for my other books and articles on information technology.

Whatever wisdom and useful information might be found in this and the other writings grew out of the conversations, interviews, seminars, courses, and other personal relationships I have had the fortune to be a part of as a result of these many opportunities. Responsibility for content is solely mine.

Introduction: The Internet as a World Enterprise

The unprecedented technical innovations that resulted in the Internet have been written about from many different perspectives, primarily by engineers and computer scientists, but a significant aspect of the Internet's success—the creation or evolution of management and governance arrangements that have enabled the interconnection of geographically dispersed computer networks over much of the globe—remains something of a puzzle. How have government officials, technocrats, businesspeople, and other leaders from diverse sovereign nations been able to effect cooperation—in a very short period of time—to create and implement rules and procedures for the relatively smooth operation of the Internet, within complex commercial and legal frameworks, at the international level? To what extent and in what ways is this an exception to the usual depiction of international relations as an anarchic activity? How strong are the basic elements of cooperation that have made the global Internet possible?

This study seeks to develop preliminary answers to such questions by examining the Internet from the perspective of the international relations discipline, with a particular focus on the usefulness of international regime theory. For several decades political scientists have successfully used the concept *international regimes,* in Robert Keohane's words, "as a way to understand international cooperation."[1] The idea has also been adopted by economists and international business researchers to help explain the increasing integration, linkages, and interrelatedness of the world economy and by legal theorists interested in its application to international law.[2] A leading study of international regimes from a business/economics perspective, led by Lee Preston and Duane Windsor, concluded that the world economy is being integrated by three interrelated types of linkages: trade and investment flows, multinational enterprises, and international policy regimes.[3]

The formation of international regimes generally proceeds through three fairly distinct and distinguishable stages, identified by Oran Young as agenda setting, negotiation, and operationalization.[4] Although not confined exclusively to international regime theory, the present study explores the development of the nascent international regime for the Internet in terms of these three stages of growth, beginning with the negotiation and implementation of technical standards and protocols in Chapter 1 and Internet governance and management in Chapter 2. Chapters 3 and 4 detail a number of activities in economy-related arenas that seek to create frameworks for global business, including attempts to develop international rules and procedures for conducting electronic commerce, building cooperative transnational arrangements for coordinating various national data-handling systems, coordinating a variety of different national Internet taxation policies, establishing norms for Internet-related international investment, and protecting intellectual property over the Internet on a worldwide basis.

While Chapters 1–4 cover areas of Internet development in which one can identify the shape of rudimentary regime principles and norms, Chapters 5 and 6 focus on subject areas in which regime outlines are still inchoate and regime formation is at a much earlier stage of development. Chapter 5 discusses some of the challenges to both international law and various domestic legal systems that have resulted from widespread use of the Internet across international boundaries, particularly in matters involving personal privacy and questions of jurisdiction. Chapter 6 analyzes the potential impact of a number of proposals for building international cooperation to protect Internet security on a worldwide basis.

Although the formation of the international regime for the Internet has taken place largely in the advanced information technology (IT) societies, some of the most formidable challenges to its continued operationalization and future development are now emerging in the less developed countries (LDCs). The People's Republic of China (PRC), perhaps the most advanced computer society among the LDCs, is representative of a number of nation-states attempting in various ways to create something of a "firewall" between themselves and the rest of the world's Internet infrastructure in such a way that computer networking within national boundaries would take on characteristics akin to the more secure and restricted "intranets" of large private corporations.[5] At the opposite end of the spectrum from China, the challenge to the global Internet regime for the least developed LDCs does not result from sophisticated efforts to wall the Internet off but rather from the inability of poorer societies to find the wherewithal to provide meaningful connectivity between their citizens and the digital world.

Summary discussions of LDC regime challenges are found at various points in this book, particularly in the concluding chapter, but space constraints have made it necessary to restrict the present study essentially to the growth of the global Internet regime among the advanced IT societies.[6] In a companion volume to this one, the relationship between the Internet and international relations is examined in five world regions—Africa, Asia, the Middle East, Eurasia, and Central/Eastern Europe—where LDCs predominate.[7]

■ INTERNATIONAL REGIME THEORY, "SOFT LAW," AND "PRIVATE AUTHORITY"

A major landmark in the development of international regime theory was the publication of a special issue of *International Organization* on the subject in 1982, in which the contributors agreed on a definition of international regimes as "principles, norms, rules, and decisionmaking procedures around which actor expectations converge in a given issue-area."[8] Empirical examples of major international regimes that have been studied among the several dozen that can be identified are those for balance-of-payments financing, regulation of trade, the international postal network, and international air transport. In all of these cases, and in most of the discussion of international regimes since 1982, the focus of research has been the role of sovereign states in developing and maintaining regime dynamics in an international setting where one international organization has played a predominant role (in the four cases mentioned here, these were, respectively, the International Monetary Fund [IMF], the World Trade Organization [WTO, formerly the General Agreement on Tariffs and Trade (GATT)], the International Postal Union [IPU], and the International Association of Transport Airlines [IATA]). In recent years, however, a number of studies have attempted to use regime theory to better understand the relationships between formal and informal aspects of institutionalized interaction between *private* and *public* international actors, in some cases in settings where no one predominant international organization is shaping the regime.

Inclusion of private authority as a key component of modern international regimes is essential for understanding of late twentieth- and early twenty-first-century dynamics. As has been pointed out by the editors of a 1999 study of private authority in international affairs, "The definition [of international regimes developed in the Krasner volume] and its utility in explaining certain forms of cooperation does not require the relevant actors to be states. Issue areas can be organized and institutionalized as private regimes or as mixed public/private ones, where the private actors can be either firms or non-governmental organizations."[9] Particularly in an era of unprecedented globalization, international regimes are increasingly products of the interaction between public and private authorities, who negotiate and jostle with one another to formulate rules and procedures ("rules of the game") that can effect workable global cooperation in an issue area where conflict or potential conflict exists. This process will frequently produce what A. Claire Cutler has described as "soft law" (e.g., voluntary and formally nonbinding agreements) to govern regime activities and behavior.[10] Cutler defines soft law as informal law and commitment rules whose authority is not traceable to the command of a sovereign or, necessarily, to the sanction of the state. Soft law includes "statements of principles, guidelines, understandings, model laws and codes, and declarations that . . . are neither strictly binding norms of law, nor completely irrelevant political maxims, [operating] in a grey zone between law and politics."[11]

The inclusion of private authority and soft law as essential or important elements in conceptualizing international regimes makes it possible to escape from the more restrictive state-centric theories of regime dynamics and to build bridges between research efforts from several academic disciplines. The "commitment rules" Cutler refers to, for example, are commonly used in the commercial world to create decentralized authority relations and are analogous to Max Weber's notion of the "law of cooperation," governing the private sphere, which Weber distinguished from the "law of subordination," governing the public sphere.[12] The work of the economist Ronald Coase—exploring ways private actors seek to deal with market failures by concluding agreements independent of government—has influenced regime theory, as has the new "institutional economics" with its focus on transactions costs, intrafirm hierarchies, and principal-agent issues.[13] Finally, the inclusion of private authority as a key element in conceptualizing international regimes is particularly appropriate during a period of history when the social and political activities organized by nongovernmental actors have been expanding. As the editors of *Private Authority and International Affairs* pointed out:

> The enhanced global influence of private actors corresponds with current developments at the domestic level. The large-scale privatization of state holdings, the delegation of regulation to industry associations, and the increased reliance on market forces in general characterize domestic developments in many states—and increasingly [are] creeping into the international sphere. . . . It is particularly important to acknowledge the degree to which this represents a private source for authority within international society.[14]

■ THE INTERNET AS A DECENTRALIZED GLOBAL NETWORK

The principles, norms, rules, and decisionmaking procedures that have evolved to make possible the international cooperation necessary for the functioning of the global Internet can be conceived as either an international regime itself, in the process of formation, or a key part of larger global communications or information technology regimes. The development of broad rules of governance for the Internet fits the definition of an international regime in many ways, but the Internet has no central governing authority and the principles, norms, rules, and decisionmaking procedures around which actor expectations are converging to manage it are evolving from the interaction of, among others, a wide variety of private business firms, governments, universities, and scientific, professional, and epistemic communities spread across the globe. The research questions being asked in the international regime literature become particularly interesting when one explores the place of the Internet "regime" in that literature. What is the relationship between basic factors in international relations (e.g., power, interest, and values) and the international regime governing the Internet? To what extent might the international Internet regime help shape international cooperation, and to what extent is it dependent on the maintenance of cooperative relationships in other issue areas?

As a technological breakthrough, the Internet is a set of standardized *protocols* or *conventions* by which data, files, and programs can be sent from one computer to another over various carriers (e.g., telephone lines, cable TV wires, satellite channels) without each computer having to be linked to the other computer through a dedicated cable.[15] Originally designed and supported by the U.S. Department of Defense (DOD) and the National Science Foundation (NSF), the Internet was functioning among a small community of scholars, scientists, and government and defense officials by the 1970s, but it then required a cumbersome and complex process of decoding (in many different computer languages) until electronic mail was invented and became widely available in the 1980s.[16] When the World Wide Web arrived in the 1990s, it created a space (now known as cyberspace) where, in the words of the leading founder of the Web, Tim Berners-Lee, "information could permanently exist and be referred to."[17] Perhaps the most revolutionary aspect of the Web resulted from Lee's conception, which was to create a system with "one fundamental property: it had to be completely decentralized." In the vision of Berners-Lee:

> That would be the only way a new person somewhere could start to use it [the Web] without asking for access from anyone else. And that would be the only way the system could scale, so that as more people used it, it wouldn't get bogged down. This was good Internet-style engineering, but most systems still depended on some central node to which everything had to be connected—and whose capacity eventually limited the growth of the system as a whole. I wanted the act of adding a new link to be trivial . . . there would be no special nodes, no special links. Any node would be able to link to any other node. This would give the system the flexibility that was needed, and be the key to a universal system.[18]

In the initial years of the Web's functioning, Berner-Lee's ideal of a highly decentralized universal system has been shared by tens of millions of people around the world who have appreciated and marveled at an invention that makes it unexpectedly easy for anyone with a computer to connect with anyone else with a computer, anywhere in the world, and to store and send information almost at will. But the Internet and the Web have also moved to the center of attention for governments, business leaders, lawyers and judges, police forces and military establishments, and anyone else dependent on the rule of law and authority structures in modern society. This is a result of the ability and tendency of Internet users to simply skirt or leap over many of the rules and institutions designed to maintain order in the pre-Internet world. Previously designed rules and legal structures enacted for slower-paced, relatively public tangible transactions in a world rimmed everywhere with borders (local, provincial, national) suddenly were challenged as never before when the Internet made it physically conceivable to carry out transactions of almost any kind in a manner simultaneously immediate, anonymous, inexpensive, and seemingly borderless.

■ OPERATING THE GLOBAL INTERNET'S INFRASTRUCTURE

Having moved to the center of attention of authorities throughout the world, the Internet is being transformed from a relatively free and open new technological wonder to an increasingly controlled public institution, governed by an evolving set of rules and laws. It now requires extensive reconciliation of interests among thousands of worldwide Internet Service Providers (ISPs), which are run by governments and private companies (some of the largest are MCI/British Telecom, Sprint, and UUNet). ISPs set their own rules for users of their services but only within the boundaries of network agreements that make it possible for them to maintain linkages to the Internet worldwide. Many ISPs have gotten together to create regional associations that closely follow, on a day-to-day basis, developments related to the Internet, both to promote regional cooperation and to ensure that regional interests are represented in key world decisionmaking arenas. The European ISPs, for example, have created the Reseaux IP Européens (RIPE). InterNIC (owned and operated by a private company in the state of Virginia, Network Solutions, Inc./VeriSign) continues to be the major regional organization for U.S. ISPs, and some Asian ISPs have formed the Asia Pacific Network Information Center (APNIC). Regional networking and trade associations—such as the North American Networks Operators Group, the European Operators Forum, and the Asia Pacific Networking Group—are also of significance in worldwide Internet organizational affairs.

Responsibility for overall operation of the Internet's technical infrastructure was originally located within the Internet Activities/ Architecture Board (IAB) in the Defense Advanced Research Projects Agency (DARPA) of the U.S. Department of Defense, but a civilian component of the infrastructure was willingly given over to NSF by DOD in the 1980s. Particularly after the invention of the World Wide Web, NSF found it impossibly time-consuming and costly to try to administer burgeoning world computer networks, with the result that operation of different facets of the Internet's physical infrastructure was contracted out to private businesses and nonprofit associations in the 1990s, with the U.S. government retaining ultimate authority to renew or cancel contracts. U.S. government agencies also continued to fund a range of activities, including the Internet Assigned Number Authority (IANA), which until 1999 determined how parameters would be uniquely assigned by code to connect computers and networks on a global basis. But in 1999 the Clinton administration "tentatively" handed over the Internet's domain name system from the government-backed IANA and other contractors to a newly formed and totally private international organization called the Internet Corporation for Assigned Names and Numbers (ICANN).[19]

ICANN was set up largely under the direction of one of the Internet's founders, the late Jon Postel, and was initially governed by an "interim board" that was "appointed" by a group of Internet founders put together by Postel. Although the Clinton administration presented the proposal to turn Internet coordination over to ICANN as having "the support of a broad consensus of Internet stakeholders, private and public," several organizations and governments have complained that it was selected in secret sessions and lacks proper fiscal controls and appropriate checks on the powers of board members. Although five of the founding ten appointed interim board members were Americans, control of the board shifted as a result of late 2000 and 2001 elections, in which the U.S.-dominated interim appointed board was replaced by nine elected board members (five were elected in 2000 and four will be elected in 2001), with elections held over the Internet on a worldwide basis (for details, see Chapter 2). In addition to the nine elected at-large board members, nine additional members were elected in 1999 from three supporting organizations of ICANN:

1. ICANN's Address Supporting Organization (ASO), designed to oversee the Internet's Internet Protocol (IP) addresses that uniquely identify networked computers, is made up of representatives from ISPs and is commonly referred to as ICANN's business constituency (the three original ASO board members, elected in October 1999, are Jonathan Cohen, a lawyer from Canada; Pindar Wong, the founder of an ISP in Hong Kong; and Rob Blokzijl, chairman of the European Forum for IP Networks, from the Netherlands).
2. ICANN's Protocol Supporting Organization (PSO) is made up of

ICANN's technical constituency (the three original elected PSO board members are Jean-Francois Abramatic, chairman of the World Wide Web Consortium, from France; Philip Davidson, a British telecommunications executive; and Vinton Cerf, one of the leading founders of the Internet, from the United States). The PSO is concerned with the assignment of unique parameters for Internet protocols (the technical standards that allow computers to exchange information and manage communications over the Internet).

3. ICANN's Domain Name Supporting Organization (DNSO) represents the commercial and trademark constituency (original elected DNSO members are Ken Fockler, an Internet consultant from Canada; Amadeu Abril iAbril, a law professor from Spain; and Alejandro Pisanty, director of academic computing at a university in Mexico). The DNSO translates hierarchically structured, easy-to-remember names (like www.ibm.org) into IP addresses assigned to specific computers at Internet locations.

In addition to the ICANN at-large board and supporting organizations, other international organizations are involved in the evolution of an international regime for the Internet. These include the World Intellectual Property Organization (WIPO) and the Internet Trademark Association, both concerned with intellectual property matters, and other organizations looked to as authorities that can help set standards in particular subject areas. A major world organization expected to be increasingly involved in negotiating principles, norms, and procedures affecting the operation of the Internet, especially on matters related to e-commerce, is the WTO, which is heavily influenced by private corporations involved in information technology and routinely negotiates international understandings on Internet-related issues. Major international organizations that have played a more general role include the following.

The Internet Society (ISOC) grew out of DARPA as a nonprofit, tax-exempt organization to support research and academic networking. The ISOC has since grown to include more than 150 organizational members and more than 6,000 individual members in over 100 nations. Its mission is to "provide leadership in addressing issues that confront the future of the Internet and [to be] the organizational home for the groups responsible for Internet infrastructure standards, including the Internet Engineering Task Force (IETF) and the Internet Architecture

Board (IAB)." ISOC members are companies, government agencies, and foundations involved in the creation of the Internet and its technologies.[20]

The Internet Engineering Task Force, organized under the umbrella of ISOC, developed some of the standards for the Internet, particularly in its early years, while avoiding involvement in day-to-day operations. The IETF operates a system based on requests for comments (RFCs) developed in work groups that meet thrice yearly to discuss proposed solutions to technical problems. Everyone is invited to respond to RFCs, and the IETF board then tries to find ways to put these responses together in a rough consensus that can become a working code to promote interoperability. As has been pointed out in a leading article on international governance of the Internet, the IETF has increasingly had difficulty reaching internal consensus on critical issues, while new industry forums and private companies have been active in establishing de facto standards.[21] The Asynchronous Transfer Mode (ATM) Forum, the Frame Relay Forum, and the Network Management Forum are "vendor-driven" consortiums working to set standards.[22]

The Centre Européen pour la Recherche Nucléaire (CERN) Laboratories in Switzerland, part of the European Organization for Nuclear Research, played a major role in creating and developing some of the major building blocks of what would become the World Wide Web, including Hypertext Transfer Protocol (HTTP), Hypertext Markup Language (HTML), and Universal Resource Locator (URL)—all brought together in 1991 in the system coinventors Berners-Lee and colleague Robert Cailliau christened the World Wide Web.[23] Researchers at CERN have continued to be leading figures in the creation and refinement of new protocols, including an advanced level of interconnection CERN calls "the Grid" (rather than the Web), which might eventually enable standard personal computers (PCs) to access and store data on original supercomputers, thereby solving a number of data storage and transmittal problems of the existing Internet.[24]

The World Wide Web Consortium (W3C) was founded in 1994 by Berners-Lee at the Massachusetts Institute of Technology Laboratory for Computer Science, in collaboration with CERN and with funding from DARPA and the European Commission, for the specific purpose of refining common protocols (e.g., in three versions of HTML subsequent to the original: HTML 3.2 in 1997, HTML 4.01 in 1999, and XHTML1.0 in 2000) to promote the evolution of the Internet and assure its interoperability. The W3C has also developed new protocols, such as, among many others, Extensible Markup Language (XML) 1.0, which allows individual communities around the world to design languages that suit their particular needs and integrate them into a general infrastructure, and the Platform for Internet Content Selection (PICS), a mechanism allowing users to select and filter labeled Web content. The W3C has more than 400 member organizations and several affiliated offices around the world. Its overall mission is to facilitate and promote the decentralized nature of the Web's infrastructure and eventually achieve universal Web access and high levels of legal, commercial, and social trust in global Internet transactions.[25] The W3C is widely considered the authority on the HTML, Hardware Markup Language (HML), and URL protocols that propel materials over the World Wide Web to interconnected computers around the globe.

The International Telecommunications Union (ITU), often described as the first truly international organization, was established in 1865 and has grown into a very large bureaucracy, now loosely affiliated with the United Nations. Responsible on a global level for, among other things, telecommunications infrastructure standards, coordination of radio frequencies, satellite orbits, and the settlements system for telephone calls between countries, the ITU is dependent for effectiveness on building consensual solutions to problems and is powerless to impose decisions on any country. Because its concerns overlap so many functions essential to the operation of the Internet, the ITU, as well as the International Organization for Standardization (ISO), has been and will undoubtedly continue to be involved in the evolution of the international regime for the Internet (the roles of both are described in more detail in Chapter 1).

Finally, the major private companies that have been instrumental in producing computer hardware, software, and network infrastructure will clearly play a major role in determining the Internet's international regime. Michael Borrus and John Zysman have tried to conceptualize this form of industrial authority by using the concept *Wintelism,* derived from the *Wintel* (Windows + Intel) coalition representing the combined power of Microsoft's operating systems and Intel's microprocessors in setting the architectural standards for personal computers.[26] Applying this concept to the literature on international governance, Sangbae Kim and Jeffrey Hart have argued that Wintel's success in winning the technological competition among modern computer firms has conferred material capabilities Wintel has translated into a form of "structural power" to determine international "rules of the game" in the global computer industry.[27] Kim and Hart suggested that three Wintel strategies have established the context for the evolution of the modern computer business: (1) control over technical standards, (2) rapid and constant innovations that give Wintel the edge in competition, and (3) assiduous intellectual property protection.

With regard to the Internet, the Wintel coalition has been a significant force in developing some of the rules of the game for international networking, if only because of Wintel's position in the international computer industry. But a number of other private firms have used the same Wintel formula—control of standards in particular areas, constant innovation, and protection of intellectual property rights to their inventions—to significantly influence the regime as well.[28] In her classic work *State and Markets,* Susan Strange identified this kind of "structural power" as particularly significant in the modern world.

> Structural power . . . confers the power to decide how things shall be done, the power to shape frameworks within which states relate to each other, relate to people, or relate to corporate enterprises. . . . Whoever is able to develop or acquire and to deny the access of others to a kind of knowledge respected and sought by others; and whoever can control the channels by which it is communicated to those given access to it, will exercise a very special kind of structural power. . . . Today the knowledge most sought after the acquisition of relational power and to reinforce other kinds of structural power (i.e., in security matters, in production and in finance) is technology.[29]

Although large corporations have and will continue to play a major role in shaping regime parameters through the development of technology, their innovations must necessarily be within the confines of worldwide interoperability, and their products must be chosen and bought by users in 190 different sovereign nations. These limitations impose constraints on the ability of large corporations to gain overwhelming dominance of the global Internet regime and impel them toward a certain degree of cooperation with one another and with governments and international organizations. As is indicated in the pages that follow, the exercise of effective private authority and structural power by corporations is dependent on a combination of consumer trust and solid working relationships with governments and international authorities.

■ **CONCEPTUALIZING THE ISSUES INVOLVED**

In addition to an appreciation of the number of actors with interests in developing an international regime for the Internet, it is important to conceptualize the range of issues that must be resolved if the existing embryonic regime is to mature and become more robust. Following an outline developed by the European Union (EU) in 1998, with some embellishments, one might classify these issues into three categories, which conform roughly to the first three-quarters of this book. First, those issues that have been addressed at the international level for the longest period of time have been the *technical issues* related to the interconnection and interoperability of diverse world networks. The development of the minimal set of principles, norms, rules, and procedures for technical standards and protocols, discussed in Chapter 1, has produced an incipient international regime for the Internet, even though it has been impossible to develop an equally robust worldwide consensus for *governance or management of the Internet's global infrastructure.* Issues related to Internet governance and management are discussed in Chapter 2.

Apart from technical and governance issues relating to basic interconnection and interoperability of the Internet is a second set of *commercial issues,* generated primarily by large transnational corporations, multinational enterprises, and governments seeking what EU leaders call an international "enabling framework" for fair market access and competition in the many diverse and promising aspects of Internet-related business and economic activities. These include e-commerce, online banking and trading of stocks, use of the Internet for business-to-business (B2B) transactions, privatization of Internet-related companies in formerly socialist or statist telecommunications environments, and much more. The commercial aspects of Internet development became increasingly apparent to companies and governments on an international scale in the mid-1990s, once the World Wide Web began to become fully operational and Internet commerce started to attract massive international investments. Specific commercial issue areas that have generated intense discussion include customs and taxation, electronic payment systems, possible elaboration of a uniform commercial code for electronic commerce, intellectual property protection matters, telecommunications infrastructure and information technology development in poorer parts of the world, and a host of standards issues.

Some of the agenda items put forth by various governments and private-sector leaders for negotiating international principles and norms to deal with Internet-related commercial issues on a regularized basis are explored in Chapters 3 and 4. These include the Clinton administration's 1997 proposals, set forth in its *Framework for Global Electronic Commerce,* calling for private-sector leadership at the global level without "undue government restrictions on electronic commerce." The agenda items also include a variety of recommendations—emanating primarily from other governments—for different types of regulatory frameworks that would not allow market forces to play as prominent a role as is suggested in the Clinton administration proposals. Regardless of the positions taken by various national governments and large corporations on the need for government regulatory actions, however, there is a widely recognized need for the negotiation and implementation of international principles and norms to provide for orderly global commercial online transactions into the future. To quote from the conclusions adopted at a 1999 EU summit: "The global electronic marketplace requires an appropriate framework. [That framework] does not need to consist of detailed and harmonized rules on all relevant aspects, [but] global uncertainty surrounding different national and regional responses to these challenges will hamper the further development of the electronic marketplace."[30]

A third set of concerns related to the growth of an international Internet regime has to do with *legal issues* relating to such wide-ranging matters as jurisdiction and liability in cyberspace, authentication and encryption of online correspondence and signatures, laws governing censorship, data protection, consumer protection, protection of privacy, personal and national security concerns, and a host of other matters involving the rights of individuals and the potential roles of governments in cyberspace. Almost all of these legal issues are closely related to the commercial issues mentioned earlier, but many Internet-related legal concerns go beyond commercial considerations and have ramifications for almost every aspect of life in almost every nation. Attempts to set agendas for negotiation of international regime principles and norms related to legal issues form the basis of Chapters 5 and 6.

It should be clear that the formation of an international regime for the Internet is an ongoing process, and this process is exceedingly complex, involving myriad actors—public and private—from around the world representing many of the most powerful technological centers, businesses, and governments. The goal of this volume is to gain a preliminary understanding of the ways in which key actors—public and private, from many nations—have negotiated issues that have thus far emerged on the international agenda. This should in turn help gauge the degree to which one can identify both the parameters of the existing international regime for the Internet and the prospects for its future development.

■ **NOTES**

1. Keohane, "The Analysis of International Regimes," p. 23. International regimes as a concept originated in international law as early as the 1920s (see, for example, de Visscher, *Le Regime Nouveau des Detroits*). See also Leive, *International Regulatory Regimes.*

2. In 1989 Kenneth Abbott published an article calling on international lawyers to read and master regime theory while suggesting that a "joint discipline" of legal, business, and political science scholars be created to bridge gaps among the disciplines. See Abbott, "Modern International Relations Theory," pp. 335–411.

3. Preston and Windsor, *The Rules of the Game in the Global Economy,* pp. 6 ff. See also Slaughter, Tulumello, and Wood, "International Law and International Relations Theory," pp. 367–392. There have been several attempts to identify and analyze international regimes related to information technology and communications. Some of these are summarized in Zacher with Sutton, *Governing Global Networks.*

4. See chapter 1, "The Stages of International Regime Formation," in Young, *Creating Regimes,* pp. 1–28.

5. Published attempts to describe China's Internet firewall concept include Yurcik and Tan, "The Great (Fire)wall of China"; Tan, Foster, and Goodman, "China's State-Coordinated Internet Infrastructure," pp. 44–52; and Lovelock, *E-China.* See also Franda, "China and India Online"; Smith, "Ambivalence in China on Expanding Net Access," p. C3; and Chapter 7 in this book.

6. A detailed study of the PRC's challenges to the regime appears in a book-length work by the author being published separately. Franda, "China and India Online."

7. Franda, *Launching into Cyberspace.*

8. Krasner, *International Regimes,* p. 1. This volume originally appeared as an issue of *International Organization,* 36: 2 (spring 1982).

9. The quote is from the introductory chapter in Cutler, Haufler, and Porter, *Private Authority and International Affairs,* p. 14.

10. See Cutler, "Private Authority in International Trade Relations," in ibid., pp. 283–332.

11. Quoted from the concluding chapter by Cutler, Haufler, and Porter in ibid., pp. 367–368.

12. Onuf, *World of Our Making,* pp. 208, 215.

13. For more detail on this point see Cutler, Haufler, and Porter, *Private Authority in International Affairs,* pp. 13–15, and the related citations in that volume, including especially Coase, *The Firm, the Market and the Law,* and Soltan, Haufler, and Uslaner, *Institutions and Social Order.*

14. Cutler, Haufler, and Porter, *Private Authority in International Affairs,* p. 15

15. This definition is adapted from a discussion in Berners-Lee with Fischetti, *Weaving the Web,* pp. 17–18.

16. The word *Internet* was first used by Vincent Cerf in a 1974 research paper. The first public demonstration of Internet capabilities took place at the Hilton Hotel in Washington, D.C., in October 1972. See Gunn and Pappas, "What a Short, Strange Trip It's Been," pp. 72, 74; and McHugh and Kahn, "Packet Man," pp. 328–329.

17. Berners-Lee with Fischetti, *Weaving the Web,* p. 18.

18. Ibid., p. 16.

19. The process to be followed in handing over the Internet's domain name system to ICANN is outlined in Clausing, "Private Takeover of Internet Administration to Begin." See also the twenty-four-page document published by the United States Department of Commerce, *Management of Internet Names and Addresses,* and the ICANN website at http://www.icann.org.

20. For more information visit the ISOC website at http://www.isoc.org.

21. Foster, Rutkowski, and Goodman, "Who Governs the Internet?" p. 17. I am indebted to the authors of this article, particularly Will Foster, for their insightful contributions.

22. Ibid.

23. CERN refers to itself in English as the European Organization for Nuclear Research and gets its acronym from the Centre Européen pour la Recherche Nucléaire. The CERN Convention of 1954, originally signed by twelve states, was one of Europe's first joint ventures, with state-of-the-art laboratories located on the Franco-Swiss border near Geneva, Switzerland. More than 6,500 scientists (half of the world's particle physicists), representing almost 500 universities in eighty countries, are in some way currently affiliated with CERN projects. More information is available on the CERN website at http://cern.web.cern.ch/CERN.

24. See "Information Technology in the News," pp. 4–5. See also Segal, "A Short History of Internet Protocols at CERN," in-house CERN document, available at http://cern.web.cern.ch/CERN.

25. Much more information about W3C is available on its website at www.w3.org.

26. Borrus and Zysman, "Wintelism."

27. Kim and Hart, "The Global Political Economy of Wintelism." Windows has been able to establish its dominant position because it was

installed in almost 90 percent of the world's personal computers by 2000. Intel is the world's largest semiconductor manufacturer, with 73 percent of the global microprocessor market in 2000.

28. In late 2000 a number of analysts opposed the merger of Time Warner, a leading cable provider, with America Online, which sees cable as the future of broadband Internet access, arguing that the merger would compromise the promise of the Internet and test the commitment of federal regulators to the principles of openness that produced the Internet because it would create a Wintel-type structural power coalition. See, for example, Lessig, "Straitjacket on the Internet?" p. A31.

29. Strange, *State and Markets,* pp. 25, 31.

30. Quoted in Malawer, "International Trade and Transactions," p. S40. See also Timmers, "Electronic Commerce Policy," pp. 195–200.

International Connectivity

There is no single reason international regimes come into being, although a number of political scientists have tried to find single-causal explanations. In the early years of regime analysis there was a tendency to link international regimes to the needs of hegemonic state actors trying to impose a form of order, or perhaps an ideological agenda, on an anarchic world. In this view an international regime might be brought into being because a single dominant world power either provided the economic thrust necessary for the regime to function effectively or simply imposed the regime on other world actors by using a combination of sanctions and incentives, all as a matter of hegemonic self-interest.[1] More recently, a number of theorists have speculated that the primary reason for the proliferation of international regimes in the twentieth century was the need for world leaders to find ways to develop policies and make decisions about highly complex scientific and technological matters in an increasingly interdependent world.[2] From this perspective, international regimes come into being because "technological innovations devalue traditional strategies [of statecraft], and social change redefines the parameters of international relations."[3] The "knowledge-based" theories of regime formation that stem from this latter perspective almost always assign a central role to the actions and ideas of epistemic communities, defined as groups or networks of specialists with recognized expertise in the regime's subject area(s). Knowledge-based theories of governance have been popular, if not predominant, in explaining how the Internet was created and operated, particularly in its early years.

More comprehensive than single-causal explanations is the work of Oran Young, one of the founders of modern international regime theory, who has spent a good part of his professional life trying to develop what he calls a "multivariate analysis" of international regime formation. Young proceeds from the assumption, developed over many years of study, that "the process through which new institutional arrangements come into existence virtually always encompasses several distinct stages and . . . the political dynamics characteristic of the different stages are by no means the same."[4] Young has identified three distinct stages that occur in the process of international regime formation, which he calls agenda formation, negotiation, and operationalization.[5] Very early in his work, Young also identified three types of external pressures that influence and result in regime change, which he described as internal contradictions, shifts in underlying power structures, and exogenous forces.[6]

The pages that follow represent an attempt to work with these six major variables to see if they can help us better understand whether, and in what ways, an international regime for the Internet is being created. What significant *agendas* have been developed for bringing into being principles, norms, rules, and decisionmaking procedures that might assure international cooperation in Internet-related issue areas into the future? What *negotiations* have taken place or are in progress to move internationally toward these goals? To what extent has effective *operationalization* of an international Internet regime occurred? Once these questions are answered, we should have some idea of the *various stages* at which the nascent international regime for the Internet is proceeding. We can then turn to an analysis of factors external to the regime that have influenced (and might influence in the future) regime formation and change.

Some of the most useful aspects of Young's work that help to explain international organization of the Internet are those relating to the formation of international regimes in the Arctic, which, like the Internet, is an extremely valuable part of the world not under the control of a single sovereign. The absence of a single sovereign in cyberspace has led a number of observers to conclude that an international regime for the Internet is not possible. And yet agendas are being set, negotiations are taking place, and attempts are being made to operationalize principles, rules, norms, and procedures for building multilateral cooperation for use of the Internet in much the same manner as has been the case for the use of resources in the circumpolar North. Young's work, for example, reveals two notable features that distinguish international regimes in the Arctic from most other international regimes, and these two features are also prominent in the evolving international regime for the Internet: (1) regimes in both areas have been heavily dependent on "soft law" arrangements (rather than legally binding treaties or conventions), and (2) regimes in both areas are centered on, in Young's words, "the initiation of programmatic activities expected to give rise to increasingly complex social practices rather than on the articulation of a collection of regulative rules."[7] Young's description of the process by which international regimes were created, in the Arctic and elsewhere, might well have been written about the Internet as well:

> Efforts to form international regimes may make it through [one stage] but stall at the next stage. Some issues fail to capture an acknowledged spot on the international political agenda. Others have difficulty achieving a high enough priority on the agenda to trigger the initiation of explicit negotiations. Still others stimulate negotiations in which the participants are unable to reach closure on the terms of a regime. Even signed agreements sometimes become dead letters. Only by successfully navigating all three stages can a regime that has real consequences for the nature of collective outcomes come into existence. . . . Because the three stages of regime formation differ from one another with regard to their political dynamics, efforts to explain success or failure . . . on the basis of propositions or models that assume a seamless or uniform process are doomed to failure. A satisfactory account of regime formation . . . will require separate but interconnected propositions concerning the several stages of the overall process.[8]

▪ TCP/IP PROTOCOL AND "OPEN STANDARDS"

Although the history of the Internet itself can be traced to the 1960s or perhaps even earlier, the development of the *international* regime for the Internet began with the acceptance of the first Transmission Control Protocol/Internetwork Protocol (TCP/IP) as a de facto worldwide standard in the 1980s and 1990s. In its earliest years—before it became international—the Internet was a single experimental network serving a dozen sites in the United States and a related set of innovative computer-based communications techniques that made possible some networking experiments with advanced computer sites in Europe.[9] But the reach of the original Internet was limited because networks could initially be built only between specific and highly reliable computer systems.

By the early 1970s computer networking capabilities had expanded to the point where many founders of the Internet could conceive of building a *worldwide* network of subsidiary computer networks and even individual computers.[10] The major problems involved in building an overall international network had to do with, first, the lack of a practical design for a universal host protocol that would work on both reliable and unreliable networks and, second, methods of attaching specific networks—located in almost 200 countries—to each other. Although communication by e-mail among computer users was becoming more common in the mid-1970s, a person could still only send a message to another person who was connected to a *single* discrete network. The key breakthrough in creating the possibility of connecting all networks and computers throughout the world occurred at a meeting organized by Vinton Cerf at Stanford University in 1973 when all academic, government, military, and commercial groups with substantial interest in computer networking at that time were able to assemble in one place and, in Janet Abbate's words, "to find enough common ground to define an approach on which most of them could agree."[11]

The internationalizing approach agreed to at Stanford in 1973 was to accept a particular host protocol—Transmission Control Protocol (TCP)—as the standard that could provide an orderly, error-free flow of data from one host computer to another, both within and between networks. The TCP was chosen from a number of other options and was distinguished because it provided for the most open and, in the words of its designers, "seamless" system. In Cerf's words, "We wanted to have a common protocol and a common address space so that you couldn't tell, to first order, that you were actually talking through all these different kinds of nets."[12] The alternative to TCP would have been a system (or systems) of networking that would have required various mechanisms for translating among them, most of which were the proprietary interests of commercial companies. Such an alternative would have been anything but seamless.

Agreement to use the original TCP protocol was further refined at a January 1978 meeting at the University of Southern California (USC) when Cerf, Jon Postel, and Danny Cohen proposed that the then-existing TCP protocol be split into two separate parts: a host-to-host protocol (TCP) and an Internetwork Protocol (IP). The pair of protocols, known collectively as TCP/IP and now used almost universally throughout the world, allowed a streamlined overall system in which the IP protocols passed individual packets between machines (from host to packet switch or between packet switches) while the TCP ordered packets into reliable connections between pairs of hosts.[13] As new versions of Internet protocols were developed in subsequent years, gateways became increasingly easier to connect and could be located faster because they ran only IP and did not have to duplicate host functions (which were confined to TCP as a result of the 1978 meeting). Both IP and TCP protocols have advanced considerably since 1978, but the goal of all advanced TCP/IP protocols has been to further the universality and decentralized nature of worldwide computer networking.[14]

Most important from the perspective of building a global network, the TCP/IP innovation in 1978 put far fewer demands on member networks than the original TCP. Thus the larger networks became much more readily accessible to those around the world whose computer and telecommunications systems were poorer in quality and less reliable than those at the U.S. Department of Defense, NSF, CERN in Switzerland, or the other high-quality computer laboratories where the Internet had originated. The Defense Department liked the innovation because it lengthened the odds that when networks were less reliable (under conditions of war, for example), they might still be functional using the TCP/IP. This feature of the Internet brought it potentially within reach of anyone with access to a computer anywhere in the world.

If one conceives of the adoption of TCP/IP as the first building block in the evolution of the international regime for the Internet, then the meetings at Stanford in 1973 and at USC in January 1978 can be viewed as the beginning of the *agenda-setting* stage in Young's formulation for regime creation. Those who met at Stanford in June 1973 represented all of the major actors with interests in exploring the vision of an international network of computers, and all agreed at the time to a vague consensus that they would develop a particular network protocol as a worldwide standard. *Operationalization* of this decision still required considerable *negotiation* among the wide variety of interests that became increasingly involved with the Internet in succeeding years. But the eventual outcome of those negotiations led to the acceptance of TCP/IP as a worldwide standard and eventual operationalization of the Internet on a global basis in the 1990s.

The process of negotiating acceptance of the TCP/IP protocol was politically charged, and its outcome was by no means certain. Companies not initially involved with the development of the Internet began to develop a number of rival networking protocols to compete with TCP/IP as the potential significance of a worldwide computer network began to come into focus in the 1970s. IBM produced its Systems Network Architecture (SNA) in 1974; Xerox Network Services and Digital Equipment Corporation's Digital Network Architecture (DECNET) came out in 1975. Honeywell, Sperry, Burroughs, and other companies produced similar systems. All of these were designed to be used and to work only with the manufacturer's computers, their technical specifications were subject to intellectual property law and were held secret, and for all company-designed systems, license fees were charged for use of the protocols. These company systems contrasted sharply with the TCP/IP protocol, which was not subject to fees for use and was not the preserve of any single manufacturer or organization.

In an effort to gain an early advantage for their particular network systems in the mid-1970s, rival companies in the United States and Europe pressured standards organizations in their respective countries to create specifications favorable to the adoption of their protocols. This resulted in the adoption of a number of competing and incompatible standards in the 1970s and 1980s, thereby threatening to slow or perhaps even prevent the growth of a worldwide network of computers.[15] In 1978, in an attempt to bring about greater compatibility of network standards, concerned members of the International Organization for Standardization—from the United States, Britain, France, Canada, and Japan—formed a new committee that, somewhat confusedly, named its project Open Systems Interconnection, with an acronym (OSI) the backward opposite of that for its parent organization, the ISO. The goal of the OSI committee was to counter the proprietary interests of the large manufacturing companies that wanted to keep networking systems as "closed" as possible.[16] The OSI committee proposed, therefore, acceptance of several principles that would constitute an "open system," including the following: "technology would be non-proprietary, so that anyone was free to duplicate it; the system would be designed to work with generic components, rather than be dependent on a specific manufacturer's products; and changes to the standards would be made by a public standards organization, not a private company."[17]

The ISO was a particularly appropriate organization in which to carry out negotiations for protocol and network systems standards in the 1970s and 1980s. Founded in 1946 as a voluntary, nontreaty organization, the ISO had grown to include members from more than ninety countries by the mid-1970s and had prepared and approved several thousand standards—through the work of 160 technical committees—

covering subject matter that ranged from screw thread sizes to the properties of sophisticated electronic equipment. Not only was the ISO trusted internationally, it was also an organization whose working groups had traditionally been dominated by large manufacturers that had both strong interest in shaping international standards and the resources to send their leaders and experts to ISO working group meetings. In an environment where all major IT companies were beginning to develop international networking systems and protocols in the 1970s, private business leaders were concerned that standards be developed fairly quickly to avoid a chaotic situation where products might become so totally incompatible with each other that the entire Internet enterprise would become dysfunctional. It was perhaps for this reason, particularly when coupled with the fact that negotiations were being carried out within a trusted organizational framework, that the work of the OSI committee significantly influenced future directions of the IT industry.

The principal impact of the OSI committee, however, was not made by a set of specific standards. Indeed, acceptance of the committee's conclusions was promoted by the conservative way in which its findings were promulgated, which left considerable room for companies to continue to pursue their proprietary interests. Rather than set forth a particular standard or set of standards that might prematurely cut off exploration of some avenues of innovation, the committee simply proposed a general framework for future standards development. This framework was a model that consisted of seven layers of protocols that fit together to form a complete network system.[18] The OSI committee suggested that the model be used to define the services the various protocols would provide and the manner in which they would interact, but the specific standards that would be fit into the model could be proposed by later interested parties and organizations and decided upon by ISO member-based procedures. In other words, the OSI committee model would be a metastandard that would set "a standard for creating network standards."[19]

As Abbate has pointed out, the work of the OSI committee gave rise to an Open Systems Interconnection movement that "significantly shaped the way computer science professionals thought about networks."[20] In the 1980s and 1990s, textbooks were organized around OSI's seven-layer model, and manufacturers, even if they continued to use their own proprietary protocols, revised their network systems to conform to the OSI framework. The idea of an OSI metastandard was endorsed by standards organizations in all countries then involved with computer networking.[21] Even the U.S. Department of Defense joined the OSI movement by adopting a policy of using the OSI framework in its networking activities and declaring in 1987 that OSI protocols would eventually be adopted as military standards.[22] Support for the OSI movement has not resulted in a set of clear and universally accepted standards for the Internet, but it has established the OSI framework and the idea of building open systems as a major preference, particularly among computer users, researchers, and academics.

▪ NETWORK STANDARDS NEGOTIATIONS AND GOVERNMENT MONOPOLY TELECOMMUNICATIONS COMPANIES

An outstanding issue in computer network standards negotiations in the 1970s and 1980s stemmed from an entirely different developmental model than that contemplated by the OSI committee. This alternative model was supported by the leading government monopoly telephone carriers in Europe, Canada, and Japan (also known as Post, Telegraph, and Telephone [PTT] companies), which in 1974 and 1975 announced plans to create public data networks that would serve computer users with world standard protocols. Working through the Consultative Committee on International Telegraphy and Telephony (CCITT) of the International Telecommunications Union (ITU), the PTTs put together a set of three protocols designated "Recommendation X.25" (X is the CCITT code for data communications standards). Canada's Datapac adopted X.25 in 1977, France's Transpac in 1978, and Japan's DDX and the multinational Euronet in 1979. A U.S. company, Telenet (a spin-off from DARPA), incorporated X.25 into its developing data networks in 1976, and other U.S. companies—IBM, Digital, Honeywell, and others—eventually offered X.25 software for their machines.

The international computer networks envisaged by the PTTs in the 1970s were based on the government monopoly telephone systems that had existed for many decades and were conceived as a third alternative to TCP/IP and proprietary networks. The X.25 protocols were based on the assumption that each country would have a single public data computer network that would interconnect with adjoining networks at national borders, just like the telephone companies whose lines and cables were controlled by government-run companies of sovereign states. In this vision computer owners would attach their machines directly to government-run networks, which would all be based on X.25 protocols. Although private networks might be allowed to exist in some countries, they would be licensed by the government and expected to conform to standards established by governments and embodied in the X.25 protocols. In contrast to the TCP/IP protocols, designed to operate an open system that would originally provide identifiers for more than 16,000 large networks (those with hundreds of thousands of hosts) and more than 2 million small networks (128 or fewer hosts)—which eventually grew to millions of such identifiers—the CCITT addressing scheme was based on the notion that most countries would require only 10 network addresses (the United States, with its abundance of existing networks, was allotted a "generous" 200 network addresses in the X.25 protocols).

Although the X.25 protocols and TCP/IP are not mutually exclusive and can be combined in a single network, they were viewed as rivals in the 1970s and 1980s, and the X.25 recommendation was widely seen as having been established in direct opposition to the open systems movement. The key difference between the two approaches was that X.25 was designed as a public utility that could guarantee quality of service over a single network in return for access charges, whereas TCP/IP literally privatized and totally decentralized responsibility for the establishment, control, accountability, maintenance, and costs of building and maintaining computer networks. The designers of the PTT carriers expected that every network in their system would be required to use X.25 protocols, whereas the designers of the Internet had created TCP/IP specifically to accommodate a diverse set of protocols and networks. In Abbate's words:

> The carriers intended to create a centralized, homogeneous internet system in which network operators controlled network performance; they also tried to perpetuate their monopoly on communications by making it difficult for private networks to connect to the public systems. This system design would ensure the carriers a large and profitable market for high-quality data communications services. Computer owners, recognizing that the X.25 system would limit their options for customizing network service to meet their military, research, or business objectives, demanded the freedom to choose the level of the service they would purchase from the public networks and to build their own private networks using a variety of techniques.[23]

The standards debates in the 1970s and 1980s can be considered the *negotiation* stage for the establishment of one key aspect of the international regime for the Internet—the model of internetworking that would be used to link computers internationally. Each of the three major groups represented in the debates—government carriers, private companies, and the original Advanced Research Projects Agency (ARPA) group of academic and military computer scientists and researchers—had its own models based on its own interests. By the early 1990s TCP/IP had clearly become the de facto network standard, both in the United States and abroad, but government network operators continued to use X.25, and OSI continued to develop standards under its seven-layer framework. OSI's seven-layer metastandard model gained wide acceptance, particularly outside the United States, but it also encountered several problems because of its complexity and eclectic nature. Two of the standards layers it outlined—the session and presentation layers—had no counterpart in the Internet or in most commercial networks, so essentially they were simply ignored. In other layers—in the physical, link, and network layers, for example, where most computer company products fit—ISO adopted a policy of approving several different protocols as standards, so long as the protocol already had a large constituency of users and its developers were willing to give up proprietary control over it.

Although the debate about internetworking protocols did not result in a single standard, it did produce wide acceptance of two principles: (1) that authority for operationalizing the Internet would be decentralized internationally and (2) that the process for developing international technical standards would be inclusive rather than proprietary or government directed, and two norms: (1) that operation of the global Internet would be designed to handle diversity at all network levels and (2) that the Internet would be characterized by interoperability and heterogeneity both within and among networks.[24] Based on these principles and norms, the PTTs tended to implement only those protocols that conformed to their model of networking, including X.25 and the transport protocol TP0, but the PTTs emerged as only a small number of networks in a vast sea of private and public networks spread throughout the world. Because OSI was willing to sanction multiple protocols in its various layers, key features of different company networking systems—created by Xerox, IBM, and General Motors, for example—were adopted as OSI standards. But manufacturer resistance to X.25, even though it was approved as one of the OSI standards, contributed to heterogeneity among networks and thwarted the hopes of government carriers to establish a uniform system based on government controls. The TCP/IP not only became the de facto network standard because of widespread use in an international regime characterized by diversity and heterogeneity of networks, but some versions of it were also eventually sanctioned by the ISO.[25] All of this eventually, in Abbate's words, "neutralized the standards controversy by paving the way for convergence—or at least accommodation—between [the various] systems."[26]

<h2>■ PRINCIPLES AND NORMS OF
THE GLOBAL INTERNET REGIME</h2>

Principles and norms lie at the heart of international regime theory and are usually distinguished from agreements.[27] Agreements are ad hoc, often one-time arrangements, but the concept of regimes "implies not only norms and expectations that facilitate cooperation, but a form of cooperation that is more than the following of short-run self-interest."[28] The purpose of regimes is to facilitate agreements. Although international regime principles and norms may not, like many agreements, be enforceable in a court of law, the principles and norms of an international regime must embody some sense of general obligation. In a security regime, for example, states would accept *reciprocity* as a principle, meaning they would sacrifice short-term interests with the expectation that other actors would reciprocate in the future.[29] When the principle of reciprocity is no longer accepted, a security regime would either break up or collapse.

The principles and norms of international regimes must be distinguished from regime rules and procedures. Whereas principles and norms provide, in Krasner's words, "the basic defining characteristics of a regime," rules and decisionmaking procedures are simply operational features of a regime that assure consistency with the regime's principles and norms. Rules and procedures within a regime can change without affecting the nature of the regime, but changes in principles and norms result in changes of the regime itself.[30] In this sense, acceptance of the principles of decentralized authority and inclusive technical standards, particularly when coupled with the norms of operational diversity and heterogeneity both within and among networks, is a fundamental feature of the present international regime for the Internet. Should adherence to these principles and norms for networking be abandoned or replaced by other principles and norms, international regime theorists would argue that the present regime would in that case either be replaced by a new one or this particular international regime for international networking would simply disappear.

The potential for robust growth of the present global internetworking regime is clear from the way in which the Internet has spread so quickly internationally. This was made possible by a number of technological breakthroughs in the 1980s and 1990s that were able to take advantage of the Internet's decentralized authority and the operational diversity and heterogeneity of its internetworking. In the 1980s, for example, computer scientists at the University of Delaware created a system that made possible a low-cost network using dial-up telephone links—the Computer Scientists Network (CSNET)—that enabled schools and colleges, nonprofit organizations, state and local governments, and other groups to access the Internet without having to incur expensive investments in hardware or software. Using funds from NSF to build a network based on TCP/IP protocols, CSNET set up the first e-mail gateways to research networks in Australia, Finland, France, Germany, Israel, Japan, Korea, Sweden, and the United Kingdom.[31]

The spread of civilian networks with access to the U.S. military's ARPANET, the original computer network of ARPA, became more feasible after 1983 when the Defense Department created a new Military Network (MILNET) for classified and military sites, leaving ARPANET for civilian research. This development occurred at approximately the same time the growth of local area networks (LANs), spurred by the development of the personal computer and other aspects of the computing revolution of the 1970s and 1980s, made possible the explosive growth of the Ethernet system, developed initially by Xerox researcher Robert Metcalfe in 1975. The Ethernet system provided a simple and inexpensive way to network computers within a local area and was commercialized by Metcalfe in the 1980s when he left Xerox to form the company 3Com. Ethernet products made it possible for people to build their own LANs for Unix workstations and personal computers, with only two technical requirements: the site had to run TCP/IP on the local network, and it had to set up a gateway (also called a router) between its network and the ARPANET. But ARPANET itself encouraged these developments by providing funding to vendors to develop TCP/IP products for Ethernet and by publishing in 1984 its own official standard for transmitting IP packets over Ethernet.[32] By the mid-1990s, according to Metcalfe's estimate, there were more than 5 million Ethernet LANs in operation.[33]

Principles of decentralized authority and inclusive technical standards, as well as regime norms for diversity and heterogeneity within and among networks, were considerably strengthened by the invention of the World Wide Web, first distributed over the Internet by CERN in 1991. The Web did not grow out of the U.S. Defense Department or the research community but was created by Tim Berners-Lee, Robert Cailliau, and others at CERN. As Abbate has pointed out, the computing tradition on which Berners-Lee and his colleagues drew was the "hacker counterculture" that "urged ordinary people to learn to use computers rather than leaving them in the hands of the 'computer priesthood.'"[34] One of the goals of Berners-Lee and his colleagues was to create "a pool of human knowledge" that could be accessed by anyone anywhere in the world.[35] A second goal was to make it possible to transmit images (photos, drawings, graphs and charts, and other images) as well as text, making it possible to network internationally the significant advances being made in the image orientations of personal computers. In later aspects of their work, the designers of the Web added audio and video.[36]

The evolving international regime for the Internet was such that it encouraged the development of the World Wide Web and related inventions.[37] Abbate has described the interrelatedness of this process of invention as follows:

> The layered structure of the Internet meant that Berners-Lee could build his new application on top of the communications services provided by TCP/IP. His group designed the hypertext transfer protocol (HTTP) to guide the exchange of information between Web browsers and Web servers. To enable browsers and servers to locate information on the Web, there also had to be some uniform way to identify the information a user wanted to access. To address this need, they created a universal resource locator (URL)—a standard address format that specifies both the type of application protocol being used and the address of the computer that has the desired data. An important feature of the URL was that it could refer to a variety of protocols, not just HTTP. This would make it possible to use the Web to access older Internet services, such as FTP [File Transfer Protocol], gopher, WAIS [Wide-Area Information Server], and Usenet news. The accommodation of all Internet services—present and future—within a single interface would be an important factor in making the Web system versatile and user friendly.[38]

■ NEGOTIATION-STAGE ISSUES
IN INTERNATIONAL REGIME DEVELOPMENT

By the mid-1990s the basic outlines of an embryonic international regime for the Internet had emerged. There was general agreement on the principles of decentralized authority for technical operations internationally and inclusive standard setting and on the norms of diversity at all network levels, with networks characterized by interoperability and heterogeneity both within and between networks. These principles and norms had been reinforced by the pattern of IT invention that mushroomed in the 1980s and 1990s, most of which either emphasized or was consistent with ideas of decentralization, inclusiveness, diversity, and heterogeneity. This pattern received perhaps its greatest initial boost from the debut of the personal computer in 1975 and its incredibly rapid adoption over the next two decades, making it possible to decentralize networks down to the level of the individual computer station. The invention pattern reached its zenith when the creation of the World Wide Web extended the Internet to millions (and potentially billions) of individual computer stations in every corner of the globe in the 1990s. Marking the occasion of the Internet's initial big lunge into the international arena was the first International World Wide Web Conference, at CERN in Geneva in May 1994, and the second International World Wide Web Conference, held in Chicago in October that same year.

But the operationalization of the Internet on an international level did not mean that a robust international regime had suddenly emerged full-blown in the 1990s. As Young has pointed out, international regimes are social institutions that take time to develop and become robust. The Internet first became operational internationally in the 1990s on the basis of widespread initial agreement on principles and norms for technical standards, but it was also clear that a full-blown international regime for the Internet could be fleshed out in the future only if principles and norms for technical standards held up over an extended period and if additional principles and norms could be developed for newly emerging aspects of the Internet, including especially those relating to matters of commercial development and legal/governance issues. In addition, rules and procedures—the other two elements (in addition to principles and norms) essential to the definition of a regime—had to be negotiated for technical operations and other emerging aspects as well.

The ultimate test of whether the present embryonic international Internet regime will survive and continue to grow along lines resembling its present form will depend on factors similar to those found in other regimes, including especially the ability of leaders across the world to adapt to rapid change and to continue to build conjunctions between, on the one hand, divergent expectations for the Internet and, on the other, even more divergent global patterns of cultural, political, social, and economic behavior and practices. In Young's formulations, "The major features of international regimes, as of other social institutions, can be expected to acquire a life of their own in the form of operative social conventions . . . [but] the rise of conventionalized behavior is apt to engender widespread feelings of legitimacy or propriety [only] in conjunction with specific institutional arrangements."[39] This does not mean all actors will always comply with the terms of regime conventions, since deviance or nonconformity is common in all social institutions. What it does mean is that international regimes, like other societal institutions, will be maintained only by the cooperative interactions of large numbers of individuals and groups. Although any given regime will reflect the behavior of all those participating in it, any given individual actor can typically expect to exercise limited influence, on her or his own, over the character of the regime, no matter how influential the person. Constant change can be expected to take place within regimes as in any complex social institution, but planned or guided change is exceedingly difficult to engineer and is therefore rare. To quote Young again,

> Given the extent and severity of conflicts of interest in the international community, it is fair to assume that the convergence of expectations around new institutional arrangements will often be slow in coming. This problem is well-known at the constitutional or legislative level (consider the law of the sea negotiations as a case in point), but it is apt to prove even more severe with respect to the behavior of individual actors who are expected to be subjects of any new or modified regime.[40]

Although a number of people have argued that the Internet will—either on its own or in conjunction with other forces—usher in a new age in which the sovereignty of nation-states will be eroded, at least for the present sovereignty remains a pervasive aspect of modern international relations and is having considerable impact on the evolution of Internet governance.[41] In other areas where no state is sovereign—in the

Arctic regions or in outer space, for example—governance functions are carried out by international regimes that exhibit different degrees of strength and vulnerability. In other international regimes constituted for such areas, sovereign states continue to play a major role in the international regime even if no one of them has sovereignty over the specific area. This is so because, in Krasner's words, "sovereignty designates states as the only actors with unlimited rights to act in the international system." Assertions of sovereignty by any organization or agency other than states are, as is demonstrated in the following pages, subject to challenge. Or to quote Krasner again, "If the constitutive principle of sovereignty were altered, it is difficult to imagine that any other international regime would remain unchanged."[42]

In this context it might be interesting to compare the early years of the international air transport regime with international beginnings of the Internet, although a detailed comparison goes well beyond the scope of this study. In the decades after the age of aviation was launched in 1903 by the development of flightworthy engine-powered planes by the Wright brothers in the United States and Captain Louis Ferdinand Ferber in France, there was speculation that international air travel might erode the sovereignty of nations, but both government and private organizations in the various nation-states were involved from the beginning in the negotiation of regime principles and norms and have continued to be involved to the present day.[43] To create and maintain the international air transport regime, large numbers of government, industry, and international organizations—such as the International Association of Transport Airlines (IATA) or the International Civil Aviation Organization (ICAO)—have interacted over the years to initiate and refine normative structures for the free movement of commerce and passenger service, subject to the internal political control of states. At the same time, principles have evolved that have regularized or conventionalized rules and procedures for such significant and recurring issues as transnational damage control, access to markets, and conduct over the high seas.

Although intense conflict has occurred in recent decades over many air transport issues—including prices, market share, competition rules, liability limits, safety and protectionist practices at airports, and government subsidies—the international air transport regime has exhibited a number of strengths. This is so, ultimately, because the major actors involved—states, airlines, related industries and organizations, epistemic communities associated with aviation, and international organizations involved with flight—are all concerned and determined to promote the rapid and safe international movement of goods and people regardless of differing interests or in some cases because widely divergent interests could otherwise lead to irreconcilable conflict and a breakdown of international air transport systems. To quote a leading study of the international air transport regime, "The flow of commerce is promoted not just by the reduction of barriers imposed by the policies of airlines and governments, but also by the reduction of uncertainty in the costs that they face and of the resources that they expend on negotiating accords. In the area of jurisdictional rights the key provisions promoting commercial openness are the right of free access to air space above the high seas and the right of innocent passage."[44]

Experience with a wide variety of international regimes over the past century or more—including those for air transport and communications—leads to the conclusion that to be strong and successful, the international regime for the Internet will require widespread international commitments not only on the part of governments but also by private, epistemic, professional, and international organizations, similar to those exhibited for many decades in the air transport field (and in other fields as well). Although vast differences exist in the technologies, economies, and political environments of air transport and the Internet, the need for key regime actors to desire cooperation is essential to regime creation and maintenance in both issue areas.

Considerable evidence indicates that those leaders most intimately involved in updating computer protocols and standards are both well aware and supportive of the principles and norms crucial to maintaining the technical aspects of the existing Internet regime. The processes used by leading organizations responsible for developing and maintaining new protocols reflect such awareness. This is particularly true of the IETF and the W3C, both of which represent large multinational communities of network designers, operators, vendors, and researchers involved in the evolution of Internet architecture—most of whom are zealously committed to preserving its decentralized character. But it is also true of many other Internet pioneers not directly associated with IETF and W3C. One example of many such Internet leaders is a coinventor of TCP/IP, Robert Kahn, who has been working to develop "a layer above the existing Internet infrastructure" that he calls the "handle system," which would make it infinitely easier to identify, store, and retrieve data and large amounts of information on a worldwide basis.

Kahn describes his work as simply an extension of the original principles and norms of networking inherent in TCP/IP (what he calls "the Internet notion") extended to facilitate storage and use of information files.[45]

The IETF's request for comments (RFC) process—led by IETF working groups (for routing, transport, security, and similar areas), introduced elsewhere in this book—has successfully encouraged enthusiastic participation and discussion from throughout the world in the development of new protocols while reinforcing the commitment of most computer users and architects to regime principles and norms. The process for deciding on standards in the IETF was described in mid-2000 by the *Economist:*

> [Anyone in the world], however lowly, can propose a standard to the IETF, and so start a process that is formal enough to ensure that all get a hearing, but light enough to avoid bureaucracy. Once a working group has reached a decision, it submits it to the IESG [the IETF steering group] for public review and ultimate approval. To become an Internet standard, a new technology must also operate in at least two working products, such as network routers. Decisions in working groups are not taken by formal vote, but by "rough consensus"—more than a simple majority, but not unanimity. The consensus is decided by any method the group chooses. One way is "humming" when a group meets (so nobody can tell who is in favour of a proposal and who against). Those who believe that their arguments have been ignored can appeal to the IESG.[46]

The W3C functions rather differently than the IETF, but it seeks to uphold norms of decentralization as well as the consensus principle. The founder of W3C, Tim Berners-Lee, broke away from the IETF in 1994 because he wanted to avoid what he called "endless philosophical rat holes down which technical conversations would disappear."[47] Since most of the 400-plus members of W3C are companies that pay $50,000 annual membership fees, the W3C has been criticized as "a key maker of public policy . . . that ought to start acting like one, especially by opening its membership and meetings to a broader public."[48] But Berners-Lee insists that although membership in W3C is expensive and limited, his organization is still involved with "the most grassroots and collegial side of the Web community [because all of W3C's Web code is] open source software: anyone can scoop up the source code—the lines of programming—and edit and rebuild them, for free."[49]

■ LIMITATIONS OF INTERNATIONAL REGIME THEORY

Although the identification of regime principles and norms might be helpful for understanding how cooperation has been effected to operationalize the Internet internationally, regime analysis often tends to overvalue the positive and undervalue the negative aspects of international cooperation. On this point, the admonitions of Susan Strange are important to factor into one's analysis. In Strange's view,

> [Regime analysis] encourages academics to practice a kind of analytical *chiaroscuro* that leaves in shadow all the aspects of the international economy where no regimes exist and where each state elects to go its own way, while highlighting the areas of agreement where some norms and customs are generally acknowledged. It consequently gives the false impression . . . that international regimes are indeed slowly advancing against the forces of disorder and anarchy. . . . It is only too easy . . . to be misled by the proliferation of international associations and organizations, by the multiplication of declarations and documents, into concluding that there is indeed increasing positive action. The reality is that there are more areas and issues of nonagreement and controversy than there are areas of agreement.[50]

From the realist political science perspective Strange represents, the essence of the political relationships involved in international affairs is likely to be understood by examining not only an incipient international regime that might be in the process of creation but, as she says, by looking "underneath, at the bargains on which it is based."

The goal of the remainder of this study is to incorporate Strange's concerns into an analysis of the international regime for the Internet, not only focusing on the formal principles, norms, rules, and procedures that are evolving and being negotiated to build international cooperation and coordination but discussing in some detail the large number of varied interests that provide the dynamics of regime formation and maintenance and could, under some circumstances, tear the regime apart. It is hoped this will lead us to a more complete comprehension of the ways in which a mature international regime for the Internet could promote order and stability, wealth and efficiency, justice and freedom. It should also help us, however, to understand ways such a regime might—in its entirety, in certain aspects, at certain periods of its development, or because of a massive regime transformation—lead to what Strange has identified as "all the opposite qualities—insecurity and risk, poverty and waste, iniquity and constraint."[51]

▪ **NOTES**

1. Keohane, "The Theory of Hegemonic Stability," pp. 131–162. For an elaboration and adaptations of the theory, see Keohane, *After Hegemony,* pp. 78 ff.

2. A classic study is Haas, *When Knowledge Is Power.*

3. Quoted from the chapter "Knowledge-Based Theories: Ideas, Arguments, and Social Identities," in Hasenclever, Mayer, and Rittberger, *Theories of International Regimes,* p. 140.

4. Young, *Creating Regimes,* p. 2.

5. Ibid.

6. Young, "Regime Dynamics," pp. 112–113.

7. Young, *Creating Regimes,* p. 3.

8. Ibid., pp. 2–3.

9. For a history of the Internet, on which this chapter is heavily dependent, see Abbate, *Inventing the Internet.* Also useful is Moschovitis et al., *History of the Internet.* 1999. This latter volume traces the beginnings of the Internet to 1843, when the English mathematician Ada Lovelace wrote an account of the work of Charles Babbage, who designed a "programmable automatic computing machine"—which he called the Analytical Engine—designed to "perform any calculation" (p. 7).

10. At this point, too, Americans were working with a number of colleagues in Europe (especially in England, France, and Switzerland) to develop international computing networks. On the early development of international networks, see Quarterman and Hoskins, "Notable Computer Networks," pp. 932–971.

11. Abbate, *Inventing the Internet,* p. 127.

12. Quoted from an interview with Vinton Cerf by Judy O'Neill, Reston, Virginia, April 1990, in ibid., p. 128. The interview is available in the archives of the Charles Babbage Institute in Minneapolis, Minnesota, or online at http://www.cbi.umn.edu.

13. For more detail see Abbate, *Inventing the Internet,* p. 130.

14. The latest version of IP is IPv6, which first came into use in the year 2000 in Japan. Version 6 is expected to provide virtually limitless IP addresses and to improve on its predecessor (IPv4) by expanding routing and address facilities, simplifying address autoconfiguration, ensuring greater reliability and security of transactions, and providing advanced quality of service. The potential impact of IPv6 is analyzed in Wen and Tarn, "The Impact of the Next-Generation Internet Protocol," pp. 22–28.

15. For a discussion of President Gistard d'Estaing's involvement with a French effort to counter IBM's network initiatives, see "France: Protocol-Linkup Plan," pp. 69–70.

16. The closed systems of the companies are defined by Abbate, based on OSI committee documents, as follows: "They kept the technical workings of their systems hidden from competitors, used patents and copyrights to prevent others from duplicating their technology, made it hard to interface their equip-

ment with components from third parties, and reserved the right to change their 'standards' at will." Abbate, *Inventing the Internet,* pp. 168–169. See also Passmore, "The Networking Standards Collision," pp. 98–106.

17. Quoted from Abbate, *Inventing the Internet,* p. 169. The *ISO Technical Committee Reports* (Committee 16, Subcommittees 16, N34, and 6, N1558) are available in "Provisional Model of Open-Systems Architecture," pp. 49–62.

18. For a description of the seven layers and their functions, see Abbate, *Inventing the Internet,* p. 170. See also McCrum, "Data Interchange," pp. 24–33.

19. Abbate, *Inventing the Internet,* p. 169.

20. Outlined in *Open Systems Interconnection Protocols,* quoted in ibid., p. 171.

21. In the United States the National Bureau of Standards initiated a Program in Open Systems Interconnection and in 1983 began to sponsor workshops to help computer companies develop products consistent with the OSI framework. The OSI metastandard was particularly welcomed in Western Europe for two reasons: (1) European leaders had been searching for ways to integrate the West European economies and had been unable to develop networking standards on their own, (2) European computer companies were too small to aspire to imposing their own standards and therefore saw the OSI framework as a means of gaining leverage against the dominance of the U.S. multinationals. Abbate, *Inventing the Internet,* pp. 171–172.

22. Ibid., p. 171.

23. Ibid., p. 167.

24. This outline of principles and norms differs slightly from, but is inclusive of, those found in Gillett and Kapor, "The Self-Governing Internet," pp. 16 ff.

25. Historians of the early years of the Internet have also acknowledged the valuable role of Jon Postel in documenting standards during his leadership of IETF, ending with his death in 1998. Postel assembled and posted on the IETF website almost 2,000 documents he called RFCs (requests for comments), many of which were final drafts written by leading computer scientists on a wide range of subjects relating to technical internetworking standards development. The result of this online "discussion" was often the acceptance of specific protocols or standards as the de facto lingua franca for thousands of network administrators and software designers, who found them essential for effecting compatibility between systems. In this way, some of them became binding in an informal and voluntary way, characterized by soft law. Postel and others in the engineering community occasionally patented some of these standards to avoid their being patented by proprietary interests.

26. Abbate, *Inventing the Internet,* pp. 178–179.

27. In the Krasner volume, regime *principles* are defined as "beliefs of fact, causation, and rectitude"; regime *norms* are "standards of behavior defined in terms of rights and obligations." For an elaboration of these definitions, see Krasner, *International Regimes,* pp. 2 ff.

28. Jervis, "Security Regimes," in *ibid.,* p. 173.

29. For an analysis of the role of regime principles and norms in the security regime called the Concert of Europe, which Jervis describes as the only security regime ever brought into being, see ibid., pp. 182 ff.

30. For an elaboration of the aspects of international regime theory, see Krasner, *International Regimes,* pp. 3–4.

31. Quarterman and Hoskins, "Notable Computer Networks," p. 945.

32. Abbate, *Inventing the Internet,* p. 188.

33. Metcalfe, *Packet Communication,* pp. 10–12.

34. Abbate, *Inventing the Internet,* p. 214.

35. Berners-Lee et al., "The World-Wide Web," p. 76.

36. Schatz and Hardin, "NCSA Mosaic and the World Wide Web," pp. 895–901.

37. An attempt to develop a fairly comprehensive understanding of the several hundred Internet technical standards that have been proposed, the several dozen that have been accepted, and the many standards development organizations involved is Libicki et al., *Scaffolding the New Web,* pp. 21 ff.

38. Abbate, *Inventing the Internet,* p. 215.

39. Young, "Regime Dynamics," pp. 94–95.

40. Ibid., p. 96.

41. One of the most forceful articles in this regard is Mowshowitz, "Virtual Feudalism," pp. 213–231. The thesis of this article is that "the absorption of [new technologies] and related instruments into standard operating procedures—made possible by computer-communications technology—is creating a fundamental realignment of economics and politics. The nation-state will decline in importance, sovereign power will come to be exercised by private organizations, and personal relationships will become ever more evanescent" (p. 213).

42. Quotes in this paragraph are from Krasner, *International Regimes,* p. 18. See also Krasner, *Sovereignty,* pp. 220 ff.

43. Like the early days of the Internet, the early days of flight produced countless new inventions, many carried out with support from the U.S. government for defense purposes whereas the development of civil aviation was led by private entrepreneurs (like Robert Six and Howard Hughes) who made fortunes at a very young age. Governments around the world were often confounded in their attempts to understand and control many of the consequences of the new technology. See, for example, Gidwitz, *The Politics of Air Transport,* pp. 37 ff., and Davies, *Rebels and Reformers of the Airways.* Some of the early correspondence among the Wright brothers, the U.S. War Department, and other government officials appears in Scott, *The Pioneers of Flight;* see especially pp. 137 ff.

44. Zacher with Sutton, *Governing Global Networks,* p. 125.

45. Instead of identifying the *place* where a file is located, as is the case with TCP/IP, Kahn's additional layer of network architecture assigns an identifier called a "handle" *to the information itself.* The information then becomes a digital object (e.g., a web page, a music file, a video file, a book chapter, dental

X rays) that can be readily retrieved and maintained by individual Internet users without having to endure the long delays and intricate maneuvers involved in performing the same tasks by going through IP addresses on Domain Name System (DNS) servers. For more information, see the article by Zaret, "Internet Pioneer Urges Overhaul," pp. 1–8.

46. "The Consensus Machine," p. 73.

47. Quoted in ibid., p. 74.

48. The quote is from Simson Garfinkel, a technology journalist, in ibid.

49. Berners-Lee with Fischetti, *Weaving the Web,* pp. 94–95. For a description of the process followed by the W3C in developing protocols and standards, see its process document at http://www.w3.org. One of the most recent standards developed by W3C is Extensible Markup Language (XML), which Berners-Lee describes as "the first step toward the next generation Web"—which is very much in the tradition of the principles and norms outlined for the international regime for the Internet in this volume.

50. Strange, *"Cave! Hic Dragones,"* p. 349.

51. Ibid., p. 354.

Global Internet Governance

I n the literature on international regimes, considerable emphasis is necessarily placed on the process by which issues get put on the active political agenda of policymakers. Policymaking at the international level is usually fairly different than comparable processes at the national level, where domestic constituencies add an urgency not usually present in international affairs. There are periods of war or catastrophe (or potential war or catastrophe) that focus the immediate attention of policymakers around the world on international matters or occasions where drastic changes (such as the end of the Cold War) might attract inordinate attention. In "normal times," however, issues usually become part of the active political agenda at the international level only when they acquire "champions"—leaders who will adopt an issue as their own, move it to the top of their own personal scale of priorities, and be willing to spend their political capital to try to persuade others of the issue's importance and urgency.

Even when issues force their way onto the active international political agenda, however, they seldom trigger *negotiation* of a process of regime formation. Such negotiation will take place only when an issue area clearly has overriding importance and the agenda has more or less been set for negotiations to take place. Key features of *agenda setting* have been summarized by Young as "the identification of players to be invited to participate, the setting in which negotiations will occur, the timing of the first round of negotiations, and remaining conceptual questions, like the breadth or narrowness of the items to be considered by the negotiators."[1] In the establishment of protocols and standards for the international Internet regime, the movement from agenda setting to the negotiation of regime principles and norms and their operationalization moved fairly quickly in the technical realm, largely because of (1) the immediacy of the need to establish protocols and standards if the Internet were to function with a minimal degree of effectiveness and order, (2) the relatively small number of players with sufficient knowledge and interest to be involved in the determination of Internet protocols and standards, and (3) accelerating demand—particularly in the United States, Canada, Europe, and Japan—for access to what was widely viewed as a series of dramatic new inventions, particularly after the Internet was enhanced by the World Wide Web.

Once technical protocol and standards issues had been sufficiently settled to make possible the physical operationalization of the Internet, however, there was much less urgency to immediately build a more robust international Internet regime. In the 1990s international policymakers increasingly realized that they would eventually have to deal with, among others, issues of Internet administration and governance, Internet economic and commercial matters (including especially intellectual property concerns), and a host of issues related to cyberterrorism, cyberwar, and cyberlaw. But most policymakers exhibited initial reluctance to put international Internet issues at the top of their political agendas, for a variety of reasons: (1) the Internet entailed subjects about which they knew little; (2) to the extent policymakers were concerned about the Internet, they were busy trying to sort out its domestic impact without trying to deal with its international ramifications; and (3) the Internet seemed to be growing so dramatically and doing so well that most policymakers were either in awe of it or were trying to cope with personal and staff efforts to get themselves and their offices up and running online.

In the key area of *Internet governance,* however, events moved rather quickly in the late 1990s to force the issue onto the agendas of international policymakers. This has resulted in the initiation of negotiations among a wide variety of international actors designed to establish principles and norms that are beginning to be operationalized as rules and procedures for Internet governance. This chapter is an attempt to better understand the agenda-setting and negotiation stages for the development of the Internet governance aspects of the international regime by analyzing the diverse interests of some of the key champions and actors involved.

■ PRIVATIZING INTERNET
MANAGEMENT AND GOVERNANCE

Prior to 1986 the Internet backbone was directly owned and controlled by the U.S. Department of Defense (DOD) or its contractors.[2] The creation of the National Science Foundation network (NSFnet) in 1986 provided both a backbone with much higher-speed capabilities to extend and improve DOD's ARPANET and a means for universities and research institutions not funded by DOD to gain access to Internet resources. During the next six years (1986–1992) Internet governance and management functions became divided between DOD and NSF, with a number of private associations playing various roles (discussed later). Core funding was provided not only by DOD and NSF but also by the National Aeronautics and Space Administration (NASA) and the Department of Energy.

Throughout this early period NSF and other U.S. government agencies, like DARPA before them, worked closely with a core group of computer scientists and engineers on network design and related inventions. Although governance patterns were changing, considerable continuity was provided by two key leaders—Vinton Cerf and Robert Kahn—who had been part of ARPANET's original Network Working Group (NWG) in the 1960s (Cerf was DARPA's Internet program manager). When the NWG disbanded in the early 1970s, Cerf and Kahn set up an advisory group of network experts called the Internet Configuration Control Board (ICCB) to coordinate discussion of technical questions among government and private groups and to "oversee the network's architectural evolution."[3] The ICCB was replaced in 1985 by the Internet Activities Board (IAB), chaired by David Clark of the Massachusetts Institute of Technology (MIT) for many years, with core members from DOD and MIT; from the acoustic and computing firm Bolt, Beranek, and Newman (which had built the infrastructure of the original ARPANET); from the University of Southern California's Information Sciences Institute; and from the Corporation for National Research Initiatives (a private-sector computer networking think tank formed by Cerf and Kahn).

The IAB, which changed its name to the Internet Architecture Board in 1992, set up a unique procedure for discussion and resolution of governance issues by opening its membership to anyone anywhere in the world with technical knowledge and related interests and with sufficient time to invest in the Internet Engineering Task Force's (IETF) elaborate discussions. Discussion forums held on the Internet became so popular—with participants numbering in the hundreds—that it became necessary in 1989 to divide IAB activities between IETF, to lead protocol development and address immediate technical concerns, and an Internet Research Task Force (IRTF) to focus on long-range planning. Working groups within these task forces communicated via e-mail, held meetings several times each year, and generally sought consensus solutions to networking problems after proposed protocols were tested in practice.[4] When NSF and ARPA decided to merge their networks in the late 1980s, NSF folded its technical group into the IETF, at that time part of ARPA. In later years IETF took on members from the Department of Energy and NASA and became, in Abbate's perhaps somewhat exaggerated words, "the single arbiter of internet-working standards for the federal government."[5]

A major watershed in Internet governance took place in 1992, when NSF decided it could no longer run the backbone and "privatized" it by giving it over to public and private companies to manage. As part of privatization, the decision was also made to move the system's technical administration out of the U.S. government entirely, with the result that formal oversight of IAB and IETF was contracted to the Internet Society (ISOC), a private organization chartered by members of IETF, presumably representing the "Internet community." In fact, however, the Internet community had become so large by the mid-1990s that it was divided into several different kinds of communities; broken down in turn into many different factional groups with competing and conflicting interests in Internet governance issues. Confronted with a variety of perspectives as to how the Internet might be structured in the future, ISOC initially committed to the following agenda:[6]

- To assure discrimination-free Internet access
- To halt censorship of online communication
- To limit government control over essential elements of networking architecture
- To encourage cooperation between interconnected networks
- To guard against misuse of personal information offered on the Internet

ISOC's initial agenda represented primarily the interests of U.S. academics and computer experts. It fell somewhat flat with the other two major sets of groups with paramount interest in future Internet development mentioned earlier—commercial and business interests (in the United States and elsewhere) and government telecommunications and other Internet-related government organizations around the world. Business leaders became increasingly convinced of the significance of the Internet during the 1980s and 1990s, but they were less enthused about ISOC's initial agenda than about the potential for the Internet to fundamentally alter business practices and, more particularly, about such new developments as e-commerce, online banking, and business-to-business networks. At the same time, government-run Internet-related companies in other countries often tended to view the expansion of the Internet with alarm, fearing it would strengthen and expand U.S. dominance in the computing industry, even though they usually also realized it was in their interest (and the interests of their respective countries) to keep pace with the Internet's development. These competing interests led to a number of more specific differences when technical administration and formal oversight of the Internet were contracted out from NSF to ISOC.

■ AGENDA FORMATION FOR INTERNET GOVERNANCE AND THE DOMAIN NAME SYSTEM

Not surprisingly, concerns about privatization of the Internet focused on the Domain Name System (DNS), designed in 1983 primarily by Paul Mockapetris of the University of Southern California Information Services Institute (in RFC 882) and fleshed out in 1984 by Jan Postel in RFC 920. The DNS assigns specific names (written as unique numerical addresses) for each machine on the network, so that the act of being on the network requires being connected to a machine that has been assigned a specific name. Whenever anyone sends a message to a particular name, the message automatically goes first to a DNS server, usually operated by local Internet Service Providers (ISPs), to find the correct numerical address for the name. Each of these DNS servers then goes to one particular computer (called the "root server") to find the numerical addresses that will enable the servers to send the message on its way. Particularly valuable have been the so-called generic Top-Level Domains (gTLDs) (initially, in 1984, .com, .edu, .gov, .mil, and .org, to which were subsequently added in 1985 .net. and .int and in 2000 .biz, .info, .name, .pro, .museum, .aero, and .coop). In addition, the root server also sends message to 240 two-digit domains (equivalent to country codes) for countries and territories, called ccTLDs (e.g., .jp for Japan or .uk for the United Kingdom).

David Post has described the root server and the various domain servers that interact with it as "the very heart of the Internet, the Archimedean point on which this vast global network balances" or, alternatively, as a "passport without which passage across the border into cyberspace is impossible."[7] As Post and others have pointed out, because the root server internationally, and the DNS servers for particular networks, are *single controlling points* that could potentially be used to choke off access to the Internet, they have enormous value in political and economic terms. In the most extreme case they can be, in Post's words, "a matter of [network] life or death: if your name and address cannot be found on the 'authoritative server,' you simply do not exist— at least not on the Internet."[8] More routinely, control of the root server and the system of domain name allocation could provide a mechanism for (1) collecting fees or taxes (those who do not pay the fee or tax lose their domain name or have it suspended), (2) regulating behavior or collecting information, and (3) enforcing intellectual property rules and laws. In addition to the potential ability to use the root server and DNS to threaten suspension from, or bar access to, the Internet, the DNS system has also become important because the domain names themselves (e.g., www.ibm.com or www.newyorktimes.com) are often trademarks that have traditionally been protected by the courts.

In the early years of the Internet, the domain name and address administration was handled by the University of Southern California's Information Sciences Institute (USC-ISI), with funding from DARPA, under the direction of Jon Postel.[9] Postel created an informal organization known as the Internet Assigned Numbers Authority (IANA), which was accepted as a constituent organization of ISOC in 1992 but never had legal standing. Postel's attempt in 1994 to "charter" IANA and transfer his USC-ISI government contract to that authority was unsuccessful. Although Postel often referred to IANA as being chartered to the Internet Society, in 1994 the National Science Foundation reached a five-year cooperative agreement with Network Solutions, Inc. (NSI)—a private, for-profit corporation—to handle domain name registrations under .com and other generic Top-Level Domains (the registration service is called InterNIC). NSI originally agreed to run the InterNIC operation for a fixed payment of $1 million annually, but in July 1995 it relinquished that right in return for U.S. government approval allowing it to charge fees for domain name registrations. Collection of domain name registration fees has since provided a lucrative, multimillion dollar revenue stream for NSI.

Milton Mueller has described NSI's domain registration activities as "a commercial beachhead in the heart of Internet administration."[10] With a monopoly on the registration of the Top-Level Domain addresses—.com, .edu, .gov, .net, and .org (the other Top-Level Domains—.mil and .int—are not available to the general public)—InterNIC quickly became an extremely lucrative part of NSI's business. NSI agreed to put 30 percent of funds raised from domain registrations in an Internet Intelligence Infrastructure Fund but kept 70 percent for itself.[11] In 1996 the InterNIC monopoly was estimated by *Wired* magazine to be worth $1 billion to NSI.[12] By March 2000, VeriSign, Inc., had agreed to acquire NSI for $21 *billion* in stock, with this incredible worth stemming almost exclusively from NSI's position as the leading provider of Internet domain name registrations.[13]

During NSI's first five-year contract (1994–1998), rivalry and animosity grew between ISOC and NSI. ISOC sensed that a key feature of its long stewardship of the civilian part of the Internet was being surrendered to NSI, and many ISOC leaders resented NSI's for-profit approach and its lack of fit with the less commercially oriented orientation of the computer science and academic communities. In June 1996 the ISOC board endorsed an IANA plan, drafted by Postel, that would have replaced the NSI contract at its expiration in 1998 with competitive registration services run by many different companies. ISOC proposed that 150 new "descriptive" Top-Level Domain names (e.g., .biz, .sports, .news, and the like) be established before the end of the NSI contract and that the companies running each new registration service established after 1998 pay a fixed $2,000 fee plus 2 percent of income into a fund managed by ISOC.

The 1996 ISOC proposal went nowhere, encountering intense opposition from both international business and the leaders of the international government-run Internet infrastructure. Trademark interests objected to a vast expansion of top-level name space because they feared it would lead to uncontrollable domain name speculation and trademark infringement. From the perspective of the large public telecommunications companies that have traditionally dominated the International Telecommunications Union (ITU), the 1996 ISOC proposal, if implemented, would have made it far more difficult for governments around the world to maintain central control of the operation of

Internet activities within their own borders. But ISOC quickly recognized that it had to build an effective alliance with the international trademark community and the government organizations that made up the ITU if it were to gain legitimacy or recognized legal authority for any scheme to control the Internet's root servers. In October 1996, therefore, ISOC created an eleven-member blue ribbon international panel called the International Ad Hoc Committee (IAHC), with two representatives from large trademark associations (the International Trademark Association [INTA] and the World Intellectual Property Organization [WIPO]), two from the ITU, and two from NSF. The remaining five members of the IAHC were called "technical members," with all five coming from IETF/ISOC and all selected by Postel.[14]

The IAHC quickly put together a second ISOC-led proposal, also ultimately unsuccessful, based on the model used by the British Internet industry to manage the .uk Top-Level Domain. This proposal was based on a conception of Internet domain name space as "a public resource" that would be organized as a single monopoly registry administered on a nonprofit basis, but the registry would be co-owned by many different competing "registrars" that could all register names in all of the TLDs. In contrast to the 1996 ISOC proposal, IAHC proposed only seven new TLDs (.web, .info, .nom, .firm, .rec, .arts, .store), a concession to trademark interests that saw this limited expansion as much easier to police than the several hundred TLDs that would have been added under the previous proposal. The IAHC proposal also envisaged extraordinary powers for trademark interests by recommending a sixty-day waiting period for a new domain name to be approved, during which time the application for the name would be subject to review by WIPO administrative challenge panels. The IAHC's recommendation for a complex Internet governance structure was outlined in a document known as the Generic Top-Level Domain Memorandum of Understanding (gTLD-MoU), which led to the establishment of a nonprofit Council of Registrars (CORE), incorporated in Geneva, even though the governing structure CORE was to administer never came into existence. In the IAHC plan, the governing authority within CORE was to be a Policy Oversight Committee (POC) whose membership was similar to that of the IAHC itself (two members each to be appointed by ISOC, the IAB, IANA, and CORE; one member each appointed by ITU, INTA, and WIPO).

The IAHC proposal met with more widespread criticism than the first ISOC proposal, particularly after ISOC and the ITU organized an "official" signing ceremony in Geneva in March 1997. Critics pointed out that neither the IAHC nor any of its constituent representative organizations had any legal claim or formal authority over the Internet root. U.S. secretary of state Madeline Albright wrote a memo, published in the Congressional Record, criticizing the ITU secretariat for acting "without authorization of member governments to hold a global meeting involving an unauthorized expenditure of resources and concluding with a quote international agreement unquote."[15] The NSI launched a lobbying campaign against the gTLD-MoU shared registry model, many Internet user groups criticized the IAHC proposal as a sellout to the trademark interests, the European Commission opposed the plan as "too U.S.-centric" because it lacked EU representatives, and the eighty or more companies that had paid fees upward of $20,000 to become CORE registrars became increasingly upset and regretful over their investments in the venture.

At this point (mid-1997), many argued that no progress had been made in developing a viable plan for the future of either Internet governance or domain name registration. In the parlance of international regime theoreticians, however, the governance issue had been pushed to the top of the agendas of both international policymakers and Internet leaders. This happened because the two IANA/ISOC proposals were so controversial that they sent representatives of the various interests scurrying to contact government and corporate leaders in more than a dozen countries whose leaders were already intensely alert to the implications of Internet governance for their future interests. This was significant for understanding the formation of the Internet's international regime because it signaled the onset of a transition from the agenda-setting to the negotiation stage of regime formation in Internet governance.

▪ REGIME NEGOTIATIONS ON INTERNET GOVERNANCE

The negotiations stage of international regime formation requires some form of explicit agreement among major actors in the issue area concerned. International regime negotiations do not necessarily have to result in legally binding conventions or treaties but can instead be imbedded in other forms of international agreement, such as ministerial declarations or even a variety of soft law arrangements that spell out the terms of a constitutive contract. Unwritten side agreements, informal deals or tacit understandings, and other informal elements that might promote the success of a regime as a result of social practices over time can all be important parts of the negotiation phase of regime formation as well. Although international regime negotiations entail hard bargaining and attempts by the parties involved to exploit whatever bargaining leverage they can muster, there is also, in Young's words, "a creative component to this process":

> The participants seldom have a clear picture of the payoff possibility set when they embark on negotiations; much of the negotiation process is exploratory in nature and involves efforts to expand the range of possibilities available. What is more, the agreement eventually reached often does no more than set a regime in motion, with the expectation that it will evolve and take on more substantive content as a response to experience with the regime in practice.[16]

It is in this context that the onset of the negotiations stage for international Internet regime governance might be said to have been initiated in the late 1990s. More specifically, the initiation of the negotiations phase might be traced to the decision by the Clinton administration to remove responsibility for the negotiations from NSF and place them squarely with the Commerce Department's National Telecommunications and Information Administration (NTIA). The announcement of this transfer of responsibility came on July 1, 1997, in a presidential executive order authorizing the secretary of commerce to "support efforts to make the governance of the domain name system private and competitive and to create a contractually based self-regulatory regime that deals with potential conflicts between domain name usage and trademark laws on a global basis."[17] In this presidential executive order, the U.S. government asserted its ultimate authority over the Internet root, but it also indicated its willingness to negotiate with international stakeholders about future Internet governance.

The position of the U.S. Commerce Department on Internet governance issues is spelled out in a white paper it released on June 3, 1998, which emphasized the importance of electronic commerce to the future world economy, advocated the principle that the private sector should lead Internet development, and called on governments to avoid placing undue restrictions on electronic commerce while facilitating its development by enforcing a "predictable, minimalist, consistent, and simple legal environment."[18] Rather than try to suggest or create a governance structure itself, the authors of the white paper announced that the Commerce Department expected "the private sector" to be able to somehow develop a consensus within the next four months that would result in the formation of a private corporation that could in turn carry out the negotiation process with Internet stakeholders and eventually reach a worldwide agreement on Internet governance. The white paper also provided for the formal involvement of WIPO in the negotiations process, requesting that WIPO initiate an investigation of trademark conflicts for the purpose of making recommendations as to how disputes might be resolved and how the creation of new TLDs might affect trademark holders.

In what might be viewed as a classic regime negotiation stance, the 1998 white paper attempted to respond to what its authors perceived to be a variety of domestic and international interests. To satisfy a widespread feeling that Internet governance should not be in the hands of any one government or be the subject of an overarching formal treaty (a feeling that resonated with particular intensity in the computer engineering and other academic communities), the white paper's authors chose not to create a new government organization or suggest any new laws or treaties. But to satisfy the business community the white paper promised continued government involvement to ensure the stability of the Internet and protect trademark holders while allowing "industry self-regulation." Responding to pressures from the European Community and concerned organizations in a few other parts of the world (a number of Australians and Japanese were active in the discussions at a very early stage and remain active), the white paper suggested ways for formal international involvement in the negotiations process. Included in this aspect of the white paper's recommendations was the prominent role for WIPO, a formal treaty organization based in Geneva with a strong international membership and tradition.

Although the white paper provided a focus for negotiations for all key actors with interests in Internet governance issues, its rather open-ended invitation for private-sector leadership to emerge within four months led to calls for an open process and new forms of online democracy. A number of meetings, forums, and conferences (most of which took place online) were "self-organized" by a wide variety of individuals and groups, many of which came together in a series of four international meetings in July–August 1998—in Herndon, Virginia (where NSI is located), Geneva, Singapore, and Buenos Aires—collectively called the International Forum on the White Paper (IFWP). IFWP leaders often referred to these meetings as an "Internet Constitutional Convention," and some maintained substantial records of their attempts to develop "consensus points."[19] Other significant groups that became involved in the discussion were the Open Root Server Confederation (ORSC), representing a number of "alternative" domain registries that had support from NSI; the Boston Working Group (BWG), which was generally critical of ISOC and the white paper process; the Commercial Internet eXchange (CIX); CORE; and the World Internet Alliance.

At the October 1998 deadline, NTIA received three proposals for the new private corporation that would conduct negotiations for Internet governance—one from the BWG, a second from ORSC, and the third from the ISOC-led coalition. In contrast to the IFWP and other groups pursuing an open process, ISOC had spent the previous four months working with a relatively small group of leaders from around the world, representing key constituencies, to draft articles of incorporation and bylaws for a new corporation and to establish a board of directors. U.S. Commerce Department leaders and presidential policy adviser Ira Magaziner were part of these discussions, which were spearheaded not only by IANA/ISOC but also by IBM and the European Commission. Although the ISOC-led coalition was strongly criticized for its unwillingness to submit to a completely open process of negotiation, it could and did argue that it had built a rudimentary consensus among major world government leaders and corporate interests, which was not the case for the BWG or ORSC proposals. In addition to support from the European Commission, which had been critical of previous ISOC efforts, the 1998 ISOC-led coalition's proposal was endorsed by organizations with official backing from Japan and Australia, as well as world trademark interests and major e-commerce corporations (with IBM taking a lead role). A key factor in bringing this coalition of interests together was the desire by all of the partners to isolate NSI and end its monopoly over the domain name registration system.

In the final stages of the white paper process in September 1998, the IFWP attempted to bring IANA/ISOC, NSI, and other Internet stakeholders together to draft a consensual constitution for the new private corporation, but IANA/ISOC rejected the approach. Instead, IANA/ISOC entered into negotiations with NSI in September 1998, emerged with a joint draft agreement, and then backed away from that agreement.[20] In early October 1998, at the same time it submitted its proposal to the Commerce Department, IANA/ISOC formally incorporated the new private corporation outlined in its proposal, the Internet Corporation for Assigned Names and Numbers (ICANN), with headquarters in Marina Del Rey, California. IANA/ISOC also unilaterally announced its selection of the nine "interim" board members who would build the new corporation.

The creation of ICANN was clearly the result of a negotiating process led by the IANA/ISOC coalition in conjunction with Ira Magaziner and the U.S. Commerce Department. ICANN's initial active board members were drawn from IANA, the gTLD-MoU coalition, and IBM; the first chief executive officer (CEO) of the new corporation was Mike Roberts, a charter member of ISOC and, in Mueller's words, "a fierce gTLD-MoU partisan."[21] ICANN produced controversy in the way it was created and immediately faced downright hostility from critics who argued that ICANN—if legitimized by NTIA—would have tremendous powers with no accountability, would be soft on civil liberties issues, and especially did not represent the full spectrum of Internet users. The atmosphere among Internet users was particularly charged when Jon Postel died, at age fifty-five on October 18, 1998. Two days after Postel's death NTIA "tentatively" accepted the IANA/ISOC proposal, with the proviso that it be "refined" in consultation with "groups and others who commented critically on [it] to try and broaden the consensus."[22] In response to NTIA's concerns, the ICANN interim board made a number of changes in its articles of incorporation and bylaws, committing itself to the creation of an open membership structure. With those changes, ICANN was accepted by the U.S. Commerce Department on November 25, 1998, as the private corporation that the Clinton administration would work with to build the governance aspects of the international Internet regime.

Shortly after its creation, ICANN became involved in what many observers called a series of "DNS wars." It has since faced constant criticism from key people and groups in various Internet communities who have charged that ICANN has reneged on its promise to build an open, at-large membership and democratic processes of decisionmaking. It has often been accused of putting results over fairness by developing rules and procedures for control of the Internet root and domain name system without first building consensus on the principles and norms to be followed in the rule-making and procedure-building processes. Nonetheless, ICANN has been able to strike bargains with the Commerce Department, NSI, trademark interests and large corporations, and foreign governments to establish new domain name policies consistent with the goals of the white paper. In 1999, for example, ICANN worked with WIPO to create a global, uniform dispute resolution procedure to resolve disputes between trademark holders and domain name registrants (this activity is discussed in detail in Chapter 4). In addition, ICANN has struggled to develop policies in three areas.

First, ICANN has worked with NSI and the Commerce Department to build a *shared registration system* that has opened up the .com, .net, and .org TLDs to competing registrars. Beginning in April 1999, NSI lost its monopoly over domain name registrations when ICANN accredited five other companies to register domain names in the .com, .net, and .org TLDs as part of a "test-bed" phase of a "shared registry."[23] By October 1999 ICANN had accredited eighty-seven additional companies as registrars to register domain names ending in .com, .net, and .org and had expanded the Shared Registry System to extend to all accredited registrars willing to sign the standard test-bed registrar agreements with NSI and meet technical certification requirements.[24] Although implemented by ICANN, this "shared system" was the result of direct intervention by the U.S. Commerce Department, which effected the system in its contractual agreement with NSI and imposed price regulations on NSI and other registrars. As Mueller has pointed out, the complicated arrangements Commerce concluded with NSI and ICANN in April 1999 did not introduce a completely open-ended competition but instead resulted in a system wherein NSI agreed to be regulated and NTIA offered "regulated discounts to a special class of businesses that paid ICANN for the privilege of accreditation." In Mueller's words,

> The real impact of the changes was to put authority over registrars in ICANN's rather than NSI's hands, and to allow ICANN to exploit its government-created gateway into the .com, .net and .org database as a source of revenue. Furthermore, by reducing the price of dot com registrations and creating an expanded sales force for NSI's .com, .net and .org domain names, the shared registration system reinforced rather than undermined the market dominance of the NSI generic TLDs. Not surprisingly, NSI was willing to go along with this step in the transition.[25]

The Commerce Department's actions with regard to domain names competition have reflected both its representation of the Clinton administration's goals for ICANN (to build a private corporation for managing Internet domain names and addresses with the "consensual support" of "the Internet community") and the department's charge to promote U.S. and international business. In 1999 Commerce was concerned that NSI had a monopoly as a registrar of domain names, which enabled NSI to develop enormous market power, but Commerce was also aware that an indiscriminate opening up to competition by the addition of new TLDs would add considerably to the difficulties already encountered by business firms in their efforts to protect their trademarks and other intellectual property in cyberspace. An indiscriminate opening up of TLDs to competition would also have entailed risks that the Department of Commerce might surrender control of the Internet governing process without putting in place a new system of governance capable of protecting intellectual property online. In 1997, therefore, when NSI responded to criticisms of its monopoly by requesting that the Clinton administration add new TLDs to the DNS root, Commerce refused to accede to the request, even though the proposed measure had the solid backing of NSF. At that point Commerce had readied its own proposal to add only five new TLDs to the root, but it did not go forth administratively with the idea in 1998 in deference to pressures from almost everyone (trademark interests, foreign governments, and ISOC) to leave decisions on TLD additions to the new corporation being created, which eventually became ICANN.

Many computer users viewed the long delays by the U.S. Commerce Department in allowing the addition of new TLDs as a setback to the principle of decentralized authority that had been widely accepted by the engineering community in establishing the technical protocols and standards that first made the Internet operational. The same delays, however, were generally viewed by trademark interests and governments—including country code TLD registries and large businesses with an established stake in the .com TLD—as supporting their efforts to design a robust and competitive international Internet regime for e-commerce and e-business. In this atmosphere, the introduction of registrar competition in three existing TLDs was considered to be relatively insignificant in comparison with the major trademark and e-business issues being negotiated on other fronts. A discussion of those issues forms the basis of Chapter 3.

In the second area, ICANN established *centralized control over the registration process* by concluding a series of agreements among itself, the Commerce Department, and NSI.[26] The core features of these agreements are as follows:

1. It was noted in the agreements that although the Commerce Department "may" at some point in the future transfer "management of the authoritative root" from NSI to ICANN (or its successor), "the Department of Commerce has no plans to transfer

to any entity its policy authority to direct the authoritative root server."[27] The insertion of this clause in the agreements made clear the determination of the U.S. government to retain authority over the basic infrastructure of the Internet, at least until a satisfactory alternative can be devised and implemented.[28]

2. ICANN was recognized in the agreements as the *authority accrediting registrars* for the gTLD registry, with the explicit proviso that its policy authority (designated to ICANN by the Commerce Department) could be terminated if ICANN did not succeed in bringing other registries into the new centralized registration process.

3. ICANN agreed to contract NSI as the gTLD registry for four years (2000–2004), with the further understanding that the contract would be extended for another four years (2004–2008) if NSI fully divested itself of at least 75 percent of its stake in either its *registry* or its *registrar* functions within eighteen months.

4. It was agreed that NSI would continue to operate the authoritative root server system in accordance with directions provided by the U.S. Commerce Department. NSI also agreed to accept domain name registrations only from ICANN-accredited registrars and agreed not to deploy an alternative DNS root server system.

5. In a move designed to give NSI leverage over ICANN's taxing policies, the fees ICANN was allowed to impose on registrars were required by the agreements to be "equitably apportioned" and approved by a combination of registrars who were paying two-thirds of the fees (at the time, NSI controlled three-quarters of the world's domain name registrations, so it was able to meet the two-thirds requirement all by itself). The yearly amount of the registrar fees NSI paid to ICANN was set at $1.25 million initially and capped at $2 million. The amount NSI could charge other registries (its so-called wholesale price) was capped at $6 per name-year, whereas retail prices (i.e., what any ICANN-accredited registry could charge for use of a domain name) were deregulated and therefore subject to open competitive pricing.[29]

The successful conclusion of negotiations among ICANN, NSI, and the Commerce Department in September–November 1999 laid the groundwork for a system of Internet governance designed to last for at least an eight-year period. The 1999 agreements reconciled a number of differing positions on key issues that had produced the DNS wars the previous decade. Although ICANN was recognized by the U.S. government to manage the Internet address system and to foster the growth of registries that would be competitive with NSI, the NSI had been able to prevent ICANN from gaining complete oversight. By agreeing to a new competition in which it was the only registry with the additional charge of running the root server and with some approval power and a head start on registrations built up over the previous six years (NSI had already registered more than 5 million names by 1999), NSI could now plan for the next eight years with solid assurances that it would be able to build even more lucrative revenue streams for both its retail and wholesale domain name businesses. Although NSI was required by the agreements to unload 75 percent of its stake in either its registry or its registrar operations, business analysts were universally agreed that the remaining 25 percent of one or the other (it turned out to be the registry) would still make NSI an extremely valuable company. The extent to which there was agreement on Wall Street was indicated when NSI stock increased in value by 17 percent in the first few days following the announcement of the agreements.[30]

For ICANN the September 1999 agreements were equally appealing because they enabled the organization's leadership to reach an accommodation with NSI in which NSI—for the first time—formally acknowledged ICANN's oversight authority (derived from the U.S. government) over both the root server and the domain name accreditation process. The agreements also outlined orderly procedures by which domain name registrations would be handled, which involved the widespread participation of companies in many different parts of the world. ICANN also received a much-needed financial boost from the agreements in the form of the $1.25 million in fees NSI would pay up front, along with other lesser fees built into the agreements. Although the agreements did not solve all of the problems confronting ICANN and the Commerce Department in their efforts to build an international Internet governance mechanism, they did produce what one observer called a "cease-fire" in the DNS wars, which enabled ICANN and Commerce to spend more time than would otherwise have been the case on other issues.[31]

Finally, ICANN has experimented with a number of different ways to develop an *at-large membership and democratic processes of decisionmaking*. This matter is likely to be of crucial importance to

ICANN's future because of the unusual nature of the organization. As Jonathan Zittrain has pointed out,

> A mere trade association model does not capture the breadth of ICANN's responsibilities and intended structure, both because of the diversity of Internet stakeholders and because of the powerful, quasi-regulatory decisions that ICANN will make. ICANN is supposed to act in the public interest, not beholden to any one stakeholder. It is as if a private "International Communications Commission," comprised of all interested parties with a vested stake, were to attempt to allocate radio spectrum that had never been explicitly designated a public resource.[32]

Throughout the white paper process that led to the creation of ICANN, the Commerce Department and a number of Internet constituencies demanded that the new corporation be structured in such a way that it would act much like a *public* organization while at the same time being incorporated as a *private* organization with private management virtues. This dual mandate was outlined in the white paper as follows:

> The new corporation should operate as a private entity for the benefit of the Internet community as a whole. The development of sound, fair and widely accepted policies for the management of DNS will depend on input from the broad and growing community of Internet users. Management structures should reflect the functional and geographic diversity of the Internet and its users. Mechanisms should be established to ensure international participation in decision making.[33]

To implement the mandate described here, the white paper proposed, and the Commerce Department later directed ICANN's interim board of directors to establish, a system for electing future boards of directors on a regular basis in a manner that "reflects the geographical and functional diversity of the Internet, and is sufficiently flexible to permit evolution to reflect changes in the constituency of Internet stakeholders." The white paper went on to suggest that "nominations to the Board of Directors should preserve, as much as possible, the tradition of bottom-up governance of the Internet, and Board Members should be elected from membership or other associations open to all or through other mechanisms that ensure broad representation and participation in the election process."

These Commerce Department mandates could be interpreted as a negotiating position designed to influence the governance aspects of the emerging international regime for the Internet in the direction of three principles long a part of democratic traditions: openness, representation, and due process procedures in organizational deliberations. The principle of *openness* was specifically stated in the white paper's admonitions that the new corporation should operate for the benefit of "the community as a whole," that its management should include "input from the broad and growing community of Internet users," and that board members should be elected through processes "open to all." The principle of openness was later affirmed by Commerce's insistence--at the end of the white paper process, as a condition of ICANN's being selected—that ICANN develop an open membership as the basis of its organizational structure. The principle of *representation* was outlined in the white paper with regard to both international geographical representation and representation on the basis of functional diversity (meaning representation from the various constituencies affected by ICANN's policies), with both forms of representation mandated in the white paper for ICANN's membership structure *and* for selection of its board of directors. An obligation by ICANN to follow the norms and procedures of *due process in its organizational deliberations* were inferred in the white paper's stated expectations that the new corporation would practice "widely accepted" and "sound" policymaking procedures characterized by "fairness" and a "flexible" approach that would "permit evolution to reflect changes," would "ensure participation," and would be in accord with the Internet's "tradition of bottom-up governance."

Although the publiclike features demanded of ICANN by the U.S. Commerce Department—and even more vociferously by some of ICANN's constituencies—have centered around the basic democratic principles of openness, representation, and due process, each of these principles has occasionally appeared to be in conflict with other aspects of ICANN's mandate. Nonetheless, ICANN has persisted in its efforts to meet the expectations of the Commerce Department with regard to all three principles.

▪ Openness

Under continuing pressure from the U.S. government and other constituencies, ICANN has sought a formula for developing an open membership and agreed in the summer of 1999 to open its board meetings to the public. It has also experimented with a number of other "sunshine" practices that might enable the organization to arrive at more transparent consensual decisions. At the same time, ICANN has been charged with effecting viable and enduring contractual arrangements among a wide variety of interests—with hundreds of billions of dollars at stake—often involving complex political issues related to the central concerns of the domestic politics of the world's nation-states and major international organizations.[34] An appreciation of the difficult and ambiguous position that has confronted ICANN as a result of these two divergent aspects of its existence can be gained from the conclusions reached by leading modern-day political scientists who have studied previous attempts to create democratic processes and procedures within organizations. In the political science literature, an idealized model that posits open memberships arriving at consensual decisions has worked only for some small communities and organizations for relatively short periods of time, but the overwhelming evidence is that governance of large organizations has conformed to the "iron law of oligarchy," first articulated by Robert Michels in 1912, which observes as part of the human condition that "he who says organization says oligarchy."[35]

Perhaps neither ICANN nor the Commerce Department nor most of ICANN's constituencies are convinced that the new corporation will ultimately be able to escape Michel's iron law of oligarchy, but a persistent attempt has been made to find ways to build a more democratic and responsive organization and governance structure for ICANN during its early years of development. The ICANN bylaws originally provided for four organizational units with different forms of membership, with three of these units (the so-called supporting organizations [SOs]) representing ICANN's major "functional interests." The three SOs are as follows:

1. The Address Supporting Organization (ASO)—also known as ICANN's business constituency—draws its membership from the regional Internet registries (APNIC, the American Registry for Internet Numbers [ARIN], RIPE, the Network Coordination Centre [NCC]) that coordinate ICANN's oversight of the distribution of IP addresses. Members of ASO are empowered to elect three of the eighteen members of the ICANN board of directors and did so for the first time in October 1999 (the three members elected were from Canada, Hong Kong, and the Netherlands).

2. The Protocol Supporting Organization (PSO), or technical constituency, is made up of members from the standard-setting and engineering protocol bodies, such as the IETF, the World Wide Web Consortium, and telecommunications groups. Members of the PSO also elect three members to the ICANN board and did so in October 1999 (the three original PSO board members were from France, the United States, and the United Kingdom).

3. The Domain Name Supporting Organization (DNSO) represents the commercial and trademark constituency, which includes primarily large companies with interests as Internet registries, registrars, trademark holders, or other Internet-related interests. Because the DNSO is so large and consists of a wide diversity of interests internally, it has its own DNSO General Assembly, which meets yearly, and chooses its own governing Names Council. Members of the DNSO General Assembly can nominate representatives to ICANN's board of directors, but the DNSO Names Council ultimately decides which of the three nominees are chosen (the three DNSO representatives elected to the ICANN board in 1999 were from Spain, Mexico, and Canada). The Names Council chooses its own chairperson, and only the Names Council can propose DNSO-related actions to the ICANN board of directors.[36]

The fourth elected ICANN unit in ICANN's original bylaws was to be an at-large membership council that would act in a manner akin to an electoral college to choose the replacements for the first nine at-large interim members of ICANN's board of directors. The nine interim directors plus the chairman of the board had simply been named by the coalition that organized ICANN in September 1998, with Jon Postel playing a major role in putting together the list of names. After the election of nine board members by the SOs in 1999, the ICANN board had reached a total of nineteen members (nine elected by the SOs plus the nine interim members plus the chair). The terms of the nine interim members were to expire in September 2000, when they were to be replaced by nine new at-large board members elected by an At Large Membership Council acting as an electoral college.[37] The At Large Membership Council was to be the first of the at-large bodies to be elected, with open membership elections scheduled to take place in September 2000. ICANN's leadership hoped this arrangement would "ensure adequate representation, on a worldwide basis, of all Internet users."

The organizational structure outlined in ICANN's original bylaws met with a barrage of criticism during ICANN's first year of existence.

In the period preceding ICANN's first open meeting, held in Chile in August 1999, the new corporation was besieged by online criticism and e-mail messages from Internet users who felt they had not been informed by ICANN of agenda items, did not have the funds to attend the meeting in Santiago, and believed the complex electoral structure was an attempt by ICANN leaders to create a closed and undemocratic organization. The August 1999 meetings were attended largely by representatives of large corporations, trademark law firms, and professional associations, which had the resources to travel to Latin America, but large numbers who could not attend made their presence felt by the barrage of criticism leveled at ICANN's plans for electing an At Large Membership Board to serve as an electoral college. Much of this criticism was subsequently organized behind a series of reports on ICANN's governance structure carried out by a variety of organizations, all of which found the original voting plan "plagued by conflicting goals, a lack of accountability, and the absence of safeguards against capture by special-interest groups."[38]

In response to widespread criticism, the ICANN board agreed at its March 2000 meetings in Cairo to substantially revise the ICANN electoral system. Instead of electing nine At Large Membership Board members by indirect methods in September 2000, the board agreed to stagger the terms of the nine at-large members, with five to be elected by direct election of the membership before November 1, 2000, and the other four to be elected a year later (in November 2000 the ICANN board voted to postpone the November 2001 elections for six months— to May 2002—to allow more time to study and improve the voting procedures of the October 2000 elections). This meant four interim members of the board would remain on as interim members until the 2001 elections (later postponed to 2002). It was not decided at the March 2000 meetings which of the four interim members would remain and which five would be replaced in the 2000 elections; nor was it decided exactly how the direct elections of board members would take place, but the willingness of the ICANN board to change course with regard to election procedures did create at least a temporary coming together of leadership and its critics in March 2000. The ICANN board argued that its unanimous decision to reverse itself on election procedures demonstrated its determination to be a bottom-up organization that could carry out the consensus views of Internet users. In March 2000 the executive director of CDT, Jerry Berman, who had played a major role in writing a report critical of ICANN jointly with Common Cause, agreed that "they [the ICANN board] listened to the people's voice and they gave the people a voice."[39]

The October 2000 election for ICANN's first five at-large board members has often been billed as the very first experiment in a totally online global election. Using funds from a $500,000 grant from the Markle Foundation, ICANN hired the organization Election.com to administer the balloting and announced as eligible to register to vote anyone sixteen years or older with valid e-mail and mailing addresses who became an ICANN member before July 31, 2000. More than 158,000 people registered, but only 21.5 percent of those registered (34,000 or so) actually cast a ballot. This disappointing turnout was explained in part by lack of interest but also by confusion among those registered, who did not know that to have their votes count they needed to activate their ICANN membership by entering online a personal identification number sent to them via surface mail. An ICANN nominating committee proposed slates of candidates for each of five world regions and invited members to nominate candidates as well. In the end, 161 candidates were nominated, and the number of voters who cast ballots varied enormously from region to region. The North American seat was won with only 1,738 votes, and a German won the European seat because more than 61 percent of those registered throughout Europe were Germans.[40]

ICANN was widely criticized for its handling of the October 2000 election because it refused to reveal the names of those registered to vote, thus making it impossible for any of the candidates to campaign among the entire electorate.[41] In this milieu, the winners of the five seats were candidates who could organize the largest number of friends, fellow workers, and clients at very local levels rather than more well-known candidates who had broad regional contacts and knowledge. The North American seat was won by Karl Auerbach, a researcher in the Advanced Internet Architectures group at Cisco Systems, Inc.; the European seat by Andy Mueller-Maghuhn, a twenty-eight-year-old hacker and founder of the Chaos Computing Club in Berlin; the Asia/Pacific seat by Masanobu Katoh, an employee of Fujitsu of Japan who at the time was based in the United States; the Africa seat by Nii Quaynor, an employee of Network Computer Systems in Ghana; and the Latin America/Caribbean seat by Ivan Moura Campos, CEO of Akwan Information Technologies in Brazil. The president of the Markle

Foundation, Zoe Baird, was perhaps more positive about the election than anyone when she said, "This election had its problems. It was by no means perfect. But it is a very important experiment."[42]

▪ *Representation*

ICANN's first experience with the principle of representation was the October 1999 election of nine members from the SOs to the ICANN board of directors (three each from the ASO, PSO, and DNSO). The voting procedure used in that election was similar to methods used in parliamentary governments to elect party and government leaders. In the case of the DNSO election of three members to the ICANN board, for example, constituency organizations initially nominated nineteen candidates for the three positions through special mailing lists to represent North America, Africa, the Asia Pacific, Europe, and Latin America. To be elected to one of the seats, a candidate had to get a majority endorsement (ten of the nineteen votes). The procedure the Names Council adopted to elect the three successful candidates from the SOs to the ICANN board was a series of rounds of runoff ballots until one person received ten or more votes in a particular round, with the lowest vote getter in each round dropped off the list.[43] Between rounds of voting, supporters of particular candidates had opportunities to lobby the voters for support. In the 1999 election the first person elected from each SO was named to a three-year term, after which the rounds of voting continued until the second and third persons could be elected with ten votes (the second person to get ten votes was given a two-year term and the third person a three-year term). With three-year terms being staggered for three members for each SO, in future years only one person will be elected to the ICANN board from each SO. ICANN required both candidates and voters to "have a knowledge of and an interest in issues pertaining to the areas for which the DNSO has primary responsibility, and who are willing to contribute time, effort, and expertise to the work of the DNSO, including work involving proposal development, discussion of work items, draft document preparation, participation in research, and drafting committees and working groups."[44]

Despite efforts to assure geographical representation, the nine members finally elected by the SOs to the ICANN board in October 1999 included four Europeans, two Canadians, one American, one Asian, and one Mexican. Thus eight of the nine elected board members were from Europe and North America, a distribution that rankled with people from unrepresented regions of the world. The distribution was also criticized by members of the U.S. Congress, who noted that only one of the nine board members (Vinton Cerf) was from the United States. In response to charges by members of the U.S. House of Representatives Commerce Committee that the Clinton administration was "giving away an American resource" by allowing the ICANN board to be dominated by non-Americans, ICANN's leadership pointed out that five of the ten interim at-large members of the board were Americans and that there was a good chance that several interim members might be elected or replaced by Americans in the October 2000 elections for at-large board members (in fact, as described earlier, only one of the five board members elected in October 2000 was a U.S. citizen). In addition, some ICANN supporters argued that the outcome of the October 1999 elections may have been the best thing that could have happened for future U.S. relations within ICANN since the results could be used to put to rest the argument that the United States had structured the organization to promote its hegemonic position in Internet-related matters.[45]

Aside from the engineering and academic communities, the two other major categories of ICANN constituents—the governments of nation-states and the multinational business community—generally held different conceptions of what was meant by representation. For business people generally, the idea of a board member's representation is not the public representational function of someone duly authorized by an election or other legitimizing process to speak for a large constituency. Rather, it is the idea that someone will know and understand a specific business interest and be able to speak for that interest in forums where such interests are being challenged. Business interests in the Internet and in Internet-related issues are explored in detail in Chapters 3 and 4, but suffice it to say here that the international business community was generally somewhat impatient with the problems ICANN encountered in 1998, 1999, and 2000 in its efforts to create a more democratic and open organization. Jonathan Zittrain has described the nub of the business approach to ICANN's organizational efforts:

> Those who want a piece of the domain name registration action—among them are those with competing claims to slices of it—may only support ICANN if they think it will generate responsive policies. At the very least, people trying to build or maintain a business like to

know where they stand and they like to have it in writing. They prefer to have what one would call "calculable rules" so that they can build a business on predictable forces as opposed to a "hum" that can be heard one way or another. Thus the authority to modify the root file, or veto attempts to change it, is something that almost every stakeholder agreed needed more systematic handling.[46]

ICANN's other large international constituency—the governments of nation-states—has also felt strongly that ICANN's management of the root file needs to be dealt with in a more systematic manner to be responsive to its interests. The governments of thirty-three nation-states with substantial interests in the functioning of the Internet have banded together to form a Government Advisory Committee (GAC) to "represent" the interests of those governments to the ICANN board. In almost all of the thirty-three member nations of GAC, the delegation to ICANN represents a government-monopoly telecommunications company or its successor or leaders from standards organizations in the states concerned who have grown professionally in an environment where government-run companies have dominated telecommunications in their countries. The major concern of GAC has been to gain greater say in the administration of the ccTLDs (e.g., .uk for the United Kingdom, .il for Israel, .cn for China), which nominally "belong" to the country concerned but have, from the beginning of the Internet, been administered by independent contractors rather than governments. GAC has established a tradition of holding its meetings at the same time and in the same location as ICANN meetings, so the two sets of meetings have become linked organizationally. But GAC has insisted that its meetings be conducted in secret, behind locked doors, with the results of the meetings remaining confidential except for carefully worded communiqués distributed following the meetings. This manner of functioning has rankled many ICANN members and leaders.

Unlike the Top-Level Domains of .com, .net, and .org (the gTLDs), which were managed exclusively by NSI until 1999, the 240 ccTLDs have been managed by a number of entities—ranging from one-person volunteer operations to government-sanctioned consortia to start-up companies that have made profits from the domain registration business. Although the ccTLDs were often handed out in consultation with the governments of the countries concerned, ultimate control over who was allowed to operate them rested with Jon Postel when he ran IANA. Postel had invented and fathered the ccTLD system, deriving the 240 country codes from the list of codes historically used by the International Telecommunications Union. Postel had a written policy for administering the country codes known as RFC 1591, in which priority was given to "government interests" but final decisions were made on the basis of "what was best for development of the Internet and the international Internet community as a whole."[47]

Shortly after Postel passed away in October 1998, ICANN wrote a letter to the Commerce Department (in response to Commerce's request as to how ICANN proposed to handle authority over the ccTLDs) stating that it would "respect each nation's sovereign control over its individual top-level domains."[48] Mention of "sovereign control" in the letter sparked a number of debates over who has the right to administer the ccTLDs and what the role of specific governments should be for each domain. In the case of .tw, for example, should the government of Taiwan or Beijing have any right to the administration of the .tw ccTLD? Should Palestine have a separate country code, as was decided in 2000, or should computers in Palestine have the ccTLD assigned to Israel (.il), as was the case before 2000? Postel insisted in RFC 1591 that "the IANA is not in the business of deciding what is and what is not a country," so he simply based the ccTLD domains on the list of country codes used by the ITU.

Responding to questions concerning the mention of sovereign control in the ICANN board's October 1998 letter, ICANN's interim president Mike Roberts has insisted that changes in Postel's policies, as outlined in RFC 1591, are not on ICANN's agenda. Roberts has also stated that any change in policy regarding ccTLDs would come "only after broad international public input was given on the domain name system as a whole." The chair of the interim ICANN board from 1998 to 2000, Esther Dyson, however, has consistently argued that ICANN will eventually have to adopt more rules and policies over country codes than exist at present. She also described her perception of the ccTLDs somewhat ambiguously: "[The] fundamental notion is that these are at the disposition of the country they are attached to. . . . The countries may then make them commercial, they may do different things. . . . In some sense, it creates a proper sense of diversity and democracy. This is all about creating a competitive marketplace."[49]

In an effort to counter the influence of GAC and the governments of nation-states with interests in the management of ccTLDs, more than seventy of the companies and contractors presently administering ccTLDs banded together in 1998 to form the International Association of Top Level Domains (IATL), whose objective is to "guarantee continuity" in how country codes are administered. The IATL has suggested that ICANN simply adopt Postel's RFC 1591 as part of its bylaws and has argued in a variety of documents and forums that turning over the administration of country codes to nation-state governments would have serious consequences for the way Internet has functioned (for a discussion of possible consequences related to the PRC's attempt to capture control of domain names in the Chinese language, see Chapter 7). It might, for example, enable governments to invalidate hundreds of thousands of domain names already assigned in particular country codes, and it could also in many cases allow governments to negate agreements Postel often drew up with ccTLD administrators, requiring them to put certain portions of their profits from domain registration fees into consolidated funds used to reduce connection fees for Internet users and advance network development in poorer countries. In the view of IATL documents and spokespersons, the ccTLDs were never intended to be the property of governments but were instead assigned to various companies and organizations for the purpose of spreading maintenance responsibilities around the globe. In the words of Tony Rutkowski, "It was never intended that just because it had a two-letter country code that the computers were in that country, much less under some sort of sovereign ownership. . . . In fact, the sovereign ownership concept doesn't make sense because this is a shared computer network."[50]

From the perspective of GAC countries and the telecom companies in them, however, the Internet naming system is a public resource that must be administered in the public or common interest by the relevant government or public authority in any given country or territory. The ramifications of this position were spelled out in a nine-page GAC-authored document presented to ICANN in February 2000, designed to serve as the basis for discussion of the rules governing management of ccTLDs in later ICANN forums and at the annual conference. The document asserts that the "government or public authority" of any given nation-state has the power and responsibility to decide whether ccTLD administrators (called "delegees" by GAC) within its boundaries are obeying the law, living up to contracts, or enjoying "the support of the relevant local community and of the relevant government or public authority, or . . . breached and failed to remedy other material provisions of RFC 1591." In cases where the relevant government or public authority decides against a delegee on any of these matters, the GAC document suggests that it is ICANN's responsibility to "act with the utmost promptness to reassign the delegation in coordination with the relevant government or public authority."[51] In addition to sanctioning them to determine whether a given ccTLD administrator should be allowed to continue, the GAC document asserts the authority of governments and public authorities to determine the "term, performance clauses, opportunity for review, and process of revocation" of licenses and contracts for delegees. It also recommended to the ICANN board that all delegees or their administrative contracts "should be resident or incorporated in the territory and/or jurisdiction of the relevant government or public authority" and that "no private intellectual or other property rights should inhere in the ccTLD itself."[52]

Faced with widely divergent positions on the part of GAC and the present administrators of ccTLDs, ICANN has created a subcommittee of the DNSO, called the ccTLD Constituency of the DNSO, to try to reach an accommodation. The subcommittee met for the first time during ICANN's Berlin meetings, on May 25, 1999, and agreed on a set of procedures through which it would try to reach consensual agreement. Central to these procedures was the need for both parties to agree that the decisionmaking process would adhere to the principles of openness and transparency and that meetings of the ccTLD subcommittee would, "as far as practicable," be open to the public. It was expected that the matter would come to a head at the July 2000 ICANN meetings in Yokohama when the GAC presentation was to be taken up for discussion, but that discussion was inconclusive and is continuing into 2001.

▪ **Due Process and Deliberations**

A third broad area in which ICANN is beginning to gain experience is with basic organizational procedures that conform to due process and other democratic norms that ensure opportunities for people to be heard and to appeal or protest in a meaningful way if they perceive their rights are neglected or quashed. Following a study of the ICANN bylaws, Jonathan Zittrain (executive director of the Berkman Center for the Internet and Society at Harvard University) concluded that:

> The process developing within ICANN is one that struggles to adopt internal structures for guaranteeing due process and deliberation. For instance, once a policy proposal is made, it may be referred to one of ICANN's supporting organizations. In the case of the Domain Name Supporting Organization (DNSO), the proposal goes to one or more "constituencies" or cross-constituency working groups. The con-

stituencies deliberate, form views, and make recommendations to the DNSO. After allowing other supporting organizations a similar chance for comment, the DNSO makes recommendations to the ICANN Board. The ICANN Board votes and decides. At that point an internal reconsideration process can be invoked by someone who feels that the decision is contrary to ICANN's structure and bylaws. If the challenge gets past this "appeal" stage, there is a structure emerging—still not here, to be sure—for an independent board of review, which will look at the disputed issue and may require the Board to come explicitly to a new judgment on the subject.[53]

Without elaborating ICANN's organizational chart in detail, its initial efforts to create a democratic mode of functioning have clearly created what Zittrain calls "a proliferation of committees, advisory bodies, supporting organizations, working groups, ad hoc groups and other entities, each struggling to define and understand its role in relation to the others."[54] This has led to criticism from some—especially business and government leaders—that due process and deliberation within ICANN often results in frivolous claims or concerns that tend to override serious policy considerations. Others—particularly from the engineering and academic communities—often view ICANN's bureaucratic proliferation as a failure to develop a unifying and purposeful organizational structure.[55] A major task for ICANN—and for the organizational process that results from the negotiations ICANN is conducting—will be to balance its quest for organizational due process and deliberation with the pressure to resolve myriad complex issues related to IT and Internet development—one of the most rapidly changing areas of human endeavor. Zittrain concludes that "a shakeout [of ICANN's proliferation of committees] seems inevitable and healthy, presuming that what remains approximates an ability [for ICANN members and interests] to participate with a clear momentum to closure."[56]

▪ CONCLUSIONS

Although international regime principles and norms for operationalizing the technical protocols and standards of the Internet proceeded during the 1990s through the three-stage process of agenda setting, negotiation, and operationalization, such a process lagged somewhat behind for those aspects of Internet development having to do with governance and management of the Internet through control of the domain name system. The agenda-setting stage of regime formation for Internet governance and management could be said to have been in progress during the 1980s and 1990s, at a time when Jon Postel and IANA were securely in charge of the root server and the DNS system and the key actors who eventually emerged with interest in Internet governance and management were only beginning to formulate their positions. During those two decades the discussion of technical protocols and standards was proceeding at a much faster pace than the discussion of governance and management issues, although the two discussions were often on parallel (or occasionally intersecting) tracks. The sequencing of these two different facets of Internet development is understandable, since it was not possible for negotiations over governance and management to emerge full-blown until fairly widespread acceptance of the principles and norms for Internet technical standards and protocols had made the Internet operational.

The negotiation stage for the governance and management aspects of Internet development began in earnest when the U.S. government turned responsibility for control of the root server and the DNS over to the Commerce Department's NTIA and initiated the white paper process in 1997–1998. Both President Clinton (in his presidential executive order of July 1, 1997) and NTIA in subsequent pronouncements and documents asserted the ultimate authority of the U.S. government over the Internet root, but both also indicated a willingness to negotiate with international stakeholders about the shape of future Internet governance and management. Beyond that, the Clinton administration and NTIA placed on the table for negotiation several suggestions for principles and norms of Internet governance and management. These included the principle that the private sector should take the lead in the development of Internet governance and management and the concomitant norm that governments should avoid placing undue restrictions on the Internet while facilitating its development by enforcing a "predictable, minimalist, consistent, and simple legal environment." In addition, both the white paper and NTIA have tried to promote the principle of openness in the organization of the Internet's governance and management functions, with the concomitant norms that some form of at-large membership, functional and geographic representation of international stakeholders and users, and international participation in decisionmaking be built into the structure of the Internet's governing and management mechanism.

Negotiation of principles and norms for Internet governance and management have dragged out over the past few years because many key actors have been involved in the various struggles with NSI to determine short-term authority relationships relative to the root server and control of the domain names system until longer-term arrangements can be finalized and endorsed. The agreement reached by ICANN, NSI, and Commerce—for contracts that would enable NSI to run the gTLD registry on a competitive basis with other companies during the years 2000–2004, with the possibility of the contract being extended until 2008—has made it possible for both ICANN and Commerce's NTIA to declare an end to the DNS wars of the 1990s and get on with negotiations for a longer-term governance and management regime. Thus far, however, consensus on regime principles and norms for governance and management of the root server and domain names has not been reached. Negotiations have centered on several key issues that have yet to be resolved.

One of the major potential alternatives to ICANN, should ICANN's efforts to create a governance and management structure for the Internet fail, would be the creation of an intergovernmental entity of some kind, perhaps like the ITU. The U.S. government indicated clearly in the white paper that it did not consider long-term U.S. government control over the root server and DNS appropriate because of the desire that DNS registration be competitive, the need for a "more robust" management structure, and the impropriety of a single government managing an increasingly commercial and global Internet.[57] With increasing assertions by sovereign national governments that they need to gain greater control of country code domains and given their increased proprietary interests in how the Internet is managed worldwide, there has been some discussion—in U.S. policymaking circles and elsewhere—of the possibility of developing an international treaty organization (along the lines of the ITU) to provide an official forum for negotiations on global Internet governance. At present, however, such a massive change in the concept of the emerging international regime for the Internet would be considered a risk in many respects by all major stakeholders. Zittrain has summarized some of these concerns:

> It is not clear to me that [an intergovernmental treaty organization] would make policies that are any more in touch with the Internet community than those proposed by a well-functioning ICANN. More importantly, as the historical context suggests, the power of the root derives from the fact that a critical mass of system administrators and "mirror" root zone server operators choose to follow it. A drastic turn-

around in the management of Internet top-level functions—either through a sea change in favor of much more aggressive government involvement, or one that purports to literally privatize the whole system (imagine auctioning it off to the highest bidder)—could result in abandonment of the network by the technical or user community. . . . Engineers who run the domain name servers . . . might simply point the servers elsewhere.[58]

In the absence of an intergovernmental treaty, the failure of ICANN to develop widely accepted principles and norms for governance and management of the root server and DNS could mean either that there would be no international regime for the Internet or that a future regime for governance of the Internet might be built around other organizations and ideas. Existing private companies might maneuver with one another to create and manage new alternative domain name and root server systems.[59] The NSI might continue to operate the existing top-level registry, and Internet Service Providers (ISPs) might simply choose from among many alternative root authorities that could be created. At least for the present, such a prospect does not seem inviting to most Internet stakeholders and users, if only because of the enormous benefits everyone has experienced by having a single repository of domain names, a central coordinated root server, a highly decentralized authority for technical operations, inclusive standard setting, and diversity, interoperability, and heterogeneity of networks. Although ICANN and the present mode of governance of the root server and DNS are clearly not everyone's ideal (or perhaps not even anyone's ideal), it is also clear that few Internet stakeholders or users would like the prospect of shifting drastically out of an emergent regime that is providing unprecedented benefits across a wide spectrum, with which everyone is familiar, and, perhaps more important, that is the basis for everyone's existing software.[60]

In the final analysis, then, ICANN may end up being the most acceptable organization for carrying out negotiations for the principles, norms, rules, and procedures of a new governance regime for the Internet simply because it already exists, has demonstrated a willingness to be responsive to criticism, and appears to many as the best of the available alternatives. Negotiation of an intergovernmental treaty as the basis for a future regime would not elicit the enthusiasm of commercial and trademark interests, but a regime that might lead to dominance by a for-profit private company or companies would be unacceptable to many, if not most, national governments. ICANN's middle path results from its position as a private corporation that is sculpting itself to perform public-interest functions. It hopes to become (or to create through negotiation) a self-regulating organization capable of managing the Internet as a public resource, and yet remain independent of any single sovereign or bloc of sovereigns. As Zittrain and others have pointed out, ICANN's power could evaporate quickly if it fails to build a worldwide consensus around the governance regime it has been assigned to create or if the U.S. government withdraws support for its approach. If it succeeds, however, it could create a new mode of governance appropriate for a human invention as revolutionary as the Internet. In Zittrain's formulation, this "distinct mode of governance" would be "one that aspires to the best of private and public rather than the worst."[61]

■ NOTES

1. Young, *Creating Regimes,* p. 10.

2. An Internet backbone is an overarching network that does not usually serve any local networks or end users directly but to which multiple regional networks connect. The original backbone was run by DOD and transferred to NSF in 1990. On April 30, 1995, NSFnet ceased operation, and the Internet was privatized (see text for details). A combination of public and private (for-profit) enterprises has since taken over management of the U.S. Internet backbone infrastructure. There are also a large number of backbone and mid-level networks in other countries, with most Western European countries having national networks connected to EBone, the European backbone. For more detail, see MacKie-Mason and Varian, "Economic FAQs About the Internet," pp. 31 ff.

3. Moschovitis et al., *History of the Internet,* p. 104.

4. IETF findings were published, and are still being published, in the form of requests for comments (RFCs).

5. Abbate, *Inventing the Internet,* p. 207. The IETF is not a government organization and most of the people setting standards at IETF are not government employees, although many are contractors or working under government grants. IETF's influence in setting standards for the U.S. government stems primarily from the respect government agencies and contacts hold for IETF.

6. From Moschovitis et al., *History of the Internet,* p. 167.

7. Post, "Governing Cyberspace," p. 4.

8. Ibid., p. 5

9. Postel directed the establishment of the first ARPANET node—to the UCLA host computer—in the early 1970s and was editor of the RFC documents of ITEF. He was a founding member of the IAB and served actively in that capacity until his death in October 1998. Postel was the first person signed up as a member of the Internet Society.

10. Mueller, "ICANN and Internet Governance," p. 500.

11. By August 1998 the Internet Intelligence Infrastructure Fund (being used by NSF to upgrade high-speed network links and for other infrastructure improvements) totaled $60 million. It had not been used before late 1998 because four companies and nine individuals had sued NSI in 1996, claiming the fund was illegitimately derived from the fee for registering domain names, which the plaintiffs called a "tax in disguise." In April 1998 Judge Timothy Hogan of the U.S. District Court of the District of Columbia ruled in favor of the plaintiffs, suggesting that the only way the fund could be legitimized would be for the U.S. Congress to retroactively authorize a "set aside" for the fund. In August 1998 Congress authorized such a set aside, to be drawn from the fee charged by NSI. Judge Hogan subsequently rejected an appeal by the plaintiffs to the original suit, charging that Congress had acted deceptively by attaching the retroactive Internet fund measure as a rider to an unrelated emergency relief bill (H.R. 3579). See Goodwin, "Washington Briefings," p. 70.

12. Moschovitis et al., *History of the Internet,* p. 175.

13. Another reason NSI is valuable to VeriSign is that the merger combined the leading provider of Internet domain name registrations (NSI) with the leading provider of e-commerce and e-mail security (VeriSign), creating a company that started with more than 12 million subscribers worldwide in two closely related and highly significant areas of Internet operations. For an in-depth analysis, see "VeriSign Buys Domain Firm," *CNN America, Inc.,* March 7, 2000, available at http://cgi.cnnfn.com/output/pfv/2000/03/07/deals/verisi.

14. Mueller, "ICANN and Internet Governance," p. 501.

15. Ibid., p. 502.

16. Young, *Creating Regimes,* p. 12.

17. *A Framework for Global Electronic Commerce,* quoted in Mueller, "ICANN and Internet Governance," p. 503.

18. See *Management of Internet Names and Addresses.* An earlier document, called the green paper, had been issued by the Commerce Department in January 1998 for the purpose of stimulating a wide-ranging discussing among Internet stakeholders and users that would eventually result in the white paper. The green paper is called *Improvement of Technical Management of Internet Names and Addresses.*

19. The IFWP archives have been maintained by Ellen Rony and are available online at www.domainhandbook.com.

20. See Lessig, "A Bad Turn for Net Governance."

21. Mueller, "ICANN and Internet Governance," p. 507.

22. Letter from J. Beckwith Burr, associate administrator, NTIA, to Dr. Herb Schoor, executive director, USC-ISI, October 20, 1998, quoted in ibid., p. 508.

23. The five original test-bed companies were France Telecom, America Online, CORE (which by 1999 had become a consortium of registrars in twenty-three countries), Melbourne IT, and New York–based Register.com. For details on the reasons for their selection by ICANN and related matters, see Wasserman, "ICANN to Can NSI Domain-Name Monopoly."

24. "ICANN Accredits Eleven New Domain Name Registrars," available

at www.icann.org/announcements/icann=pr26oct99.htm. The additional accredited registrars included companies from Australia, Canada, China, Denmark, France, Germany, Israel, Italy, Japan, Korea, Kuwait, Norway, Spain, Sweden, and the United Kingdom, with several countries having more than one accredited registrar.

25. Mueller, "ICANN and Internet Governance," p. 511.

26. These agreements include (1) a Registry Agreement between ICANN and NSI; (2) a revised Registrar Accreditation Agreement between ICANN and all registrars in .com, .net, and .org; (3) a revised post-test-bed transition Registrar License and Agreement between NSI as registry and registrar; (4) amendment 19 to the Cooperative Agreement between the Department of Commerce and NSI; and (5) amendment 1 to the MoU between Commerce and NSI. See "Press Release on ICANN-DoC-NSI Tentative Agreements," available at www.icann.org/announcements/icann=pr28sept99.htm.

27. *Domain Name Agreements,* also available at http://www.ntia.doc.gov/ntiahome/domainname/agreements/.

28. Some policymakers and scholars have questioned whether the U.S. government should surrender its authority over the basic infrastructure of the Internet. Harvard professor Lawrence Lessig, for example, has commented: "We are creating the most significant new jurisdiction since the Louisiana Purchase, yet we are building it just outside the Constitution's review. Indeed, we are building it just so that the Constitution will not govern—as if we want to be free of the constraints of value embedded by that tradition." See Lessig, *Code,* p. 217.

29. The agreements are summarized in ibid. See also the ICANN summary at www.icann.org/agreements.htm, and Mueller, "ICANN and Internet Governance," pp. 514–515.

30. Macavinta, "Analysts," also available at http://news.cnet.com/news/0-1005-200-266300.html.

31. The term *cease-fire* is used by Perine, "ICANN Carves out a Compromise," also available at www.thestandard.com/article/article_print/1.1153,7496.00.html.

32. Zittrain, "ICANN," p. 1083.

33. This and the following quotation from the white paper are from ICANN's web page under "FAQ on At Large Membership and Elections"; see www.icann.org/general/faq1.htm.

34. In ICANN documents the ICANN board has recognized (among others) the following constituencies: commercial and business interests, ISPs and other networking and connectivity providers, noncommercial domain name holders, registrars, country code Top-Level Domains, generic Top-Level Domains, and trademark, intellectual property, and anticounterfeiting interests. See Wasserman, "ICANN Moves into Action."

35. The basis for the iron law of oligarchy is outlined in detail in Michels, *Political Parties;* see especially pp. 377 ff.

36. Oram, "Groucho Marx and Online Governance," available at request from andyo@oreilly.com.

37. This complex voting system is described in detail in "FAQ on At Large Membership and Elections." For a critique of the system, see Nader, "A Framework for ICANN."

38. Quoted in Clausing, "Internet Board," p. C14. Many of these studies were paid for by grants from the Markle Foundation ($200,000 to ICANN to help build an "open membership base" and $300,000 to several public interest groups to enable them to send members to future meetings and to finance their activities in support of a fair and open voting process within ICANN). Among the organizations that developed reports on ICANN's governance structure were the Computer Professionals for Social Responsibility, Common Cause (led by Ralph Nader), the Berkman Center at Harvard University, and the Carter Presidential Library and Center in Atlanta, Georgia.

39. Quoted in ibid.

40. Analyses of the October 2000 election are available in Hill, "Election Day on the Internet," p. A31, and Pressman, "The Changing of ICANN's Guard."

41. See, for example, Jay Tate, "Web 'Democracy' Resembles Dictatorships," *Financial Times* (London), October 18, 2000, p. 16, and Weise, "With Dissidents on Board."

42. Quoted in Stellin, "Internet Domain Administrator," p. C6. In addition to support from the Markle Foundation, three other organizations (Computer Professionals for Social Responsibility, the Electronic Privacy Information Center, and the American Civil Liberties Union) established an Internet Democracy Project designed specifically to encourage participation in the ICANN board election. See Hopper, "Groups Encourage Democracy on the Internet."

43. During the run-up to the 1999 ICANN board election, some constituents objected that NSI had three representatives on the Names Council while no other company had more than one representative. As a result, the ICANN board revised its bylaws in August 1999 so no single company could have more than one representative on the Names Council. See Niccolai, "ICANN Curtails NSI's Influence," available at www.sunworld.com/swol-08-1999.

44. Quoted in Macavinta, "Election Begins for ICANN Board Seats," available at http://news.cnet.com/news. This source provides a summary of the election process. Unmentioned in the list of requirements for candidates is the candidate's willingness and ability to support her/himself for all activities undertaken in pursuit of ICANN's work. At least one prominent figure—Ellen Rony, coauthor of the *Domain Name Handbook*—asked that ICANN institute "certification" procedures to verify that supporters of nominees met membership qualifications.

45. For analyses of the elections, see Marsan, "Domain Group Lacking

Strong U.S. Presence," and Clausing, "One American Elected to Internet Board."

46. Zittrain, "ICANN," pp. 1082–1083. Zittrain attributes the concept of "calculable rules," as opposed to a "hum," to Weber, *Economy and Society*; see especially chapter 11, "Bureaucracy," pp. 956 ff.

47. Quoted in Clausing, "New Internet Board," p. C4. For example, when one government ministry in the People's Republic of China asked Postel to allow it to administer the .cn domain, Postel instead allocated the domain to the Asia Pacific Network Information Center (a private organization located in the United States) because Postel "was unclear who the user community would be if the domain were given to the communist Chinese government." Quoted by Tony Rutkowski, a Virginia Internet consultant, in Clausing, "New Internet Board."

48. Quoted in ibid.

49. Ibid.

50. Ibid.

51. *Principles for Delegation and Administration of ccTLDs,* available at www.icann.org/gas/gac-cctldprinciples. In this document the administrator of a ccTLD (the delegee) is defined by GAC as "the organisation, enterprise or individual designated by the relevant government or public authority to exercise the public trust function of a ccTLD and *consequently* recognised through a communication between ICANN and the designated entity for that purpose." If this definition were accepted by ICANN, all of the existing administrators of ccTLDs would have to be approved by the governments in the relevant countries and then reconfirmed by ICANN, with the host country governments having the right to disapprove of any present administrator.

52. Ibid.

53. Zittrain, "ICANN," pp. 1087–1088.

54 Ibid., p. 1088.

55. See, for example, Mueller, "ICANN and Internet Governance," pp. 517 ff. After a review of ICANN's dispute resolution procedure, Mueller expresses his frustration by predicting that "if ICANN survives another five years, it will rival the ITU in size" (p. 519).

56. Zittrain, "ICANN," p. 1088.

57. *Management of Internet Names and Addresses,* p. 14. A discussion of five roles the United States might potentially play in the international development of the Internet—summarized as funder, facilitator, judge or arbiter, partner, and legitimizer—appears in McKnight, "Information Security for the Internet," pp. 443 ff.

58. Zittrain, "ICANN," pp. 1089–1090.

59. Alternative root systems that have been proposed can be located through the Open Root Server Convention, Inc., at http://www.open-rsc.org.

60. At the end of 2000, many policymakers involved with ICANN were hopeful that a new leadership would make possible a new start for the organization. Not only did Esther Dyson step down as chair of ICANN in December

2000 (she was succeeded by Vinton Cerf), ICANN's point person in the Commerce Department, Becky Burr (associate administrator for international affairs in Commerce's National Telecommunications and Information Agency), has left the government to return to private practice. In addition, the new president of the United States, George W. Bush, has appointed new leadership at the Commerce Department that is expected to look at ICANN from a fresh policy perspective. For a discussion of the contributions of Dyson and Burr under the Clinton administration, see Pressman, "A New Leader for ICANN."

61. Zittrain, "ICANN," p. 1092.

Frameworks for
E-Commerce and Taxation

The agenda-setting stage of international regime creation as regards *commercial* aspects of Internet development and use could be said to have been initiated in July 1997, when the Clinton administration released a report entitled *A Framework for Global Electronic Commerce*. This report enunciated the first consistent U.S. position firmly in support of the idea that the commercial aspects of international Internet development should be led by the private sector, without substantial government administration or regulation. In the words of the framework report, "The private sector should lead."[1]

Following widespread international discussion and controversy evoked by the framework report, its recommendations were revised and folded into the green paper released by the Commerce Department in January 1998, which was further amended and amplified in the white paper of June 1998, as detailed in Chapter 2. The white paper process that brought the discussion of Internet governance to the agenda of world leaders (as outlined in Chapter 1) was paralleled by a framework report process that set the pace for the agenda-setting stage for the commercial aspects of international regime creation. The framework report process was initially instrumental in agenda setting at the international level primarily because it prompted the EU to initiate a series of high-level meetings designed to formulate a European response to what was viewed as a rather extreme and potentially threatening U.S. stance on electronic commerce development.

The White House–supported framework report also elicited high-level discussion of the commercial aspects of a global Internet regime among several other countries that had become seriously involved in electronic commerce, most of which, like Europe, had historical traditions in which the private sector had never been assigned as large a role in communications and telecommunications as had been the case in the United States. In those countries, where telecommunications and other communications regimes had always been either run or substantially regulated by government, considerably greater domestic adjustment would be necessary if local populations were to subscribe to the idea that the private sector should lead on Internet commercial and economic matters.

By the early 1990s both European and U.S. leaders had begun to realize the Internet's enormous potential for commercial, business, and economic development, but before June 1997 little formal or specific international discussion had occurred on how countries and firms might build international economic cooperation in cyberspace.[2] U.S. and European government personnel had been familiarizing themselves with the Internet and its implications for business and society at the national and state or provincial levels while struggling to develop specific policies on commercial Internet-related issues in their domestic political environments. In the early years of the Clinton administration, for example, its focus (under the leadership of Vice President Al Gore) was on the development of a National Information Infrastructure (NII) within the United States. A White House Intellectual Property Working Group, headed by Bruce Lehman, considered international issues and in 1995 recommended even stronger protection for intellectual property holders on the Internet than had been provided historically to educators and writers in the print and publishing media, but the proposal was considered by Congress in 1995–1996 and was never reported out of committee.[3]

In Europe, the celebrated Bangemann Report of June 1994, drafted by a distinguished panel of high-level representatives of industry and government from all over Europe, recommended a major role for the private sector and substantial modernization of IT industries, telecommunications, and Internet-related infrastructure so Europe might remain competitive with the United States in e-commerce and other commercial aspects of cyberspace.[4] But the EU responded to the Bangemann Report by initiating discussion of action plans in four areas, a move that immediately led to postponement of some aspects of the report and alteration of others, although the report did eventually have a major impact on Internet development throughout Europe.

At the international level, in December 1996 the World Intellectual Property Organization (WIPO) passed two treaties designed to establish protocols specifically for digital productions (one for performance and sound recordings, the other for copyright), but a frequently quoted assessment of the treaties by John Browning concluded that the 1996 WIPO conference would be remembered "not so much for what it did as for what it did not do. It did not give copyright holders many of the new legal powers they asked for—mostly because delegates feared that they would use those powers to force the future into the mold of the past, and so rob the Net of its potential to create change."[5] Similarly, the World Trade Organization (WTO) had been reluctant before 1997 to enter into areas involving intellectual property and the Internet, even though the WTO (formerly GATT) mandate had been expanded in the early 1990s to include the protection of intellectual property.[6]

In this atmosphere, the strikingly direct position of the Clinton administration in the 1997 framework report—that the private sector should lead Internet development in all respects—provided a focus for discussion of regime principles and norms that had not existed previously. In addition, the framework report proposed four corollary recommendations consistent with the "private sector should lead" principle: (1) governments should avoid undue restrictions on electronic commerce; (2) where government involvement is needed, it should support a predictable, simple, and consistent legal environment for commerce; (3) governments should recognize the unique qualities of the Internet; and (4) electronic commerce over the Internet should be facilitated on a global basis.[7]

▪ U.S. AND EUROPEAN PERSPECTIVES ON ELECTRONIC COMMERCE

The U.S. position assigning the lead role for Internet regime creation to the private sector had been heavily influenced by the way in which the personal computer and software industries had amassed large amounts of capital for start-up companies by closely protecting and charging for use of patented products, trademarks, copyrights, and other intellectual property. The origin of this pattern is often traced to 1974, when a young Bill Gates (just before he dropped out of Harvard University) and Paul Allen (then a systems programmer at Honeywell in Boston) wrote a programming system for the first small commercial personal computer (PC)—the Altair 8800—in BASIC, a high-level computer language developed at Dartmouth College in the 1960s that could be readily used by nonexperts. The Altair 8800 had been developed as an affordable computer for individuals (a PC) by Ed Roberts, founder of Model Instrumentation Telemetry Systems (MITS), using Intel Corporation microchips, but this first PC was dependent for its huge business success in the late 1970s on the software program written by Gates and Allen.

In spring of 1975 Gates and Allen founded Microsoft and immediately became embroiled in controversy because of their insistence on patenting software and other Microsoft products. Gates's insistence on fierce protection of intellectual property immediately produced a strong contrary reaction—in the United States and elsewhere—in many different ways, fueling the open software movement based on the notion that "information should be free." Supporters and participants in this movement have often championed open-source operating systems such as Linux, which allows millions of users to log on and encourages them to help each other solve technical problems without imposing a patent or other intellectual property regulations on their involvement.[8] Gates's implementation of a maximalist position on use of intellectual property, particularly when coupled with a fiercely aggressive competitive business style, led eventually to the ruling by U.S. District Judge Thomas Penfield Jackson on April 3, 2000, that Gates's Microsoft had violated the Sherman Antitrust Act, "maintained its monopoly power by anticompetitive means," and attempted to illegally monopolize the Web browser market.[9] On April 28, 2000, the Justice Department and seventeen state attorneys general asked the judge to break Microsoft into two parts, one to develop and market the Windows operating system and the other to develop Microsoft's other software and Internet holdings. Microsoft is appealing Jackson's ruling.

Coming as it did when the personal computer industry was just getting started, the Gates-led software flap in 1975 established intellectual property as a basic feature of both hardware and software development, not only in the United States but throughout the world, eventually leading to an almost universal acceptance by world business leaders of the idea that intellectual property protection was essential to the incredible growth of the "information economy" and Internet-related industry.[10] Gates's advanced position on intellectual property also induced in its train industry-led policing groups for intellectual property protection such as the Software Publishers' Association (SPA), which in 1998 alleged that more than $11 billion was being lost annually to illegal duplication of computer programs.[11] Support for a maximalist position on intellectual property protection has increasingly come as well from trademark interests, which in the 1990s became involved in a series of legal battles (discussed later) to protect the use of trademark names and associated property in cyberspace. Support for maximalism has also come from nonsoftware copyright holders and from a number of U.S. politicians and officials.[12]

Europe's response to the July 1997 framework report and the European Community's (EC) negotiating positions on the economic aspects of Internet regime issues have reflected a number of cultural differences between U.S. and European perspectives on the role of commercial development in society, as well as the diversity of European experiences with business competition and government regulation. Since the adoption of the Maastricht Treaty in 1992, the EC has adopted dramatic and sweeping proposals designed to provide open access to computer networks, including interoperability and interconnectivity along lines consistent with the principles and norms of the international regime, as outlined in Chapter 1. In response to the challenges of U.S.-led IT development, the EU has also established general, legal, and economic principles for the application of competition rules within Europe and between Europe and the rest of the world, designed to build and maintain European competitiveness in global markets, particularly with regard to electronic commerce. And yet, the European approach to open access and private-sector–led competition is markedly different from that of the United States. A leading study of the liberalization of Internet-related aspects of the European economies has identified several characteristics of information infrastructure initiatives that set the EU experience apart from that of the United States:

1. The idea of *universal service,* which imposes noncommercial obligations on private companies, has been accepted by the EU in sharp contrast to the more market-oriented approach in the United States, where U.S. legislators almost universally avoid imposing noncommercial legal responsibilities on private-sector firms. Indeed, the treaties that established the EU, including the 1993 Treaty of Rome and the Maastricht Treaty (also 1993), include what are often called "guarantees" that the EU shall promote "economic and social progress which is balanced and sustainable" (Maastricht, Title I, Article B) and a high level of social protection, the raising of the standard of living and quali-

ty of life, and economic and social cohesion and solidarity among Member States."[13] EU acceptance of treaty guarantees for universal service obligations on the part of private firms has resulted in extensive regulatory frameworks for tariffs and quality of service of Internet-related activities in Europe, as well as the establishment of "procedures for consumer monitoring, defining access [to services] for all social sectors, establishing funding mechanisms [for services], and including provisions for higher thresholds of minimum services."[14]

2. In matters of *competition policy* (similar in some respects to what Americans think of as antitrust policy), the EU has adopted what it calls a "reregulatory approach" that links privatization of telecommunications and other traditionally government-controlled enterprises and the freeing up of restraints on competition directly to community law and the performance of public service. For example, the EU rules of competition retain legal constraints on such activities as commercial alliances, joint ventures, partnerships, and mergers, but the strict application of those constraints "will be waived for communications carriers, providers and distributors who perform services (frequently non-commercial or low-profit services) in the public interest as part of their cost of operation. In order to meet the criteria of the public service regulatory model, industries must agree to either restrain their size and thus their profitability and freedom to consolidate capital ownership structures and reduce risk, or else assume an array of less profitable public interest obligations."[15]

3. European institutions—including the European Parliament and the European Court of Justice—continually consider and have often adopted measures to protect the rights of consumers by *restricting socially harmful content* in information or media outlets or by shrinking the limits of advertising, mandating a certain basic level of educational programs for children, requiring that citizens groups be represented on the governing boards of infrastructure and content industries, and even transforming information services into a civil right. Both the degree and frequency with which these regulatory measures are considered and adopted by the various nations in Europe and by the EC contrast markedly with the United States. As Shalini Venturelli has pointed out, only some of the numerous regulatory proposals have been accepted in Europe, and many have been considered and subsequently rejected, but "the balance achieved between the [various] approaches [to content regulation] . . . at any particular time, and on any single issue, will deter-

mine market conditions for investment and competition in a given communications sector."[16]

In the period since 1997, Western Europe has lagged behind the United States in IT and Internet development, with only 12 percent of European homes connected to the Internet in early 2000, compared with 45 percent of U.S. homes (in mid-2000 it was estimated that only 5 percent of Europeans were regular Internet users, compared with 30 percent in the United States).[17] Western Europe has also trailed the United States in job creation and other aspects of IT growth, with European unemployment in 2000 hovering around 10 percent, compared with less than half that figure for the United States. By the year 2002, the EU estimates that there will be a 1.6 million shortfall in skilled workers for IT firms in Europe, a figure EU economists admit is at least partially related to a lack of incentive for some Europeans to aggressively seek employment or skills when they are assured a fairly decent minimal standard of living from the entitlements the EU and its member nations provide. European leaders are convinced that Europe can compete with and even outstrip the United States in IT and a number of Internet-related areas, but they are determined to do so while imposing a much more extensive regulatory framework on private industry than is the case in the United States.[18] At a "dotcom summit" of European leaders in Lisbon in March 2000, for example, the president of the EU, Portuguese prime minister Antonio Guterres, said the goal of the EU was to develop "an entrepreneurial business culture to rival the US, but to keep Europe's cherished social safety net too." Speaking at a news conference after the summit, Guterres said, "We have a model of civilization we do not want to give up in any way."[19]

■ **EU RESPONSES TO THE FRAMEWORK REPORT**

The March 2000 dotcom summit in Lisbon marked the end of almost three years of negotiations—between the United States and the EC and within the European Community—on a number of issues growing out of the 1997 White House framework report. The result of these negotiations was a compromise between the maximalist notion of a self-regulatory regime for Internet commerce articulated by the White House's Bruce Lehman and, at the other extreme, the preferences of traditionalist Europeans that private-sector involvement in Internet commerce be subject to the same kinds of regulations that had governed previous technologies in Europe. The acceptance of this compromise by both sides, in a series of agreements that began to be concluded in 1999 and 2000, could be said to have at least tentatively established two regime working principles: (1) that the private sector shall play a lead role in the development of electronic commerce on a global basis and (2) that regulatory and other government activities should avoid undue restrictions on Internet commercial activities while facilitating the development of international electronic commerce by the private sector. One might also identify two working regime norms that grew out of the 1997–2000 negotiations: (1) that diverse sets of national rules and procedures governing Internet commerce will be accommodated at the international level by soft law arrangements designed to promote global cooperation and expand commercial activities and (2) that regional and international organizations will play a major role in facilitating the growth of the Internet on a global basis.

Compared with the White House framework document of June 1997, this compromise iteration of working regime principles and norms tones down the maximalist assertions of the Clinton administration regarding private-sector leadership and the setting aside of government regulation and provides for both greater accommodation of national rules and procedures and a role for international and world regional organizations. Among European leaders this approach accepted the basic thrust of what the White House framework document had tried to accomplish—to place leadership of Internet development squarely with the private sector—while at the same time retaining what the Europeans called "a light regulatory touch."[20] From the perspective of U.S. business and government leaders, Europe's acceptance of the concept that the private sector shall lead was considered crucial to U.S. interests, whereas the need for U.S. private-sector interests to come to terms with the rest of the world's national, regional, and international regulatory authorities had long been recognized as essential for building a robust global commercial electronic network.

Willingness on the part of the EC and most EC nations to subscribe to this compromise version of regime principles and norms stemmed primarily from the widespread recognition within Europe that it needed to become more competitive with the United States if it were to stop falling further behind in electronic commercial fields. In 1999, for example, the EC estimated e-commerce revenues for the fifteen EC nations at only $16.8 billion, compared with $71.4 billion (more than four times European revenue) for the United States alone. The EU commissioner for enterprise and telecoms, Erkki Liikanen, stated, perhaps a bit melodramatically, that the EU had "three to four years to catch up with the US before the gulf becomes unbridgeable." EU leaders were also concerned with the rapid development of e-business and e-commerce in Asia, as outlined in an article that appeared in October 1999—widely circulated in Europe—in which Oracle vice president Paul Burrin was quoted as saying, "Asia is behind, but not far behind."[21] In the article an International Data Corporation (IDC) study was quoted to the effect that e-business revenues for the five leading Asian nations (Australia, South Korea, Taiwan, New Zealand, and Hong Kong) totaled an estimated $21 billion in 1999 (compared with only $16.8 billion for the EC countries), and the IDC projected that the figure would grow to over $400 billion by 2003. The study also noted that the People's Republic of China was likely to become a much more significant e-commerce nation, both within Asia and on a global basis, in the immediate years ahead.

Discussion of the framework report within Europe during the 1997–2000 period revealed a number of differences between and within European nations on the future development of e-commerce. Britain, Ireland, and France favored a set of common standards with the United States that would be based on principles of self-regulation by the private sector, and Germany eventually joined the advocates of this position. Germany had originally sided with Austria and the Netherlands in advocating the extension of European domestic commercial legislation over e-commerce, but most European nations rejected this view on the assumption that a single set of rules for the European e-commerce market would be much preferable to an alternative situation in which companies would have to comply with the diverse and often conflicting rules of every EC member nation. This sentiment was forcefully articulated by Patricia Hewitt, the UK minister responsible for e-commerce, when she told an EC gathering in December 1999: "It is immensely important that we get agreement if possible. There is a big prize to be won and that is a single market in e-commerce. That prize is within our grasp." Echoing that sentiment, the president of the European Commission, Romano Prodi, called the EC's eEurope initiative, launched in December 1999, "the most important project to follow the creation of the single market and launch of the euro."[22]

Lobbyists within the EC countries—on behalf of trade unions, consumers, the legal profession, and others—weighed into the discussion of e-commerce during the 1997–2000 period, as did private-sector firms involved in Internet-related business. A number of companies warned that if Brussels tried "to tie them in knots with rules," they would move their businesses to other locations where they would be subject to less government regulation. Robbie Vann-Adibe, the head of Viant (an Internet consultancy firm in London), told the European press in 1999 that "politicians and administrators need to be very aware of exactly how mobile this community is and if they step on too many toes, these people will just go elsewhere."[23]

Responding to the sense of urgency that had emerged in EC and other European discussions of electronic commerce during the period 1997–2000, the dotcom summit of European leaders in March 2000 endorsed the EC recommendation of an ambitious agenda to pass seven proposed EC directives and pieces of legislation by the end of 2000 on the following topics: (1) copyright protection, (2) distance selling of financial services, (3) electronic money, (4) e-commerce, (5) data protection, (6) attempts to set up simple online procedures for settling contractual disputes rather than rely on elaborate procedures under the Brussels and Rome Conventions that allow the public to routinely bring legal cases against Internet Service Providers (ISPs) in the EU, and (7) simple and effective dispute settlement procedures for e-commerce.[24] In addition, the dotcom summit agreed to support European Commission attempts to develop a better risk capital market in the EU, where the number of new companies lagged far behind the United States and East Asia.

The EU reached its first set of substantive agreements on e-commerce rules when it passed a directive in December 1999 that provided for recognition of electronic signatures on contracts. At the same meetings EU ministers also agreed to proposals allowing wider use of electronic money, in the face of opposition from the European Central Bank that more regulations needed to be put in place before such action was undertaken. A second set of substantive agreements in the direction of government deregulation was reached at the Lisbon dotcom summit in March 2000, when the EU heads of state signed up to introduce greater competition into local telecommunications networks by the end of 2000—which would considerably reduce the cost of Internet access.[25]

■ **THE EU-U.S. DATA PROTECTION
AGREEMENT AND REGIME FORMATION**

Differences between the United States and Europe on commercial aspects of Internet regime–related issues are perhaps best illustrated in their contrasting approaches to data protection for the vast files of personal information on individuals that banks, insurance and credit card companies, brokerage houses, and other financial service companies accumulate and pass back and forth in conducting business on the Internet. In the context of international regime formation for the Internet, it was extremely important that in early 2000 the United States and Europe were able to negotiate a means for reconciling the two sharply contrasting approaches traditionally used on the two continents. A major test for maintaining the commercial aspects of the nascent international regime into the future will be the ability of U.S. and European leaders to extend some of the ideas for reconciliation of differences developed in the data protection negotiations (such as the concept of safe harbors, discussed later) both to other areas of commercial developments in cyberspace and to other parts of the globe.

Before the Internet, there was rather limited need (or physical possibility) of transferring massive amounts of personal data across the Atlantic quickly or dramatically, and so the U.S. system of self-regulation of personal data files by private companies had come into conflict with the EU system of government regulation only in restricted and relatively limited ways. All that changed when the growth of Internet commerce made it necessary to transfer larger and larger sets of data files on a much more frequent basis—and in cyberspace time—creating concerns about rights to privacy and a host of other legal matters. The matter came to a head on October 25, 1998, when an EU Directive on Data Protection was scheduled to take effect that would have prevented the EU's fifteen member states from transmitting personal data about their citizens into any country that failed to have what the EU considered "adequate" privacy protection.[26] Since EU officials had declared that the United States had inadequate privacy safeguards, the EU directive threatened to cut off all electronic exchange of information between the United States and Europe.[27]

Negotiations on regime norms and rules for handling different approaches to data protection had been initiated before the October 25, 1999, deadline (when the EU directive was scheduled to take effect), and they continued until mid-2000, when the United States and Europe reached an accommodation. Negotiations were facilitated by divisions within the EU (on the October 25, 1999, date only Greece, Portugal, Sweden, Italy, Belgium, and Finland had implemented the privacy directive, and self-regulatory approaches were being considered in defiance of the EU directive by Germany, the United Kingdom, the Netherlands, and the Scandinavian countries).[28] The agreement between the United States and the EU reached in March 2000 and ratified by the EU countries and the relevant U.S. government agencies later in the year is based on what are called "safe harbor" arrangements, which U.S. companies can subscribe to voluntarily as long as they agree to subsequently be bound by those arrangements.[29] Under the safe harbor accommodation, the United States does not have to change its own laws for U.S. companies to take advantage of whatever safe harbor arrangement a given company reaches with the EU, but the U.S. Federal Trade Commission and other U.S. agencies have agreed to oversee enforcement of the voluntary soft law embedded in the arrangement.[30] Once agreed to with the EU, U.S. companies have the opportunity to join whatever safe harbor arrangement is negotiated, giving them assurance that they can transmit and receive data to and from Europe without interruption and without having their data subject to review by "data police," as is commonplace in some parts of Europe (e.g., Germany and Italy). At the same time, when dealing with U.S. companies in cyberspace, European consumers receive forms of protection of their privacy that they have been familiar with for many years in Europe.[31]

Successful bilateral negotiations between the United States and the EU on data protection have encouraged negotiators across the Atlantic that a new generation of agreements for settling trade disputes and other potential international electronic commerce conflicts might be possible. The U.S. deputy secretary of commerce for trade who led negotiations on the safe harbor arrangement mechanism, David Aaron, for example, stated when he retired in April 2000 that he conceived of traditional methods of international trade and commercial dispute resolution changing radically in the future, with business playing an increasingly major role in settlement. This new generation of agreements would be modeled on the safe harbor data privacy pact and would enable negotiators, in Aaron's words, to "work around differences in their legal systems, increasingly using their private sectors to find convenient solutions."[32] Aaron and many of his European negotiating partners are convinced that the safe harbor concept negotiated bilaterally between the United States and the EU can be extended to multilateral negotiations with other parts of the world into the future.[33] Many policymakers and negotiators working at the international business–national government interface are also hopeful that the concept can help bridge differences between nations in other areas of international electronic commerce development where complex issues exist, including international taxation and attempts to tax transactions in cyberspace across international boundaries.

■ INTERNATIONAL TAXATION OF THE INTERNET AS A REGIME ISSUE

If the United States and Europe can be said to differ substantially with regard to their legal cultures on the issue of data protection, differences between them are even more substantial when it comes to taxation. An indication of the unique U.S. legislative environment on international taxation of the Internet was the October 1999 vote in the House of Representatives (423-1) in support of a resolution calling for the Clinton administration to seek a *permanent moratorium* on international e-commerce tariffs at WTO meetings. The resolution (later passed in a slightly different version in the Senate) also asked the Clinton administration to lobby the Organization for Economic Cooperation and Development (OECD) to implement a ban on "special multiple and discriminatory taxation of electronic commerce and the Internet" and to oppose a UN proposal for the establishment of a "bit tax" on electronic transmission of information.[34] These recommendations reflect widespread support within the U.S. Congress for a total ban on Internet taxes, whether domestic or international. Consistent with such support, both the Senate and the House passed the Tax Freedom Act in 1998, which imposed a three-year ban on all e-commerce taxes within the United States and established an Advisory Commission on Electronic Commerce (composed of political and government leaders, as well as representatives from private companies) to study alternative strategies for taxing the Internet and proposals to establish a permanent ban on domestic Internet-related taxes.

The Advisory Commission on Electronic Commerce was composed of nineteen members, drawn from state governors, members of the Clinton administration, representatives of citizen tax groups, and leaders of e-commerce business firms. Embroiled in the politics of the 2000 presidential election race during a period when the legislative and executive branches of the U.S. government were controlled by different political parties, the commission was unable to muster the "supermajority" (thirteen of the nineteen members) it needed to officially recommend to Congress any specific plan for future taxation of electronic commerce. In its April 2000 final report, therefore, the commission simply passed on to Congress (at the request of Congress) its consensual view that the 1998 ban on new Internet taxes should be extended for another five years (to October 2006). The commission also recommended that Congress pass laws to prohibit taxes from being imposed on Internet users for gaining access to computer networks, and that digitized goods (such as music and software) be declared off-limits to taxation. Other recommendations included a proposal to repeal and phase out the 3 percent federal excise tax on telecommunications that had been in existence in the United States for more than a century.[35] The sole commission recommendation on international electronic commerce was that Congress enact a permanent ban on all international e-commerce tariffs.

Major U.S. opposition to a complete ban on Internet-related taxes and tariffs has come from thirty-six of the fifty governors of U.S. states, who are concerned that such a ban would deprive the states of the massive potential sales tax revenue if taxation of electronic commerce were allowed. Some states are currently taxing Internet transactions in the same way they have been allowed to tax mail-order business and other "remote vendors" under the terms of a 1992 Supreme Court decision known as Quill (*Quill Corporation v. North Dakota,* decided May 26, 1992). That decision allows U.S. states to require remote vendors to pay taxes only if the vendor has a physical presence, such as an office with desks and such, in the particular state. Where there is no physical presence, the state can ask the vendor to pay the tax voluntarily, and some vendors have "voluntarily" paid state taxes on transactions out of concern that they may face state audits if they do not do so. In its 1992 decision, the Supreme Court recognized the constitutional authority of the U.S. Congress, as regulator of interstate commerce, to require Internet retailers to recoup unpaid state sales taxes, but Congress has thus far refused to exercise that authority.[36]

The sensitivities associated with the taxation issue in the United States were dramatized when the governor of Texas and Republican candidate for U.S. president in 2000, George W. Bush, did not join the thirty-six state governors opposing a ban on Internet taxes. Although

Bush has not come out unequivocally in support of the idea that the Internet should be a "tax-free zone," his principle rival in the quest for the GOP nomination, Senator John McCain, was a key congressional champion of the movement to ban taxes on electronic commerce.[37] The Democratic Party candidate for president, Vice President Al Gore, refused to support proposals for federal taxes on electronic commerce but was guardedly receptive to allowing taxation by states.[38]

Governments in several countries other than the United States have developed positions on taxation issues related to electronic commerce, but in few of those countries have national, provincial, or local leaders faced as intense an aversion to Internet taxes as is found in the United States. The European Commission director of tax policy, Michel Aujean, for example, has pointed out that existing European "consumption taxes" (similar in some respects to U.S. state sales taxes) have been and, he predicts, "will be modified to apply to e-commerce without great protest."[39] Aujean also pointed out that many European governments rely heavily for revenue on a value-added tax (VAT; a series of indirect sales taxes paid on products and services at each stage of production or distribution of service that are folded into an all-inclusive price when the product is retailed to the customer). The manner in which the VAT is collected, in Aujean's view, makes it easier for European governments to collect Internet-related taxes and would make it more difficult for opponents of such taxes to sort out from the total product or service package those portions of the item being sold that are Internet related.[40]

Outside of Europe, U.S. support in the WTO for a global ban on e-commerce tariffs has been opposed by many developing nations (and some relatively developed nations as well) because leaders of those nations view taxation of Internet-related activities as both a potentially lucrative source of future revenue and, in some instances, a means of paying for domestic Internet infrastructural costs. In 1999 India's Finance Ministry initiated exploration of ways it might tax electronic transactions, and the minister of taxes and levies in the Russian Federation, Aleksandr Pochinok, said in April 2000 that "if the Europeans do this, we will be forced to introduce a similar mechanism here simply because otherwise the revenue from the Russian part of the Internet will go elsewhere in Europe."[41] In February 2000 the Japanese newspaper *Nihon Keizai Shimbun* reported that the Ministry of Finance in Japan was planning to levy taxes on large Internet transactions involving business-to-business exchanges and to impose a "consumption tax" on online purchases of software, music software, and images sent into Japan by overseas vendors.[42]

Several proposals have also been made within the United Nations for UN-imposed taxes on Internet transactions to either improve world revenue streams to third world governments or create an international fund that might be used for Internet development in those parts of the world that are on the downside of the digital divide. One of the most ambitious of these schemes, devised by the United Nations Development Program (UNDP) in October 1999, calls for a tax equivalent to one U.S. cent on every 100 e-mails sent by individuals anywhere in the world, which the UNDP estimated would have generated U.S.$70 billion in development assistance for the United Nations in the four-year period 1996–2000.[43] A somewhat similar bit tax was proposed for the European Union in 1997 by influential economist Luc Soete, then director of the Maastricht Economic Research Institute on Innovation and Technology, and the tax was seriously considered for a short time by some EU leaders.[44] But international bit tax proposals have not been enthusiastically received in U.S. official, political, or business circles; nor have they been seriously considered in Europe or East Asia.

U.S.-EU negotiations on Internet taxation issues have been characterized by several ups and downs over the past few years, as EU leaders have become increasingly enamored with the idea of taxing electronic commerce. In 1997 Clinton administration negotiators seemed on the verge of an understanding with the EU that there would be no tariff barriers across the Atlantic on certain electronic goods sold over the Internet—including some types of computer software—but the negotiations were never formalized into law, treaty, or a soft law arrangement.[45] At the time, such goods accounted for less than $1 billion a year in trade worldwide, but the volume of that trade has increased enormously since then and is expected to grow at an even faster pace in the years ahead. In contrast to the cooperation developed during the 1997 negotiations, the United States suffered what the *New York Times* called "its largest defeat ever in a trade battle" in February 2000, when the WTO sided with the European Union and ordered the United States to repeal a law that had allowed U.S. companies to avoid paying taxes on some overseas sales by channeling them through offshore subsidiaries.[46] Further strains in the U.S.-EU relationship have resulted from a March 2000 decision by the European Commission to impose VATs on music and software delivered over the World Wide Web, despite protests from U.S. companies that this would be highly detrimental to the growth of electronic commerce into the future.[47]

Possibilities for conflict over international taxation issues are likely to grow throughout the world as Internet use increases in the years ahead, especially in those countries where e-commerce and e-business become prominent features of a nation's commercial environment. As more and more nations enact legislation to tax transactions over the Internet, it will be increasingly necessary to find regularized means for reconciling, at Internet speed, the laws of nations that do not tax electronic commerce at all with those that tax it at different rates or with different procedures. The possibilities for misunderstanding and conflict are enormous, but there is a widespread realization among many nations of the need for widely accepted rules and procedures at the international level if electronic commerce is to flourish in the years ahead. At this point, however, discussion of regime principles and norms for taxation has lagged behind more advanced negotiations on data protection and other aspects of the international regime for the Internet.

Efforts to move discussion of taxation-related regime issues from the agenda-setting stage to more structured negotiations have recently tended to cluster around two powerful international organizations: one (the Global Business Dialogue on Electronic Commerce [GBDe]) representing international business interests, the second (the OECD) representing the governments of those nations that account for the bulk of world trade.[48]

■ *The Global Business Dialogue on Electronic Commerce*

Founded in June 1998, the GBDe has emerged as the leading global organization of private business leaders involved in electronic commerce (U.S. secretary of commerce Richard Daley has called it the "International Chamber of e-Commerce"). During its first year, Thomas Middelhoff of Bertelsmann AG chaired the group.[49] In the second year the cochairs were Steve Case, chairman of America Online, and Gerald Levin, chairman of Time Warner, Inc. The GBDe was originally formed by 24 companies—drawn from the Americas, Asia, Europe, and Africa—interested in giving organizational shape to the principle that the private sector should lead in setting up rules and procedures for coordinating electronic commerce.[50] At its first annual conference in Paris in September 1999, leaders from more than 200 member companies (including 70 CEOs) attended, along with representatives from 23 international organizations and 110 governments of nation-states from around the world.[51] The GBDe functions through seven working groups, dealing with privacy, consumer confidence/alternative dispute resolution, consumer confidence/GBDe trustmark,[52] trade and taxation, intellectual property rights, advocacy of GBDe recommendations, and outreach.

GBDe's Trade and Taxation Working Group is chaired by the CEO of IBM, Louis V. Gerstner, with the contact point for Asia being Hiroshi Egami of Bank of Tokyo-Mitsubishi and the contact point for Europe/Africa being Lutz Kolbe of Deutsche Bank. The goal of the working group is to involve itself with governments around the world and with the WTO, OECD, EU, and other international and regional organizations to promote what it calls "a seamless global system" for international electronic commerce. The GBDe has endorsed the U.S. Congress in its attempts to bring into being a permanent worldwide ban on Internet taxes and tariffs. It defines its day-to-day activities as "collaboration with governments to target and eliminate discriminations against [global electronic commerce], or other non-tariff barriers to global trade in electronic commerce . . . in an environment unencumbered by detrimental taxation."[53]

▪ The Organization of Economic Cooperation and Development

The OECD was founded in Paris in 1961 as the successor organization to the Organization for European Economic Cooperation (OEEC) (1948–1961), which had handled the massive transfer of funds and programs from the United States to Europe under the Marshall Plan. Originally established by a convention signed by twenty European and North American states plus Turkey, the OECD had expanded to twenty-nine member countries in 2000, including Japan, Australia, New Zealand, Mexico, the Czech Republic, Hungary, Poland, and Korea. Its member nations account for more than two-thirds of the world's production of goods and services and more than three-fourths of international trade. The OECD Council meets regularly at the ambassador level to make recommendations for harmonizing world economic policies and practices. It sponsors the periodic economic summits of the so-called Group of 7 (G-7) leaders (the heads of state of Canada, the

United States, U.K., France, Germany, Italy, and Japan), which have provided world leadership on a host of substantive political economic issues.

One of the most important contributions of the OECD to the growth of the modern world economy over the years has been the work of its committees, which are composed of representatives from its member nations and supported by a staff of more than 2,000 professionals at OECD headquarters in Paris.[54] The governments of the EU, the United States, Japan, and other OECD nations are looking to the results of a three-year study of taxation issues related to electronic commerce being carried out by the OECD's Committee on Fiscal Affairs (CFA), which will make specific recommendations for the establishment of standards, rules, and procedures relating to Internet taxation.[55] The CFA recommendations will presumably be based on the five principles the OECD has already developed as guideposts for evaluating the operation of online tax systems.[56] These five principles (which would more accurately be referred to as "norms" in the political science literature on international regimes) have been outlined by the CFA as follows:[57]

1. Neutrality—Taxation should seek to be neutral and equitable among forms of electronic commerce and between conventional and electronic forms of commerce. Business decisions should be motivated by economic rather than tax considerations. Taxpayers in similar situations carrying out similar transactions should be subject to similar levels of taxation.
2. Efficiency—Compliance costs for taxpayers and administrative costs for tax authorities should be minimized as much as possible.
3. Certainty and simplicity—The tax rules should be clear and simple to understand so taxpayers can anticipate the tax consequences in advance of a transaction, including knowing when, where, and how the tax is to be accounted.
4. Effectiveness and fairness—Taxation should produce the right amount of tax at the right time. The potential for evasion and avoidance should be minimized, and counteracting measures should be proportionate to the risks involved.
5. Flexibility—The systems for taxation should be flexible and dynamic to ensure that they keep pace with technological and commercial developments.

Although no formal agreement has been reached among the major nations with significant interest in taxation of electronic commerce, sufficient discussion of various concepts of taxation frameworks has occurred to produce increasing clarity about the interests of key world actors. In the political science literature on international regimes, Oran Young has pointed out that ideas and interests interact a great deal during the early stages of regime formation, with ideas especially prominent during the agenda-setting stage and interests dominating the stage of negotiation.[58] This has clearly been the case thus far in the evolution of the commercial aspects of international regime dynamics for the Internet. Large lists of initial conceptions among actors about how international business might be conducted in cyberspace have begun to be whittled down to a finite number of specific issue areas, with more and more nations becoming involved in discussions of how the challenges in those issue areas might be met. The negotiation stage of regime formation has been reached and successful negotiations carried out in some areas, such as data protection. In other areas (e.g., taxation), discussion of a variety of ideas may have led to increasing clarity about the interests of the parties involved but has not yet moved beyond the earliest negotiation stage of regime creation.

■ **NOTES**

1. *A Framework for Global Electronic Commerce,* available at www.iitf.nist.gov/eleccomm/ecomm.htm.
2. An early collection of academic studies on the subject was McKnight and Bailey, *Internet Economics.*
3. See Moschovitis et al., *History of the Internet,* pp. 213–214, and Kahin, "The U.S. National Information Infrastructure Initiative," pp. 150–189.
4. The Bangemann Report and the EU's response to it are detailed in Hedblom and Garrison, "European Information Infrastructure," pp. 491 ff.
5. Browning, "Africa 1, Hollywood 0," p. 186. The two WIPO treaties were heavily influenced by a coalition of African and Asian nations with some European countries backed by private IT firms from Europe. The treaties were extremely moderate and established no governance mechanisms for enforcement. A third treaty proposed at the December 1996 WIPO meeting—on protection of digital databases—was tabled. The two treaties that were approved are still wending their way through the ratification processes of the 170 domestic governments that belong to WIPO (for more detail, see the section Copyright in Chapter 4).
6. Blackhurst, "The Capacity of the WTO," pp. 46 ff. The addition of

intellectual property to the WTO's mandate is of special significance, as is pointed out later in this chapter, because the WTO, unlike WIPO, has effective *enforcement* mechanisms, embedded in trade sanctions, to back up its rules in areas where its membership has granted it a mandate.

7. These recommendations appear in *A Framework for Global Electronic Commerce,* pp. 2–4, and are analyzed in some detail in Malawer, "International Trade and Transactions," p. S40.

8. Summary coverage of open-source operating systems is available in a theme issue on the subject in *FEED* magazine, February 1999, available at www.feedmag.com. The issue includes an electronic roundtable with three luminaries in the field: Richard Stallman, president of the Free Software Foundation; Eric Raymond, author of *The New Hacker's Dictionary;* and Eric Allman, president of Sendmail, a company offering commercial e-mail software built on Allman's free software version of Sendmail. See also Abreu, "Poking Holes in Linux," and Hold, "Who Pays? Who Cares?"

9. Quoted in Brinkley with Lohr, "Tangled Path," p. C6.

10. Riordan, "Patents Considered Vital," p. C39.

11. Illegal programs are often called "wares" or "warez" by computer hackers or "pirated software" by the computer industry. Wares are traded through unauthorized software rental, counterfeit software engineering, and downloading of programs from the Internet or bulletin boards without publishers' permission. For further information, see Moschovitis et al., *History of the Internet,* pp. 235 ff.

12. One of the most strident positions in support of intellectual property interests was taken by Bruce Lehman when he chaired the Clinton administration's Intellectual Property Working Group in the White House in the mid-1990s. Lehman argued that because of the ubiquitous nature of the Internet, traditional "fair use" policies for copyright protection should be replaced by much more stringent policies that would outlaw "the forwarding, duplication, or even online reading of digital materials without permission from the copyright holder." Quoted in ibid., p. 214.

13. For more detail, see Venturelli, "Information Liberalization," pp. 465 ff.

14. Ibid.

15. Ibid., p. 466.

16. Ibid., p. 468. See also Crandall and Waverman, *Who Pays for Universal Service?*

17. Figures in this paragraph are from Peter Ford, "EU's 'Dotcom' Summit." See also Karen Chan, "European Web Use Increased."

18. Europe has gained a competitive edge on the United States in the areas of mobile telephony and wireless communications, both considered vital aspects of the Internet's future. For analyses, see Borland, "Technology Tussle," and Borland, "AT&T Fights Back."

19. Quoted in Ford, "EU's 'Dotcom' Summi," p. 7. At the same summit the EU commissioner for jobs, Anna Diamantopoulou, said, "We can be a

model for the world—matching the United States on competitiveness but ahead of them with a fully modern European social model."

20. The emergence of this compromise is analyzed in Hargreaves, "Light Touch on the Web," p. 25. The quotations in this and the following paragraph, unless otherwise noted, are from this source.

21. The article by Borisuthiboun Dasaneyavaja, "Electronic Business Indicators Suggest Asian e-Business Is Up," initially appeared in the *Bangkok Post,* October 27, 1999, but was carried by or written about in the Asian Intelligence Wire of the *Financial Times* (London) and all major European wire services.

22. Eaglesham and Hargreaves, "Rules and Red Tape," p. 13.

23. Hargreaves, "Light Touch of the Web," p. 25.

24. Hargreaves, "Fast Tract for e-Commerce Laws," p. 1.

25. Hargreaves, "Brussels Acts," p. 2. In addition to opening competition among local networks, the telecoms policy endorsed by the EU heads of state in March 2000 would also deregulate and allow greater competition among private firms in the crucial "final mile connection" between the telecoms networks and subscriber homes.

26. The directive eventually came into effect only after an agreement was reached reconciling differences between the United States and EU. Under the new act, Europeans will be allowed to claim compensation for any breach of data protection law and for distress as well as direct loss, thereby expanding considerably the potential liabilities of companies, which previously could be sued only for financial loss stemming from inaccurate or wrongly disclosed data. The new directive also covers a wider range of activities, including the clear legal right to object at any time to information being used for direct marketing and stricter controls on the processing of "sensitive" data, including data on racial or ethnic origin. For more details, see "Consumers' Rights Companies 'Ignorant' of Tougher Sanctions."

27. Jane Kirtley has pointed out that different approaches to data protection can be traced in part to differences between the U.S. common law tradition, based on case law and a restricted role for the federal government, and the civil law tradition in Europe, based on codes that countenance a more obtrusive role for government. See Kirtley, "Is Implementing the EU Data Protection Directive in the United States Irreconcilable with the First Amendment?" pp. 87–91. See also Messmer, "U.S., Europe at Impasse over Privacy...," and Edgecliffe-Johnson, "Corporate Security," p. 2.

28. See deBony, "EC Takes Countries to Court."

29. The terms of the safe harbor proposals are outlined in Yerkey, "U.S., European Union Set to Begin Talks," pp. 2284 ff. The safe harbor arrangement includes sections relating to choices by individuals to opt out of databases, onward transfer rules for forwarding information to third parties, data integrity protocols to ensure data are what they purport to be, access rights to records, and enforcement mechanisms to provide redress for individuals in cases where rules are violated. An outline of the key features of the agreement appears in "EU, U.S. Hammer out Privacy Agreement."

30. In response to the concerns of U.S. editors and publishers, the EU attempted (in Article 9 of the directive) to make exceptions that would afford some protection for a journalist and his or her sources. As Jane Kirtley pointed out, application of the safe harbor principles and EU law would be both unworkable and unconstitutional if applied to journalistic endeavors in the United States. Kirtley argues, for example, that "the Notice and Choice Provisions require that individuals must be informed about the purposes for which information is being collected, and given the choice to 'opt out.' To compel reporters to identify why a particular piece of information is being gathered, and to obtain permission from the subject before writing about her, would be an unwarranted intrusion into the editorial process." Kirtley, "Is Implementing the EU Data Protection Directive in the United States Irreconcilable with the First Amendment?" p. 89.

31. To facilitate companies' use of the safe harbor agreement, in November 2000 the Internet's leading privacy seal program, TRUSTe, announced an EU Safe Harbor Privacy Seal program that would verify full compliance with the agreement, including training programs for companies, Web site certification and oversight, and facilities for online and offline dispute resolution. See "TRUSTe Unveils European Union Safe Harbor Privacy Seal Program." At the same time, international lawyers were advising companies transferring data into the United States to have their safe harbor certificates supplemented by a legally binding indemnity lest they risk being legally exposed. See Eaglesham and Mason, "US 'Not a Safe Harbour for Data Transfer,'"p. 26.

32. Quoted in Dunne and Lerner, "Role for Business in Trade Disputes," p. 12.

33. For comments by the EU's negotiator, John Mogg, on the safe harbor pact, see Clausing, "Europe and U.S. Reach Data Privacy Pact," p. C6.

34. A summary of the resolution and an analysis of its political context appear in Perine, "Congress Seeks Global E-Commerce Tax Ban."

35. Wasserman, "Tax Panel Agrees They Can't Agree."

36. An excellent analysis of the legal aspects of state taxing powers for electronic commerce appears in Tyson, "Should World Wide Web Be a Tax-Free Zone?" p. 3.

37. During his New Hampshire primary campaign in January 2000, McCain was quoted as saying, "I think the real pernicious tax that's out there is the Internet tax. My friends, that should be permanently banned. . . . I think that part of my commitment of not raising taxes should be a commitment to maintaining a permanent ban on Internet taxing." Quoted in Zimmerman, "McCain," p. 17. McCain subsequently introduced a bill in the Senate permanently banning taxation of e-commerce.

38. Wasserman has pointed out that the three Clinton administration representatives on the Advisory Commission on Electronic Commerce abstained from almost every vote on final recommendations, a strategy that "avoided tainting Vice President Al Gore as a supporter of Net sales taxes and simultaneously robbed the panel Chairman, Virginia Governor Jim Gilmore (rumored to

be a potential cabinet member or running mate to George W. Bush) of an anti-tax victory." See "Tax Panel Agrees They Can't Agree," p. 1. See also Lambro, "The Plot to Tax the Internet," pp. 77–84, 109.

39. Quoted in an Associated Press article, "Fed Panel Urged to Keep Web Tax Free," p. 2.

40. The Internet tax Germany decided to impose, beginning in September 2000, was a VAT imposed on Internet-related products, with the understanding that the proceeds of the tax would be paid to "firms that specialize in collecting royalties on . . . intellectual property, [which would] pass these fees on to clients such as authors, music, film or software companies." See "Report: Germany Plans 'Internet Tax.'"

41. "Government Planning to Tax Transactions on Internet," p. 14, and "Russia: Internet Tax Would be 'Europe-Driven.'"

42. The *Nihon Keizai Shimbun* story was summarized in English in the *Financial Times* (London), February 22, 2000.

43. Dean, "UN Proposes Global Email Tax."

44. Soete's bit tax proposal is summarized in Soete and Kamp, "Bit Tax," available by request at luc.soete@algec.unimaas.nl.

45. The terms of the agreement are detailed in Lohr, "U.S. and European Union Agree."

46. In 1999 alone, the EU estimated, large U.S. companies like Boeing, Microsoft, and General Motors had avoided paying more than $4 billion in taxes under the provision ruled in violation of WTO trade rules. For details, see Kahn, "U.S. Loses Dispute on Export Sales," p. 1

47. The issue is analyzed in Andrews, "Europe Plans to Collect Tax on Some Internet Transactions."

48. Jonathan Schwarz has pointed out that "[Internet taxation] issues involve every country, [so] tax administrations world-wide have recognised that they are unlikely to be satisfactorily addressed by unilateral action. . . . Consequently, the OECD has become the forum for addressing the challenges of e-commerce." Quoted in Schwarz, "Profound Threat to Revenues," p. 10.

49. Middelhoff was named Most Influential International Executive by the *Standard* in its April 24, 2000, issue. Information on the formation of GBDe is available on its website at www.gbd.org.

50. A summary article about the formation of GBDe and its mission appears in "CEO Group Tools to Set E-Biz Rules," p. 1. See also "E-Commerce Band to Battle Net Regulators," and "Global Group on E-Commerce Meets to Set Standards."

51. Uimonen, "Internet Privacy Issues Focus of Paris Summit."

52. The GBDe trustmark is scheduled to be awarded to commercial e-commerce sites around the world that meet the codes of conduct and standards set or endorsed by the GBDe and its member companies as a means of building consumer confidence that those websites are reliable and will protect consumer privacy and confidentiality.

53. Quoted from "Working Groups Issues Summary" on the GBDe

website at www.gbde.org/structure/working/issues.html. See also Shannon, "CEOs Lobby for E-Commerce," p. E3.

54 Analysis of OECD involvement in Internet-related issues appears in *Implications of the WTO Agreement*. See also the OECD website at www.oecd.org.

55. The CFA project originated at an informal business-government roundtable entitled "Electronic Commerce: The Challenges to Tax Authorities and Taxpayers," held in Turku, Finland, in November 1997 in conjunction with the OECD conference "Dismantling the Barriers to Global Electronic Commerce," held at the same time.

56. The CFA has established five technical advisory groups to study indirect and consumption taxes, technology and taxation, professional data assessment, business profits, and income characterization. For an analysis of the factors being considered by the CFA in preparing its September 2000 report, see Schwarz, "Profound Threat to Revenues," p. 10.

57. Articulation of these five principles was the result of a series of discussion documents circulated among relevant agencies of the twenty-nine OECD member states. Their place in the larger framework for electronic commerce is discussed in detail in *Taxation Principles and Electronic Commerce*, available at www.oecd.org, which lists the five principles verbatim.

58. Young, *Creating Regimes*, pp. 169 ff.

4

Investment and Intellectual Property

C hapters 1–3 outline the working principles and norms negotiated and agreed to by advanced information societies for the technical, governance, and commercial aspects of international computer networking, which together have made it possible to operationalize the Internet as an engineering feat and to conceive of the extension of its reach to more and more areas of life and to almost all parts of the world. But in fact, the Internet in 2000 was being accessed by a small percentage of the world's population (no more than 2 percent). Only in 4 of the 103 nations in the world's poorest regions (Africa, South Asia, the Middle East, Eurasia, and Central/Eastern Europe) did more than 6 percent of the population have access to the Internet at the beginning of the twenty-first century (South Africa, Estonia, Israel, and the United Arab Emirates are the four nations).[1] In 90 of those 103 countries, less than 2 percent of the population has access to the Internet, and in most of those 90 nations access is available to much less than 1 percent of the population.

As outlined in Chapters 1–3, the key principles identified by advanced IT societies for extending the Internet from one part of the world to another rely heavily on the role of the private sector and local, informal processes of decisionmaking and involvement, often built around soft law arrangements. Key elements of the regime include the principle that regulatory and other government activities should avoid undue restrictions on Internet commercial activities while facilitating the development of international electronic commerce by the private sector. Regional and international organizations (e.g., WIPO, OECD,

WTO) are expected to play a major role in multiplying Internet access internationally, but these organizations are not conceived to be global governments with authority over sovereign nation-states and private companies; nor are they looked to for the financial resources necessary for IT development.

Extending Internet regime principles and norms to less advanced IT nation-states necessarily entails large amounts of direct foreign investment by the private sector in Internet-related activities and the enforcement of intellectual property rights on a global basis. This is so because neither governments nor the private sector in the less advanced IT nations has the kind of available capital necessary to build extensive Internet and Internet-related IT infrastructures, whereas in the advanced information societies the primary sources of such large amounts of capital are in the private sector. But private-sector banks and other private sources of funding can be induced to invest in Internet-related ventures around the world only if substantive liberalization, privatization, and regulatory programs are effectively implemented and it is assumed that intellectual property will be protected. Protection of intellectual property on an unprecedented scale at the global level is particularly important if private sources of wealth are to achieve levels of capital formation necessary to play the lead role expected of them within the framework of the Internet's emerging international regime.

This chapter seeks to understand the role of these two key elements—international foreign direct investment and protection of intellectual property rights—in the attempt to extend the international regime for the Internet to the less developed countries (LDCs) and other nations. Promotion of foreign direct investment (FDI) is explored in two of the most prominent instances where leaders of advanced information societies have tried to extend international Internet regime principles and norms to those parts of the world with less advanced IT infrastructures: (1) the process established by the European Union (EU) to bring liberalization and privatization policies in Internet-related sectors of the economies of the ten nations in Central/Eastern Europe being considered for EU membership into conformity with the policies of present EU member states in Western Europe, and (2) attempts to facilitate liberalization and privatization of the Internet-related sectors of LDC economies as a result of the General Agreement on Trade in Services (GATS) of the WTO, negotiated in 1994. Both the EU and WTO/GATS processes are intended to promote foreign investment in those developing countries that demonstrate a commitment to privatization in Internet-related matters. The concluding section of the chapter is an analysis of some of the major attempts to strengthen intellectual property awareness and enforcement at the international level in the context of international Internet regime formation.

▪ EU INTEGRATION AND INTERNET REGIME–RELATED ASPECTS OF INTERNATIONAL INVESTMENT

Apart from attempts by the EU and its member nations to negotiate electronic commerce agreements with the U.S. government and the private sector, a separate set of EU policies has influenced both the ways in which financial investment aspects of the global Internet regime are developing and the speed at which the Internet has spread to the rest of the world, particularly to Central and Eastern Europe (CEE). This separate set of policies resulted from the confluence of two major EU decisions agreed to in the late 1980s and early 1990s, when the Berlin Wall was dramatically torn down and communist regimes throughout Central and Eastern Europe were either being toppled or self-destructing. First, the European Economic Community (EEC) green paper was finalized in 1987, requiring that EU member nations of Western Europe adopt a sequence of steps toward liberalization of their economies, including the privatization of telecommunications monopolies and other aspects of IT development that would become crucial to the spread of Internet technology and use in the 1990s. Second, following the collapse of communism, the EU initiated negotiations with ten nations in Central and Eastern Europe being considered for entry into the European Union, with the understanding that each nation would be admitted only if it adopted the same sequence of steps toward economic liberalization and privatization that had been or were being experienced by present EU members.

The aspiration of CEE nations to join the European Union therefore placed strong pressures on those countries to liberalize and privatize their economies and to adopt telecommunications and IT-related policy environments that would help them meet requirements for EU membership. The steps the EU laid down, as outlined in the green paper, include separation of government regulatory authority from the operation of telecommunications systems; open interconnection of user equipment to telecommunications lines to encourage free flow of information; liberalized use of leased lines; liberalization of licensing and other controls on private value-added networks to enable them to more readily compete with government companies and with each other; privatization of highly competitive specialized services, such as cellular and mobile; legal and regulatory tolerance or encouragement of facilities-based private networks; governmental allowance of competition in long-distance service; and encouragement of competition in basic local or regional telecommunications services.[2] These steps have been designed to encourage private-sector leadership and investment in the building of Internet-related and other telecommunications infrastructures, and they have had a major impact in this regard on both Western and CEE nations.

All of these steps are not only intimately related to the development of telecommunications and IT infrastructures necessary for the development of the Internet; they are also consistent with the two regime working principles negotiated between the EU and the United States for the development of electronic commerce as outlined earlier in this chapter and in Chapter 3: (1) that the private sector shall play a lead role in the development of electronic commerce on a global basis, and (2) that regulatory and other government activities should avoid undue restrictions on Internet commercial activities while facilitating the development of international electronic commerce by the private sector. But the confluence of embryonic international regime principles for electronic commerce and an emergent economic order in Western Europe has added an additional dimension to European Internet and Internet-related financing that in turn has had a major impact on the development of the international regime for the Internet at the global level.

Since none of the countries in Central and Eastern Europe was prepared (in a technical, financial, or managerial sense) to build modern Internet infrastructures in the 1990s, much less to become meaningfully involved in e-commerce and other commercial electronic activities, the leadership of CEE nations was neither ready nor able to be included in any significant way in the U.S.-EU negotiations on e-commerce norms, standards, rules, and procedures. This does not mean the CEE nations have been excluded entirely from discussion of regime principles and norms, but it has entailed the need for what might be conceived as a separate track in the regime formation process.[3] As a result of discussions and negotiations carried out in the 1990s, during a period when the CEE nations were first beginning to build modern Internet-related telecommunications and computer networking infrastructures, the confluence of events mentioned earlier resulted in rather firm agreement—

throughout all of Europe—on the regime principle that the costs of Internet-related infrastructural development shall be borne primarily by the private sector and the regime norm that governments shall commit themselves to economic liberalization, privatization, and regulatory programs consistent with this and other regime principles. To a considerable extent, the evolution of this principle and norm has been spontaneous rather than planned, arising primarily from the twin realizations that governments in Europe did not have the kind of capital necessary to build globally competitive Internet-related infrastructures and computer networks and that private-sector banks and other sources of the massive funding needed would be willing to invest in Europe only if substantive liberalization, privatization, and regulatory programs were effectively implemented.[4]

In addition to pressure from the EU for privatization and competition in Internet-related development, pressures on the CEE countries also emanate from policies of the World Bank and other development banks that routinely insist on reductions in the size of government operations, debt, and expenditures in sectors of the economy (like telecommunications) that have traditionally been government monopolies but where private operators and investors can be found in abundance. In addition, users and customers of telecommunications services in the new democracies of Central and Eastern Europe—individuals, organizations, and businesses—are pressuring governments to lower prices while providing more efficient service and to offer a range of services (cellular telephony, digital overlay networks, computer-enhanced or value-added services, and very small aperture terminal [VSAT] or other satellite services) government cannot afford to initiate on its own. Such pressures tend to push government and political leaders toward advocacy of privatization and liberalization as a way to quickly attract at least some significant portion of the capital, technology, and expertise needed to become seriously involved in the global cyberspace economy.

Approaches to both privatization and EU membership vary among the CEE nations, depending on a number of factors explored in the companion volume to this one. Although ten CEE nations are being considered for EU membership, the European Commission has warned that enlargement of the EU cannot be considered a forgone conclusion, particularly in light of several contentious and potentially explosive issues relating to the impact of enlargement on employment, trade, competition, and migration. Despite these warnings, a 2000 survey by the *Financial Times* (London) concluded that "many hundreds of companies have already been acting for years on the basis that it [EU enlargement] is almost certain to happen."[5] This has led a number of observers to liken the way in which economic integration has taken place between Eastern and Western Europe since the early 1990s to the process followed when the EU was created several decades ago, at which time the interests of the French and German coal, iron, and steel communities were gradually brought together—in a rather willy-nilly way—until the formation of a "community" eventually just seemed inevitable. By pursuing their own economic interests, companies and governments brought about an increasing degree of economic integration in the 1990s, particularly in areas related to telecommunications and IT. As Stefan Wagstyl has pointed out, this process is furthest along for those five countries already involved in accession talks (the Czech Republic, Estonia, Hungary, Poland, and Slovenia) and is generally less advanced for those that have just started serious negotiations (Bulgaria, Latvia, Lithuania, Romania, and Slovakia).[6]

Although progress in the accession of each of the CEE states is discussed in detail in the companion volume to this one, it should be pointed out here that the nations of Western Europe have been having difficulty meeting the standards for liberalization of the telecommunications market. In March 2000, for example, the EU started legal action against six member nations (Austria, Belgium, Finland, France, Italy, the Netherlands) for failing to implement the latest stage of liberalization by the first day of the new millennium, as scheduled.[7] A major problem was addressed at the dotcom summit in Lisbon in March 2000 when Europe's heads of state agreed to speed up deregulation of EU telecoms markets to reduce the cost of Internet access, recognizing that such costs were much higher in Europe than in the United States. Prior to the summit the EU Enterprise and Information Society Commission had addressed a second major problem in a strategy document—*Towards a New Framework for Electronic Communications Infrastructure and Associated Services*—calling for the replacement of telecom-specific legislation with practices that would allow regular European antitrust law to determine the legality of market practices and conditions. The plan also called for elimination of unnecessary bureaucratic rules and regulations within three years by reducing the number of EU telecom-related laws from twenty in 2000 to six by 2003. The six remaining laws would most likely cover the overall framework, licensing procedures, universal service requirements, data protection, Internet access, and interconnection.[8]

▪ **THE WTO AND REGIME ASPECTS OF
INTERNET-RELATED INTERNATIONAL INVESTMENT**

In the same way criteria for EU membership (and accession to membership) have helped operationalize for Europeans the regime principle that the costs of Internet-related infrastructural development shall be borne primarily by the private sector and the regime norm that governments shall commit themselves to economic liberalization, privatization, and regulatory programs, WTO membership criteria and related rules and procedures have helped operationalize the same regime principle and norm at the global level. The WTO criteria, rules, and procedures were first established in principle as part of the GATS at the end of the Uruguay Round of GATT trade talks in December 1993 and the annex to the 1993 agreement concluded in 1994.[9] The GATS addressed world trade in services, including telecommunications, for the first time in history, since GATT had always confined itself to discussion and agreements on trade goods.

Under the 1993 GATS agreement, every country in the world that wishes to be part of the GATT (now WTO) trading community is required to negotiate and file an individual schedule of commitment, indicating how and when that country is going to comply with GATS principles. These principles require (1) national treatment (i.e., the same regulatory treatment domestic firms receive) and (2) compliance with a number of GATS market access provisions (designed to open world exchange of services, including telecommunications, to competition). Among other things, the GATS provisions forbid national rules and laws that explicitly discriminate among service providers on the basis of nationality (e.g., by placing limitations on foreign capital investment or requiring that foreign providers operate through a specific legal form).[10]

The 1993 GATS agreement applied only to those telecommunications sectors WTO members incorporated in their schedules, most of which were put together by the member nations in 1994. The schedules initially contained what are commonly referred to as "enhanced telecommunications services," those in which the voice or nonvoice information being transferred undergoes an end-to-end restructuring or format change before it reaches the customer. Many of these services— such as electronic mail, online information, electronic data interchange, code and protocol conversion, and data processing—are intimately related to the functioning of the Internet, and demand for many of them mushroomed throughout the world in the 1990s. But in 1993–1994 WTO members were not prepared to commit themselves to open world competition in basic telecommunications services because, unlike enhanced services, basic services have traditionally been either state-owned or state-sanctioned monopolies in almost every country in the world.

Within the space of only four years, however—on February 15, 1997—sixty-nine WTO member nations (accounting for 93 percent of world trade at the time) were willing to sign a much more comprehensive agreement that did include basic telecommunications services: the WTO Agreement on Basic Telecommunications (ABT).[11] The significance of this agreement was summarized by Alan Cane in 1999:

> Telecommunications is in brutal, unpredictable transition. The new millennium will close the door on 100 years of the old order charac-terised by the dominance of a handful of state-owned monopolies, high prices, costly but inefficient technologies, and an innate conser-vatism. The new telecoms is virtually the reverse. It is distinguished by competition, consolidation, falling prices and an armoury of new, low-cost technologies which promise unprecedented speed and trans-mission capacity.[12]

Cane and others have attributed the willingness of the world's trading nations to negotiate a much more competitive international telecommu-nications market to the massive demand for data transmission made possible by the Internet and the expected second revolution mobile tele-phones are expected to bring to world communication networks early in the new millennium. As Cane put it in 1999: "Mobile telephones threat-en to displace the fixed variety for most voice calls within the first few years of the next century. . . . The next generation of mobile phones, known as UMTS [Universal Mobile Telecommunications System] in Europe and set for launch around 2001, will be able to receive and send text, data and video images in addition to voice. It threatens to revolu-tionise personal communications."[13]

By 1998 the leaders of the world's major trading nations were anx-ious to become part of the "twin revolutions" in telecommunications, as it had become increasingly clear that the Internet and mobile telephony were converging to make it possible for the most effective service providers to offer almost any information almost anytime almost any-where in the world. To become part of the "new telecoms"—or, in other words, for a leader to take one's nation through the "brutal, unpre-dictable transition" described by Cane—it became evident that massive amounts of capital would have to be raised and that the governments of nation-states were incapable of raising or providing such capital without the enthusiastic participation of the private sector. Since significant private-sector involvement could be assured only within national frameworks where companies were allowed to compete to provide new IT services and have access to newly emerging telecommunications markets, a number of WTO member nations agreed to commit to such a framework.[14]

The 1997 ABT set in motion a wave of privatization measures for telecommunications throughout the world, beginning in Europe, Canada, and Japan and eventually extending to other parts of the world. Within a year, for example, Canada had opened its previous government telecommunications monopoly to private partnerships and mergers, with the result that each of Canada's three dominant telecommunications carriers acquired U.S. private-sector partners.[15] Just before President Clinton and Prime Minister Ryutaro Hashimoto of Japan met at the G-8 summit in May 1998, Japan announced a number of telecom liberalization measures allowing for increased competition by private companies while reducing consumer rates and providing some hope that foreign telecom carriers might be able to enter the Japanese market.[16] Smaller nations in even some of the most remote parts of the world offered to open their telecoms sectors to foreign investment in 1998 in efforts to join the new information order, and most medium-sized and larger nations also developed liberalization policies designed to either get them admitted to the WTO or maintain themselves as WTO members in good standing.[17] In March–April 1999 China and India (as well as Taiwan) announced "sweeping new telecommunications policies that allowed greater foreign participation."[18]

Agreement by many countries to WTO guidelines for private-sector involvement in telecommunications development has not always been a smooth and continuous process. In the case of some countries, like Saudi Arabia, initial proposals for telecom liberalization made to the WTO have been unacceptable.[19] In other cases, like Japan in 1998–1999, initial commitments were agreed to by all parties but later became matters of dispute between WTO member nations.[20] As the case studies in the companion volume to this one point out in detail, the ABT agreement resulted in problems for policymakers in almost all of the world's major nations, but political and government leaders were willing to face sizable obstacles because of the enormous stakes involved. When proposals for a new round of trade talks collapsed at the Seattle meeting of the WTO in December 1999, there was substantial agreement within the organization that "it was the sheer complexity of the negotiations—and the unwillingness of countries to compromise on politically charged issues—that ultimately doomed the talks."[21]

Despite setbacks to telecommunications liberalization in individual countries and delays in initiating a new round of trade talks in 2001, there is continued optimism among trade officials and private-sector leaders that WTO negotiation processes in the telecom sector will continue and even accelerate over the next few years.[22] No one expects telecommunications, for example, to present anything resembling the intractable dead ends often encountered in the WTO and EU when discussing trade in agricultural products. With regard to telecommunications, U.S. trade representative Charlene Barshefsky suggested in late 1999 that what was necessary to resume progress was for WTO leaders to "take a time-out" following the failure of the December 1999 Seattle meetings. Chancellor Gerhard Schroeder of Germany echoed this assessment, suggesting that the WTO ministers reconvene "as soon as possible" while chiding them to "come next time better prepared."[23] In any event, the breakdown of the Seattle meetings did not lead observers or participants in WTO telecom activities to waver from the assessment that the massive world movement in the waning years of the twentieth century and the first few years of the twenty-first century toward competitive private and public telecommunications systems, backed by private-sector financing and the ABT agreement, will continue to be a major factor in shaping the world's telecommunications regime, and therefore the international regime for the Internet, for many years into the twenty-first century. In the words of Aileen Pisciotta,

> The implementation of the WTO Basic Telecommunications Agreement was a watershed event that resolved once and for all the longstanding global debate over whether competition or government planning should rule the telecommunications sector. Overwhelmingly, it is now accepted world-wide that open markets subject to reasonable and transparent regulation are not only appropriate, but necessary, for the achievement of a modern information infrastructure.[24]

■ DEVELOPING REGIME PRINCIPLES AND NORMS FOR INTELLECTUAL PROPERTY

Among the many issues involved in building the international regime for the Internet, none are potentially more significant for e-commerce and a competitive framework for future world economic development than those related to intellectual property, which has historically included patents, trademarks, industrial designs, appellations of origin, and copyright in literary, musical, artistic, photographic, and audiovisual works. This is more evident now than it was even a decade ago because, as David Kline put it, "the burgeoning knowledge economy has given rise to a new type of CEO and a new type of business competition—one in which intellectual assets, not physical ones, have become the principal sources of shareholder wealth and competitive advantage."[25] Whereas government officials and executives of private companies used to think of intellectual property as something tucked away in the offices of corporate attorneys, today intellectual property is at the top of the agenda items being discussed in the White House, Congress, and other government offices worldwide and in corporate boardrooms and offices in all trading nations. To quote Kline again, "For both traditional and new-economy businesses . . . leveraging patents properly can produce benefits such as reduced corporate risk, the ability to anticipate and react to market shifts, and, ultimately, increased shareholder value and profits."

The origins of an international framework for intellectual property protection date back to the Paris Convention for the Protection of Industrial Property, signed by 14 nation-states in 1884, and the Berne Convention for the Protection of Literary and Artistic Works, finalized in 1886. These two organizations joined together in 1893 to form the United International Bureaux for the Protection of Intellectual Property (known throughout the world for more than seven decades as BIRPI, its French acronym). In 1970 BIRPI became the World Intellectual Property Organization (WIPO) following the entry into force of the Convention Establishing WIPO, which has now been signed by 171 countries. WIPO became a specialized agency of the UN system of organizations in 1974.[26]

In its June 1998 white paper, the U.S. Commerce Department said it would "seek *international support* to call upon WIPO to initiate a *balanced and transparent process,* which includes the participation of trademark holders and members of the Internet community who are not trademark holders," to develop a series of recommendations on international intellectual property as might be related to cyberspace.[27] These recommendations were to include a uniform approach for resolving trademark/domain name disputes involving cyberpiracy, a process for protecting famous trademarks, and an evaluation of the effects on intellectual property holders and trademarks of adding new Top-Level Domain names. The white paper made clear that these recommendations were to be developed in conjunction with ICANN and other concerned organizations, with WIPO's final findings and recommendations being submitted to the ICANN board.

The designation of WIPO as a focal point for the development of rules and procedures for the intellectual property aspects of the global Internet regime is based on WIPO's respected international reputation, its wide support and membership (more than 90 percent of the world's nation-states are members), and its standing among private corporations and other organizations (many of which are involved in WIPO's various projects and training programs). Before submitting its final recommendations to ICANN in 2000, WIPO engaged in a process of information gathering and discussion on its website in three languages (English, French, and Spanish); held open meetings on the Web with participants from five continents; sent information about its thinking to more than 400 subscribers to a targeted listserve group; issued three requests for comments (RFCs) each in three languages; and received comments on RFCs from 40 governments, 4 international organizations, 74 professional, industrial, and academic organizations, 181 corporations and law firms, and 183 individuals. In its evaluation to ICANN, the final WIPO study concluded that the world had encountered a series of significant problems across the spectrum of intellectual property concerns in a wide variety of attempts to relate intellectual property to the Internet. The study warned against what it called "a wasteful diversion of resources" and a global policy environment "condemned by all" in the absence of a uniform world approach to intellectual property in cyberspace.[28]

Associated with WIPO's involvement with the white paper process was the development of what WIPO leaders called its "Digital Agenda," a two-page document distributed on the WIPO website in six languages (Arabic, Chinese, English, French, Russian, and Spanish) and approved by WIPO's 171 member states at the WIPO General Assembly in September 1999. The WIPO "Digital Agenda" is the most comprehensive and authoritative planning document for the development of an international framework for intellectual property aspects of the international regime for the Internet. It is based on the assumption that intellectual property issues in cyberspace can be resolved within existing international legal and administrative frameworks, with several modifications. The kinds of modifications needed are summarized as ten broad "agenda items."[29]

The white paper designation of WIPO as the point organization for developing rules and procedures relating to intellectual property issues in cyberspace, particularly when coupled with the development of WIPO's "Digital Agenda," moved the process of international regime formation on intellectual property matters rather quickly from the agenda-setting stage of Internet regime-related activity to the negotiation stage. Although negotiations on almost all intellectual property matters are still in progress, are dominated by the policies of national governments, and are being carried out by many different organizations in the different regions of the world, WIPO's activities in each of major intellectual property subfield (trademarks, copyright, and patents) provide a useful focus for trying to understand the dynamics of regime creation.

▪ *Trademarks*

WIPO's major accomplishment in the trademark area has been to establish a soft law procedure for settling disputes over Top-Level Domain names, or Internet addresses ending with .org, .net, and .com. The procedure (called the Uniform Domain-Name Dispute-Resolution Policy [UDRP]) was developed in association with a group of domain name registrars, including NSI, and approved in principle by ICANN at its third meeting in Santiago, Chile, in August 1999. The UDRP is designed to arbitrate settlements out of court, without the major expenses incurred in lawsuits, in cases of "cybersquatting"—where one company or individual lays claim to an Internet address another entity also claims a right to use. Following ICANN's Santiago meeting, a detailed draft of the UDRP mechanism was distributed on the Internet for public comment before being finalized by the ICANN board. The mechanism became available through the auspices of ICANN on January 3, 2000.

Cybersquatting became possible from the early days of the Internet because a domain name (such as www.ibm.com) could only be held by one person or entity, and anyone was originally allowed to purchase the rights to names on a first-come-first-served basis for a small fee. By contrast, under traditional trademark law a number of different companies might have trademark rights to the same name, as long as use of the name does not cause confusion. Moreover, under traditional law trademark names are granted only after the extended period of time (usually a year or more) required to determine whether use of the name is being contested or would involve contestation for any reason, whereas in the early days of the Internet domain names were granted almost instantaneously, usually to the first person who applied for use of the name.[30]

Those cybersquatters who purchased trademark addresses (domain names) from NSI in the formative period of the Internet for a standard biannual fee of $70 were often able to sell them later for a small fortune. In November 1999, for example, a cybersquatting speculator sold the address business.com for $7.5 million to a new firm called eCommerce, headed by Jake Winebaum, formerly head of Walt Disney's Internet operations, and Sky Dayton, founder of Earthlink—a successful Internet service provider—who used the name to start a new global business directory and considered the name to be "90 percent of the business." The $7.5 million paid for business.com was more than twice the previous record of $3.3 million paid a year earlier by Compaq for altavista.com. The entrepreneur who sold business.com for $7.5 million was Marc Ostrofsky, who had purchased the name three years earlier for $150,000 from someone who had originally registered it with NSI in the early 1990s for the $70 biannual fee. Ostrofsky at the time owned more than 100 domain names and had made a number of deals in which he sold names at an enormous profit. Earlier in 1999, for example, he sold the address eFlowers.com to Flowers Direct, an online flower shop, for $25,000 plus 50 cents in perpetuity for every transaction on eFlowers.com plus free flowers delivered to his wife every month for the rest of her life. A *Times* (of London) study in January 2000 estimated that 97 percent of the single words in *Webster's Dictionary* had been registered as domain names on the Internet, with an additional 5,000 names being registered *every day*.[31]

Use of domain names by cybersquatters has been challenged in national courts under traditional trademark law principles of infringement, dilution, and unfair competition, but the results of such cases—usually after lengthy and expensive legal proceedings—have been inconclusive. In roughly half of the cases decided before 2000, the courts ruled that the allegedly offending domain name did not infringe on an existing trademark, although in some widely publicized cases, such as that involving Harrod's of London, companies were able to successfully challenge cybersquatters. In one case in England, a cybersquatting company called One in a Million was ordered by the Court of Appeal to pay 65,000 British pounds in legal fees and to transfer domain names back to five British companies (including British Telecom and Marks and Spencer) for simply *threatening* that the domain names controlled by the cybersquatter—such as buckingham-palace.org and burgerking.co.uk, among others—would be sold to another party if the threatened company did not purchase the domain name itself.[32]

Prior to the UDRP mechanism, NSI had established a procedure wherein trademark owners could ask that domain names be placed "on hold" pending resolution of a dispute between the trademark owner and the domain name registrant. But this procedure had several drawbacks: (1) it applied only to cases where a trademark owner possessed a prior trademark *registration*, which meant it did not apply to the large number of cases where rights had been acquired by common law through extended use rather than registration; (2) NSI policy required that registered trademarks and domain names be an *exact match,* which meant the procedure could not be used to challenge domain names that combined a trademark with another term or consisted of an alternate misspelling of the trademark; (3) the on-hold solution only satisfied trademark owners who wanted to stop someone else from using their trademark name but did not provide a means for transferring the domain name back to the trademark owner (to do this, the holders of trademarks still had either to file and pursue a lawsuit in a court that might agree to hear the case or pay large amounts to settle with the domain name registrant).[33]

The UDRP mechanism has been judged a major success because it offers several features lacking in either the old NSI procedure or formal national judicial systems:

1. The UDRP process is *mandatory,* requiring a domain name registrant accused of cybersquatting to submit to a proceeding if it falls within certain classifications. A proceeding is initiated if a complainant sends a complaint to one of four arbiters (known as providers of the dispute resolution service). The four ICANN-approved arbiter providers are WIPO, the National Arbitration Forum (a neutral administrator of arbitration services based in Minneapolis), a Montreal-based consortium of academics and law practitioners specializing in trademark law known as Disputes.org/eResolution Inc., and the CPR Institute for Dispute Resolution, Inc., based in New York (formerly Center for Public Resources).[34]

2. Complaints under the UDRP can be simultaneously *more inclu-*

sive and specific than in the old NSI procedure. Complainants can submit challenges for both registered and common law trademarks, and they must allege that (1) the registrant's domain name is "identical or confusingly similar" to a mark belonging to the complainant, (2) the registrant has "no rights or legitimate interests" in the domain name, and (3) the registrant registered and used or uses the domain name in bad faith.[35]

3. Costs of the UDRP procedure are minimal (estimated at $750 to $4,500 for most disputes), and the mechanism is designed for online access, with no in-person hearings normally permitted. Decisions are expected to be handed down in forty-five days or less, with both parties reserving the right to go to court later if the UDRP adjudication fails to satisfy them.

4. Unlike the NSI procedure, which made no judgments regarding the respective rights of parties and could be invoked whenever there was a preexisting trademark registration, the UDRP mechanism is premised on the assumption that proceedings will go forth only when genuine cases of cybersquatting are alleged and that judgments about the rights and equities of the parties can be made on the basis of specific criteria within a short space of time.

Within a few months of its initiation, the UDRP mechanism was judged a success by private corporations, governments, and most others concerned with domain name trademarks. The first few decisions handed down—in favor of the World Wrestling Federation, Stella D'oro Biscuit (a Nabisco affiliate), and Telstra, the Australian telecommunications company—were handled expeditiously and were widely considered equitable.[36] The number of cases submitted to ICANN for adjudication under the UDRP mechanism jumped from 1 in December 1999 to 28 in January to 60 in February and to more than 3,100 in October 2000, with more than 1,300 websites taken away from bad faith offenders.[37] Recognizing that UDRP would quickly replace its old procedure, NSI served notice in March 2000 that the on-hold status of all websites previously so designated as a result of NSI-adjudicated domain disputes would be terminated within ninety days. This meant parties to previous NSI-adjudicated disputes would have to reach an accommodation privately, go for redress to the national courts, or use the UDRP procedure. The NSI adopted the UDRP procedure as its own as of January 3, 2000.[38]

Since most of the world's trading nations have not yet been able to enact national legislation specifically protecting trademarks in cyber-space, the use of UDRP is expected to mushroom in the years ahead. A number of surveys have indicated that most companies in all parts of the world have experienced what they perceive to be infringements on their intellectual property. A 1998 survey by Marques—the European association of trademark-owning companies—for example, indicated that 85 percent of respondent companies claimed infringements, with domain name infringements alleged by a whopping 78 percent of the companies and copyright infringement indicated by a substantial 40 percent.[39] As a *National Law Journal* article pointed out, "Unless and until anti-cybersquatting legislation is enacted in Canada and Europe, the UDRP procedure may be the only true mechanism by which to enforce the rights of Canadian and European trademark owners and to prevent and deter cybersquatting [in other countries] abroad."[40]

In the United States, the U.S. Congress moved rather quickly in the waning days of its 1999 session to enact the Anticybersquatting Consumer Protection Act, which for the first time altered traditional trademark law to explicitly apply protection to cyberspace, including imposing penalties of up to $100,000 on those who register trade-marked words or phrases as a domain name. The U.S. Congress also passed two amendments in 1999 to long-standing trademark legislation—the Trademark Amendments Act and the Trademark Law Treaty Implementation Act—"to more readily protect trademarks in the electronic global marketplace."[41] Some legal scholars suggested that Congress had simply "scrambled to get a domestic domain name dispute resolution policy on the books to prevent the shifting of control over Internet trademark disputes to an international tribunal."[42] But most legal practitioners and scholars agree that the new U.S. laws on trademarks are fully compatible with ICANN's UDRP mechanism while providing alternative enforcement authority and the possibility of large financial penalties for those complainants who want to go beyond the arbitration procedure to longer-term litigation.

▪ Copyright

In addition to its work in developing international regime rules and pro-cedures for use of trademarks in cyberspace, WIPO has led internation-al efforts to develop norms for copyrighting digital technology and works and their online dissemination. WIPO's efforts in this regard have resulted in two treaties that were approved at the WIPO Diplomatic Conference in Geneva in December 1996, designed to update the 1886 Berne Convention for Protection of Literary and Artistic Works and the 1961 Rome Convention for Protection of Performers, Producers of Phonograms, and Broadcasting Organizations. The 1996 treaties are the WIPO Copyright Treaty (WCT) and the WIPO Performance and Phonograms Treaty (WPPT). Although leaders of more than fifty nations have signed these treaties, neither takes effect until both have been ratified by the legislatures of at least thirty nations. By January 2000, eleven national legislatures had ratified the WCT and ten had ratified the WPPT (the only country that had signed and ratified both was the United States).

The two treaties together provide a fairly comprehensive but conservative set of rules and procedures for protection of copyright in the context of the Internet, with neither extending nearly as much protection as do the Trade-Related Aspects of Intellectual Property Protection (TRIPS) agreement of the WTO (discussed later) and the domestic laws of the leading trading nations. In very broad summary, the two treaties deal with rights of online transmission, computer software protection, conditions of rental, and technical protection systems. A clause outlining rather stringent rules governing production of ephemeral copies or temporary reproductions from the Internet (and in other media and formats) was ultimately dropped as too controversial. A third treaty that would have incorporated the core provisions of the EU's Directive on the Legal Protection of Databases was drafted for the 1996 Diplomatic Conference in Geneva but was not approved because of heavy opposition from within the United States.[43]

Conservative approaches to copyright matters in cyberspace have been criticized by a number of business and commercial organizations, particularly in the software and recording industries, which have often singled out copyright and patent offices in particular countries for lagging behind technology. In the United States, for example, until 1994 computer software was considered to be covered by copyright law, under which it was treated in the same manner as mathematical algorithms in a way that often made it ineligible for patents. But that approach changed drastically in the mid-1990s as the software industry became the driving force of Internet and IT development and computer code became increasingly valuable. In 1994 the U.S. Patent and Trademark Office (PTO) issued substantially new guidelines for copyright and patent procedures related to software, invited representatives from the software industry to help educate PTO staff, hired a number of software engineers to train as patent examiners, opened a new computer database of existing software technologies, and established a software reference library. In 1997 the U.S. Patent Office established a new department (Group 705) designed specifically to process patents for business-method software, a department that has mushroomed in size from twelve to forty examiners by mid-2000, with more being added at a continuous significant rate.[44] All of this has reflected a series of other transformations in the 210-year-old PTO and in the Copyright Office as well, designed to cope with changes brought about by the onset of the information age.

One particular focus of copyright infringement has been the trading, or "swapping," of music files over the Internet through services like Napster and MP3.com without providing compensation to copyright holders.[45] Lawyers in the recording industry have been pursuing ways to either halt such services or collect royalties on the digital works being traded, arguing that the practice of swapping amounts to piracy. The issue has become even more complicated in the twenty-first century with the creation of programs such as Freenet, specifically designed to make it possible for Internet users to find and acquire files without reference to a central database and thus providing no single target for prosecution by a copyright holder whose work is being traded.[46] A digital distribution program called Gnutella has the same anarchic features of Freenet, with no central directory of information contained in the system, but Gnutella goes far beyond the capabilities of Napster or MP3.com to make possible distribution of video, software, and text documents, as well as digital music files. Both Freenet and Gnutella developers have experimented with a digital "immune system" that would respond to any effort by companies to determine the location of a piece of information by automatically spreading the information helter-skelter throughout the worldwide network whenever an inquiry is received.

Proliferation of new technologies such as Freenet and Gnutella has led some legal scholars, such as Pamela Samuelson of the University of California at Berkeley Law School, to argue that "copyright law is not the right tool in the case of many of the new technologies." From Samuelson's perspective, the ability of governments and the private sector to enforce intellectual property rules and procedures in cyberspace will depend less on the specific legal framework enacted than on the development of new "countertechnologies." The founder of Freenet, a twenty-three-year-old Irish programmer named Ian Clarke, agrees with this assessment and has been quoted as saying, "I have two words for these companies: give up! . . . There is no way they are going to stop these technologies. They are trying to plug holes in a dam that is about to burst."[47]

But leaders of technology and industry associations concerned with copyright protection are convinced that a combination of new countertechnologies and patient enforcement of an ever-adapting legal and treaty framework will make it possible to meet anarchic challenges to the concept of intellectual property in cyberspace.[48] The president of Silicon Valley's Secure Digital Music Initiative, Talal Shamoon, for example, conceives of anarchic programs as "small communities" on the Internet and argues that "from a trust standpoint, the current generation of tools such as Gnutella and Freenet are a nightmare for the same reason that badly constructed social communities are a nightmare." In the long run, Shamoon and others argue, a regime based on rule of law and protection of intellectual property will prevail over anarchic systems with no inherent basis for trust that fail to provide economic incentives for invention. Ironically, despite his challenge to companies quoted earlier, Ian Clarke agrees with this assessment. Citing responses by industry and governments to past innovations, Clarke concludes on his website that "artists and publishers all adapted to those new technologies and learned how to use them and profit from them; they will adapt to Freenet as well."

Despite reservations about the potential effectiveness and some specific aspects of the two WIPO copyright treaties, their ratification by the necessary thirty nation-state legislatures is expected at some point in 2001, although in most nations legislatures are pursuing ratification at a rather deliberate pace to make sure domestic political and commercial interests are served. For example, in the U.S. Digital Millennium Copyright Act (1998), the bill designed to help implement the two treaties, the U.S. Congress added (at the behest of the Commerce Department) a "no mandate" amendment, clarifying that manufacturers of computer software and consumer electronics makers are not required to respond to specific technological protection measures used by copyright owners to have their material protected. Without the no mandate clause, the anticircumvention provisions of the act would have forced IT producers to respond to a host of technological protection measures for each copyrighted product or risk having their products outlawed as "circumvention" devices.[49] In 1998 the Canadian government committed itself to signing both treaties and has made the treaties the cornerstone of its phase III legislation on copyrights, but ratification is not expected until 2002.⁵⁰ Japan's parliament, the Diet, is also expected to ratify both treaties in 2001, but three major changes are being negotiated by the Japanese government to make this possible.⁵¹ Ratifications are also expected from a number of African nations, encouraged by the director-general of WIPO, Dr. Kamil Eltayed Idris of Sudan, who also serves as Sudan's ambassador to Switzerland.⁵²

▪ Patents

WIPO's activities with regard to patents have been built around its Patent Cooperation Treaty (PCT), which was concluded in 1970 and has been in effect since 1978. Since 1978, 107 countries have signed the treaty, which is administered through offices headed by the PCT Executive Committee at WIPO headquarters in Geneva. The principal accomplishments of the treaty have been a centralized filing procedure for international patent applications and a standardized application format (now available online). Patents can still be protected only under the laws of the country wherein protection is sought, but the PCT enables a patent seeker to file a single application at the outset and then follow up on this global application within individual countries when the process reaches what is known as the "national stage." WIPO and the PCT have been effective in helping to develop common rules and procedures for both international patent applications and dispute resolution by working closely with the WIPO member governments and with regional authorities involved in patent matters, such as the European Convention countries, the North American Free Trade Agreement (NAFTA), and the WTO.⁵³

The number of patents applied for has escalated rapidly since the early 1990s, largely because of IT—and especially Internet-related—invention. In 1999 alone WIPO reported a 10.5 percent increase in the number of patent applications under the PTC, to more than 74,000. Of these, the U.S. share was 39.8 percent (29,463), down from 42.3 percent in 1998. Germany ranked second with 14.7 percent in 1999, up from 13.6 percent the year before.⁵⁴ Mushrooming increases in patent applications have taxed the patent offices of most countries and led to severe criticism of the patent process on a worldwide basis as well. The U.S. Patent Office has been a frequent target of criticism as a result of a number of poor patent decisions made in the 1990s, described by the *Economist* (London) as follows:

The broad concern is over "bad" patents that should not have been awarded because somebody else got there first, or where the idea was too obvious to deserve protection. It has happened often, most embarrassingly in 1993 when a company called Comptons New Media was given, in effect, a patent on multimedia. Not only was the patent absurdly broad, but much of the work had been done by Xerox's Palo Alto Research Centre two decades earlier.[55]

Problems in European patent offices have been less frequent than in the United States, in part because the volume of U.S. patent applications is much smaller but also because European countries, unlike the United States, have "opposition" systems that enable competitors to challenge a proposed patent before it is approved. This process generally takes longer than is the case in the United States, but it provides more time and the benefit of different perspectives for patent examiners to consider and weigh the merits of a case. Hasty decisions are also greatly encouraged in the U.S. Patent Office because patent examiners are given bonuses for "disposal" of patent cases (disposal generally means a patent has been issued, whereas rejection of a patent may not constitute disposal because the inventor can amend the proposal and try again). What the *Economist* calls "quality, sticking-power and morale" among U.S. patent examiners are also problems, since starting salaries at the U.S. Patent Office (where entrants usually have technical, engineering, or law degrees) average around $40,000, whereas comparable salaries elsewhere for graduates with technical, scientific, or engineering backgrounds range upward of $50,000 and the starting salaries of new law school graduates are as high as $140,000 a year at East Coast U.S. law firms.[56]

Patent offices in developing countries are criticized less for the ways in which they grant patents than for their lack of enforcement, although many are just beginning to join the WIPO PCT system.[57] India, for example, announced that it would sign WIPO's Paris Convention in 1998, and Algeria ratified the PCT in December 1999. Many Middle Eastern nations just started to modernize their patent offices in the first year of the twenty-first century.[58] The most intriguing country for world business and government leaders to deal with has been the People's Republic of China, which has established what is often considered "a respectable, if not perfect, legal system for intellectual property rights [IPR] . . . while IPR violations continue [in China] on a massive scale."[59]

The introduction of the Internet has led to many calls for reform of patent offices and processes and to even more debate about whether reform is necessary.[60] As mentioned earlier, the commissioner of the U.S. Patent and Trademark Office, Todd Dickinson, has initiated a major overhaul of long-standing traditional patent-granting procedures in an attempt to adapt to new IT- and Internet-related technologies, as have patent offices in other developed countries. A number of proposed reforms of patent administration in developing countries have been aimed at two problems in particular: (1) heavy legal fees inventors must pay to acquire adequate patent protection, which often favors large corporations in developed countries over those in the developing world in the quest for secure patents on significant invention; and (2) the frequent practice in poorer countries of using scarce resources to conduct investigations of patent applications that are often redundant with investigations already completed in other countries. A project funded by the Research Foundation of the Franklin Pierce Law Center has recommended that a more effective global patent regime might be created by restructuring patent administration in developing countries around "optimum use of electronic information search and retrieval techniques, the expansion of regional digital databases, the reduction and delay of patent acquisition costs, and . . . the adoption of a 'rapid-patent system with delayed examination' in conjunction with a 'system of reference' for granting patents."[61]

At this point mild support is found among world business and government leaders for significant reform of the way patents and other forms of intellectual property are presently drafted. Rather than pursue fundamental change in the administrative or legal frameworks for intellectual property on a global scale, however, the central theme around which negotiations regarding intellectual property have revolved is the question of *enforcement* of existing intellectual property law and procedures. Although some adjustment of traditional IP rules and administrative processes is taking place throughout the world—in some cases in fairly dramatic fashion—the conclusions of the legal affairs editor of *Business Week,* Mike France, seem closer to a consensual position among world leadership than do the admonitions of those predicting or demanding sweeping change. France summarized this more moderate perception of the patent reform issue as follows:

The issue deserves to be taken seriously. But it's useful to keep in mind how . . . patent scares have played out. . . . [Ultimately], the legal system finds a way to manage the new technology, and the dire predictions [of reformers] never come true. . . . At this point, there's still ample reason to believe that the [existing patent offices] and the courts will be able to cope with the problem of Internet business-method patents. . . . Yes, the Web is unique. It tends to give first movers big rewards and therefore provides companies with a disproportionate incentive to patent everything in sight. Still, traditional patent law provides adequate tools for weeding out bogus claims. . . . It's early yet, [but] history gives plenty of reasons to be skeptical of the Chicken Littles.[62]

▪ THE WTO AND ENFORCEMENT OF INTELLECTUAL PROPERTY RIGHTS IN CYBERSPACE

Attempts to develop means for *enforcement* of existing intellectual property law and procedures at the international level have revolved primarily around what is known as the TRIPS Agreement of the WTO, which was originally adopted in 1995 and is binding on all members of the WTO as long as they remain members. The TRIPS Agreement sets minimal standards for all WTO members for the content and enforcement of intellectual property law, including trademarks, copyright, and patents. Although not initially adopted to advance a digital agenda, the TRIPS Agreement is increasingly becoming linked to the work of WIPO and to intellectual property cyberspace issues. It is comprehensive enough to cover many directly Internet-related areas, including specifically mentioned copyright and related rights, trademarks and service marks, geographical indications and appellations of origin, industrial designs, patents, the layout designs of integrated circuits, and so-called undisclosed information such as trade secrets and test data.[63] The three main features of TRIPS are:

1. Standards—The agreement sets out the "minimum standards of protection" to be provided by each WTO member and defines each of the main elements—the subject matter to be protected, the rights to be conferred, permissible exceptions to those rights, and the minimum duration of protection. The agreement sets these standards by requiring, first, that WTO member nations comply with the two main conventions of WIPO—the Paris Convention and the Berne Convention (excluding

only one clause on moral rights). Second, the TRIPS Agreement adds a substantial number of additional obligations on "matters where the pre-existing conventions are silent or were seen as being inadequate." For this reason, the TRIPS Agreement has often been called in shorthand "Berne and Paris-plus."

2. Enforcement—A second set of provisions in the TRIPS Agreement deals with the domestic procedures and remedies for the enforcement of intellectual property rights WTO members are required to follow. TRIPS contains provisions on civil and administrative procedures and remedies, provisional measures, special requirements related to border measures, and criminal procedures—all specifying in some detail "the procedures and remedies that must be available [within each WTO member country] so that holders of intellectual property rights can effectively enforce their rights."

3. Dispute Settlement and Sanctions—In cases of disputes between WTO members about member obligations under the TRIPS Agreement, dispute settlement procedures are spelled out in the agreement. But the distinguishing feature of the TRIPS Agreement is the way in which it expands the WTO's mandate—in contrast to other international economic organizations—to include an effective enforcement mechanism, that is, an effective way of sanctioning member countries found to be in violation of WTO rules or procedures or that refuse to change illegal behavior. In the words of Professor Richard Blackhurst, former director of economic research and analysis for GATT/WTO: "At the end of the WTO dispute settlement procedures, if all else fails, lie multilaterally approved trade sanctions. A desire to gain access to this enforcement mechanism is the main reason that the WTO mandate was expanded to include the protection of intellectual property despite the existence of the World Intellectual Property Organization."[64]

Although the TRIPS Agreement has been in effect for WTO members from the developed countries since 1995, its real test began on January 1, 2000, when those member nations were first required to fully comply with TRIPS. A five-year deferment for developing countries was written into the original agreement for two reasons: first, to gain experience with dispute settlement procedures and determine whether the agreement was workable among the older traditional trading partners of the developed world and, second, to allow time for the developing countries to prepare for the point at which dispute settlement procedures and sanctions would be applicable to violations in the poorer nation-states. Between 1995 and 2000 there were only twenty instances where charges of significant violations of TRIPS were formally leveled against one WTO member by another, with only five of these cases brought against developing countries on relatively unimportant issues not subject to the five-year deferment. The majority of the cases charged that required procedures for enforcement of the TRIPS Agreement were not being followed by one of the developed countries in the WTO.[65]

Because the TRIPS Agreement is the first effort to put real "teeth" into enforcement of intellectual property rights at the international level, getting it to work is expected to be the major challenge facing the WTO in the next decade or more. Particularly in the developing world, where piracy levels of trademarks, copyrighted materials, and patents are estimated to routinely exceed 50 percent and frequently rise above 75 percent of the market for Internet-related products, the question of whether conflicting national-cultural traditions relating to intellectual property rights can be accommodated to produce a set of principles, norms, rules, and procedures for the evolution of a robust international regime in this area is one of the fundamental unresolved aspects of international political economy in the early twenty-first century. What is most remarkable at this point, however, is that both developed and developing countries have agreed to the terms of the TRIPS Agreement, which requires that they all make an effort at accommodation.[66] Particularly in the late 1990s, there was considerable movement toward accommodation in an exploration of mutual interests to explore the potential commercial and other economic benefits expected from the explosion of information technology and the growth of e-commerce into the future.[67]

Since January 1, 2000, when the LDCs were first required to fully comply with TRIPS, leadership of the most influential developing countries has tried to forestall still further the day when full compliance with TRIPS will be enforceable by the WTO. At their December 1999 meeting in Seattle, WTO members were unable to reach a consensus on the date at which they would start negotiations on issues they had previously agreed to negotiate (agriculture and services), but they left all of their previous agreements about TRIPS in place. After the Seattle meeting, however, although India did not ask for a renegotiation of TRIPS, it did call for more careful "clarificatory interpretation" about implementation of the agreement while discouraging a post-Seattle WTO negotiating round in the near future—a maneuver widely interpreted to reflect a lack of political will within India for enforcing TRIPS to the letter.[68] Similarly, China has postponed its entry into the WTO, which was expected in early to mid-2000 but has been put back to an indefinite date, as its officials (particularly at the local level) have realized the wrenching changes the country will have to undergo if the PRC is to comply with WTO rules. In September 2000 the deputy director of the Development Research Center of the PRC State Council, Lu Zhiqiang, stated publicly that local governments, industrial regulators, and individual enterprises in China were "not adequately prepared" for the international competition that would result from WTO membership, citing inadequate grasp of trade laws, inexperience with foreign investment, and lack of knowledge about WTO rules and regulations.[69] Most trade analysts still consider the TRIPS Agreement basically sound and enforceable, particularly since the LDCs are highly dependent on the markets of the developed nations for economic growth. But Charles S. Levy captured the sense of urgency about moving forward with the TRIPS Agreement when he wrote in spring 2000: "We are at a pivotal time for TRIPS, when we will see whether TRIPS has achieved its pivotal purpose of bringing developing countries to a minimum level of IP protection. It is also a pivotal time for the WTO generally, when we will see whether the TRIPS model of imposing 'positive' obligations on members is a viable approach to future WTO negotiations."[70]

■ CONCLUSIONS

The material in this chapter describes some of the main features of the Internet regime related to international investment and intellectual property concerns. As indicated earlier, the guidelines for these aspects of the regime are the principle that the costs of Internet-related infrastructural development shall be borne primarily by the private sector and the norm that governments shall commit themselves to economic liberalization, privatization, and regulatory programs consistent with this and other regime principles.

The regime at this point is clearly a work in the process of creation, with considerable progress having been made throughout the world (particularly in Europe) toward privatization of telecommunications and other Internet-related IT sectors, as well as deregulation of Internet-related activities. Although many difficult issues remain to be negotiated before the commercial aspect of the regime becomes robust in any sense, most issues have moved beyond the agenda-setting stage of regime creation and are being negotiated in earnest by leading regime actors. Some negotiations have produced innovative agreements and soft law arrangements that seem promising for the future development of workable regime rules and procedures on issues that have at times appeared intractable. This is the case, for example, with the U.S.-EU agreement on data protection, outlined in Chapter 3, which has produced the safe harbor mechanism to facilitate movement of large amounts of confidential data back and forth across the Atlantic. A major question for the future is whether soft law arrangements such as the safe harbor mechanism can be negotiated for international taxation of e-commerce and other commercial issues on a worldwide basis.

Grounds for optimism exist because a number of powerful international organizations have either been created or taken on new tasks—within both the government and private sector—in an impressive display of international cooperation that includes leading figures involved in e-commerce and other Internet-related commercial activities from all over the globe. The Global Business Dialogue on Electronic Commerce (GBDe), for example, was founded as recently as 1998 and would have been unimaginable as a rather closely integrated world organization before the Internet. But the Internet has made it possible for the GBDe to link more than 200 member countries and 70 CEOs from 23 international organizations and 110 governments of nation-states into an effective private organizational structure that has already contributed substantially to both the agenda-setting and negotiation phases of the commercial aspects of international regime creation for the Internet. One of the most encouraging aspects of the GBDe's work was the formation in September 2000 of a Digital Bridges Task Force, designed to focus the attention and activities of leading business and government leaders on the need for investments in Internet infrastructure and connectivity in "that 80 percent of the world where the population has never even heard a telephone dial tone."[71] Although the GBDe can be expected to assume and exercise various degrees of private authority in future negotiations on commercial aspects of the Internet's development, its authority will inevitably be exercised in cooperation with regional and international organizations (such as the OECD, the EU, WIPO, the WTO, among others), as has already been the case on a number of the issues discussed in this chapter.

Cooperative interaction among the governments of nation-states, powerful private-sector organizations like the GBDe, and regional and international organizations has already produced a number of the incipient regime norms, rules, and procedures discussed in this chapter and Chapter 3, including the OECD's CFA "guideposts" for evaluating the operation of online tax systems; EU membership criteria based on principles of liberalization, privatization, and regulatory programs consistent with private-sector investment in telecommunications and other Internet-related activities; the 1997 WTO Agreement on Basic Telecommunications; WIPO's creation of an apparently successful soft law dispute resolution procedure (UDRP) for settling international trademark disputes over Top-Level Domain names and Internet addresses; treaty-based international rules and procedures (also developed by WIPO) for protection of copyright and patents in the context of the Internet; and the prospective gradual extension of the WTO's 1995 TRIPS Agreement as an enforcement mechanism for controlling piracy of intellectual property in the context of Internet-related activity.

Whether any of these embryonic aspects of an international Internet regime eventually takes on a fully robust character will be determined by factors involving literally hundreds of regime actors, including private-sector companies, governments, and a variety of governmental and nongovernmental regional and international organizations. Many of these factors are explored in detail in the companion volume to this one, dealing with regime relationships in some of the less developed parts of the world (Africa, China, India, the Middle East, Eurasia, and Central/Eastern Europe). From the literature on international regime formation, one would expect the strengthening of the commercial and other aspects of the international Internet regime to depend on a number of regulatory, procedural, programmatic, and generative tasks that will have to be carried out by myriad regime actors in future months and years if the regime is to survive and flourish in anything resembling its present form.

■ NOTES

1. The analysis on which these figures are based, compiled from a variety of sources, is available in Franda, *Launching into Cyberspace.*

2. These steps are spelled out in detail in discussions of the EEC green paper in Ungerer and Costello, *Telecommunications in Europe,* pp. 185–226. The summary of steps listed in the text is taken from a summary that appears in Straubhaar, "From PTT to Private," p. 15.

3. The existence of several tracks proceeding simultaneously during the

formation of international regimes is a usual pattern, since, in Young's words, regimes proceed more often "by fits and starts" than by "gradual or steady progress." Young likens regime formation in this respect to the concept of "punctuated equilibrium" developed in the field of biology to explain processes of change and development. See Young, *Governance in World Affairs,* pp. 143 ff.

4. Spontaneous and planned elements of regime formation are analyzed in Young, *International Cooperation,* chapter 4.

5. Wagstyl, "Survey," p. 5.

6. Ibid.

7. The two new rules not fully brought into force in those six countries are (1) to allow consumers to take their telephone numbers with them when they change their accounts from one provider to another and (2) measures that would allow callers to choose a new carrier without dialing a prefix. The EU Commission views both services as important measures limiting the ability of new Internet Service Providers (ISPs) to gain market share. See Hargreaves, "Brussels Acts over Slow Liberalisation," p. 2.

8. deBony, "European Union to Revamp Telecommunications Legislation," p. D62.

9. GATT was the predecessor to the World Trade Organization. Based in Geneva, GATT was formed in 1948 as simply a series of trade negotiating rounds, with 50 nation-states as members, at a time when tariffs in industrialized countries averaged 40 percent or more. By 1995, when GATT became the World Trade Organization with 134 members, GATT had organized eight worldwide trade negotiating rounds, tariffs in industrialized countries had been reduced to less than 4 percent on average, and world merchandise exports had increased by sixteen times over 1948 levels—*almost three times the growth in world output.* A summary of GATT's accomplishments appears in de Jonquie'res, "World Trade System," pp. 1, 7–8.

10. Article II of the GATS states that "each Member shall accord immediately and unconditionally to services and service suppliers of any other Member treatment no less favourable than that it accords to like services and service suppliers of any other country" (this is commonly known as most-favored nation status). Article XVI requires that "Members shall not, unless noted in their schedules: (1) limit the number of service suppliers by quotas or monopolies; (2) limit the value of service transactions; (3) limit the quantity of service output through quotas; (4) or place limits on the number of persons employed in a particular service sector; (5) adopt measures that require specific legal entities to supply a service; and (6) limit the participation of foreign capital in service suppliers." A detailed review of the GATS provisions appears in Harwood, Lake, and Sohn, "Telecommunications Law," pp. 879 ff.

11. A useful discussion of the 1997 agreement appears in *The WTO Telecom Agreement.*

12. Cane, "Out with the Old," p. 3.

13. Ibid.

14. This was the conclusion of a landmark study *Electronic Commerce*

and the Role of the WTO. In a major speech on e-commerce issues in Berlin in September 1998, WTO director-general Renato Ruggiero drew heavily on that study and concluded: "The reality of an increasingly borderless global economy means that the economic reach of nation-states is being challenged, and the ground rules of international relations are changing. Almost more than any development, it is pushing governments to work together, plan together, and pool their efforts as never before." The CEO of America Online, Steve Case, echoed these conclusions when he referred to the new international framework for e-commerce emerging around WTO activities as "the new glue that binds nations, and the new fuel that expands world and regional economies." Both quotes are from Malawer, "International Trade and Transactions," pp. S40 ff.

15. The largest Canadian company, Bell Canada, partnered with Ameritech; MetroNet Communications entered into a merger with AT&T; and GTE acquired a 27 percent stake in BCT.Telus, the western Canadian carrier. In addition, Sprint entered into a partnership with a Canadian upstart, Call-Net Enterprises of Canada. See Morrison, "Canadian Telecoms," p. 10. For details of Canadian government policy, see "Government Opens Overseas Telecommunications Market to Competition."

16. de Jonquie'res, "Japan-US Summit," p. 6. See also Sasamotou, "British Telecom Targets Golden Opportunity in Japan," p. 12.

17. Kyrgyzstan, for example, agreed in July 1998 to open its telecoms sector to foreign competition by January 1, 2003, in an effort to gain admission to the WTO (Zarocostas, "Kyrgyzstan Nears Joining WTO"). Malaysia offered in May 1998 to commit to a minimum 30 percent foreign stake in its telecom companies, with the possibility that this could be extended to 61 percent in the future (Lim, "Government Comfortable with Telecom Policy Refinement"). South Africa, Ghana, and Uganda were the first African nations to open their markets to liberalization in late 1998 (Wolffe, "US Aid for Africa Telecoms," p. 7).

18. Dodgson, "Chinese and Indian Governments Release New Telecom Policy," p. 1. See also Dickie, "Taiwan Set to Break Telecoms Monopoly," p. 10.

19. Saudi Arabia's 1998 market offer to the WTO, for example, drew widespread criticism from the United States and other WTO members because, as one U.S. official put it, telecommunications was "essentially missing" from the proposal. See "US, Others Pan Saudi WTO Market Access Offer," p. 10A.

20. In February 1999 European Commission deputy director Gerard Depayre told the Japanese government that it had "failed to live up to its international commitment" because its high interconnection charges and rules governing the right to lay underground cable "continued to obstruct competition in Japan's telecoms market." See Nakamoto, "EU Challenges Japan over Telecoms Reform," p. 5.

21. Pearlstein, "WTO Negotiators' Reach Far Exceeded Grasp of Complexities," p. A47. Pearlstein and other observers, as well as WTO insiders, agreed almost unanimously that it was the breakdown of negotiations on central issues, such as agricultural subsidies, that resulted in the failure of the 1999

Seattle meeting rather than the high-level protests carried by international television and other media, as protest leaders claimed.

22. Issues involved in organizing the next round of world trade negotiations are presented in *WTO 2000*.

23. Quoted in Pearlstein, "WTO Negotiators," p. A47.

24. Pisciotta, "International Legal Developments in Review," p. 34.

25. Kline and Rivette, "Discovering New Value in Intellectual Property," p. 54. Both quotations in this paragraph are from this source.

26. The need for international protection of intellectual property had been prompted by the refusal of the most prominent inventors to attend international exhibitions, beginning with the International Exhibition of Inventions in Vienna in 1873, for fear that their ideas would be stolen and exploited commercially in other countries. For a history of BIRPI and WIPO, see Ryan, *Knowledge Diplomacy,* pp. 125 ff. Operating out of Geneva, WIPO currently administers twenty-one international treaties while providing training, arbitration, and mediation services in cooperation with member countries, nongovernmental organizations, and other private and public organizations. WIPO's staff of 700 or so is drawn from seventy-five countries and functioned with an annual budget of 325 million Swiss francs in 1999, most of which (85 percent) came from earnings from WIPO's three major registration systems, with the rest coming from member states and sales of publications. WIPO has a reputation for being well administered and is one of the few UN agencies that is almost entirely self-supporting (the five largest contributing countries each provided less than 1 percent of WIPO's budget in 2000). For more information, visit the WIPO website at http://ecommerce.wipo.int.

27. *Management of Internet Names and Addresses,* p. 5 (italics in the original).

28. Quotations and summaries of findings in this paragraph are taken from the extensive materials provided on the WIPO website at http://ecommerce. wipo.int.

29. A drastically abbreviated version of the ten items is as follows (taken from the WIPO website): (1) broaden participation of developing countries; (2) enter into force two world copyright treaties adopted by WIPO in 1996 (discussed later); (3) promote adjustment of the international legislative framework to facilitate e-commerce; (4) implement the WIPO domain name process; (5) develop appropriate principles and rules for determining the circumstances of IPR liability of Online Service Providers; (6) promote the interoperability and interconnection of electronic copyright management systems, online licensing of digital expression, and online administration of IPR disputes; (7) introduce and develop online procedures for existing WIPO registration systems as embodied in its Patent Cooperation Treaty, Madrid System (for trademarks), and Hague Agreement (for industrial designs); (8) study and respond to international needs for global licensing of digital assets, notarization of documents, and certification of websites; (9) study and develop IPR norms for electronic commerce; and (10) coordinate with other international organizations on "hori-

zontal issues" affecting IPR, including the validity of electronic contracts and jurisdictional issues.

30. Some trademark lawyers have advised their clients to apply for a mark in Tunisia, where trademarks can be registered within two or three days, but countries with the most elaborate processes afford the most secure protection. For a comparison of traditional case law for trademark names and domain name registrations, see Mullineaux and Jakubik, "Keeping up with Developments," pp. 3–7.

31. More excesses of cybersquatting are detailed in Alexander, "Cyber-squatters Banned."

32. Taylor, "Trading in Cyberspace," pp. 19–20.

33. The NSI procedure is outlined in detail, and compared with the UDRP mechanism, in Crane, "Domain Name Disputes ICANN's New Policy," pp. 1–4.

34. Ironically, eResolution, Inc., became involved in a domain name dispute with a registrant in California over the use of eresolution.com. For details, see Akin, "Internet Adjudicator Gets into Dispute over Name," p. C6. Detailed analysis of the role of the four providers is available in Jarvis, "ICANN Sets Rules for Resolving Disputes."

35. This list is taken from Paine, "New Weapons Against Cybersquatters," p. 14. Indicia of bad faith, based on ICANN and WIPO documentation, are defined in detail in this article.

36. For analyses, see Caher, "New Rules for Domain Name Arbitration," pp. 1–3, and "WIPO Cyber Arbitration."

37. See Jarvis, "ICANN Sets Rules for Resolving Disputes," and Hong, "Getting Ready for a Cyber Court," p. 28.

38. McElligott, "A New Magistrate," pp. 3–5.

39. The Marques survey and similar data drawn from around the world are available in Wood, "Protecting Intellectual Property on the Internet," pp. 21–29.

40. Buchen and Belowich, "Global Anti-Cybersquatting," p. B7.

41. Details of these amendments are available in Welch, "Modernizing for the Millennium," pp. 43–57.

42. Grossman and Hift, "Anti-Cybersquatting Act," p. 63.

43. A detailed discussion of the content of the two WIPO copyright treaties and related issues appears in Lai, "Substantive Issues of Copyright Protection," pp. 127–140.

44. Chartrand, "Federal Agency Rethinks Internet Patents." The U.S. Patent Office has been widely criticized for issuing patents for what often appear to be common ways of conducting electronic business, as in the case of Amazon.com's one-click purchasing patent or Priceline.com's "name-your-price" method of conducting online auctions. In the context of such criticism the chief executive of Amazon, Jeffrey Bezos, has suggested that the compacted nature and transparency of cybertime and cyberspace might make it necessary for copyright and patent offices to publish applications while they are

pending and shorten the life span of copyrights and patents (to as little as three years, compared with traditional life spans of fifteen to forty years or more), particularly in areas related to business-method patents. See Richtel, "Chairman of Amazon Urges Reduction of Patent Terms," p. C4.

45. For a description of the intellectual property issues involving MP3.com, Napster, and other audio websites that have been accused of digital piracy by the Recording Industry Association of America and other trade associations, see Joseph, "MP3.com's Questionable IPO," and Penenberg, "Habeas Copyrightus." See also Doan, "NetPD Wants to Be Web's Police Department," describing a ten-person consulting firm in Cambridge, England, that has developed technology it is selling to intellectual property holders to enable them to identify Internet users who have been trading audio materials via MP3 or Napster without regard to copyright.

46. A summary article of some of these programs, including an analysis of the issue in general, appears in Markoff, "The Concept of Copyright." Quotations in this and the following two paragraphs are from this source.

47. See Ian Clark's homepage at http://www.sanity.uklinux.net.

48. For analyses of some of the legal challenges against companies that facilitate swapping and other anarachic technologies on the Internet brought by the recording and music publishing industries, see Stern, "MP3.com to Pay Universal $53 Million," p. E3; "MP3.com"; Holson, "Which Direction Now for Digital Music?" p. C1; and Taylor, "Napster Decision," p. A9.

49. "Information Technology Industry Council," pp. 59–60.

50. LeBlanc, "Canadian Government Commits to Signing Two WIPO Treaties," pp. 3–4, and LeBlanc, "Canadian Government Is Slow to Propose WIPO Legislation," pp. 43–44.

51. McLure, "Approval of Japanese Copyright Law Amendments Expected," pp. 79–82.

52. Idris is only the third director-general of WIPO, the first being Holland's Georg Bodenhausen (1963–1973) and the second Hungarian-rooted U.S. citizen Dr. Arpad Bogsch (1973–1997). See Lofthus, "Dr. Kamil Eltayed Idris," pp. 62–65. Scorecards on ratifications of the two treaties are available at http://www.wipo.org and Engelman et al., "Additional Countries Ratify," p. 20.

53. An exploration of some of the cooperative activities regarding intellectual property within NAFTA involving Canada, Mexico, and the United States appears in Flax, "NAFTA and the Patent Systems of Its Members," pp. 461–501.

54. "US Continues Lead in New Patents."

55. "Patent Nonsense." The Compton's patent was later reexamined by the U.S. Patent Office and revoked in response to industry concerns. Other prominent cases of what are widely considered bad patents include granting Amazon.com exclusive rights to the idea of buying a product online using a single mouse click and Priceline.com's software that allows consumers to bid for an item at the price they are willing to pay rather than bid against one

another in an auction. Critics of these patents argue that they are too broad, that they prevent the proliferation of e-commerce, and that they are of debatable "newness." See Marks, "US Thinks Again on Net Patents," p. 14.

56. "Patent Nonsense."

57. In 1999 only 2.4 percent (1,745) of the 74,023 applications to WIPO for international patent protection came from those nations categorized by the United Nations as "the poorer nations of the world." See Williams, "WIPO Applications Reach Record," p. 12.

58. See Jayaraman, "India Set to Allow Patents for Products," pp. 709–714, and Schnockelborg, "Book Review," pp. 347–352. See also "Algeria Ratifies Patent Treaty," p. 6, and "Qatar."

59. "Protecting IPR in China," p. 9.

60. For three perspectives on patent reform, see Mullaney, "Those Web Patents Aren't Advancing the Ball," p. 62; France, "Why We Don't Need Patent Reform—Yet," p. 54; and Roberts, "The Truth about Patents."

61. Sherwood, Scartezini, and Siemsen, "Promotion of Inventiveness in Developing Countries," pp. 474 ff.

62. France, "Why We Don't Need Patent Reform—Yet," p. 54.

63. A twenty-five-page detailed summary of the rules and procedures that have evolved from the TRIPS Agreement, including its relationship to WIPO treaties, is available on the WTO website at www.wto.org/wto/intellec/intell2.htm. Quotations explaining the agreement in this section are from this site.

64. Blackhurst, "The Capacity of the WTO," p. 47.

65. For example, the United States initiated a WTO dispute in 1997 under Article 50 of TRIPS, alleging that Swedish law did not provide for ex parte searches for pirated goods. Sweden amended the law in 1998, and the case was dropped. Similar complaints are pending against Ireland and Denmark, where legislative reforms are being considered. Trade officials in other countries are reviewing possibilities for bringing similar allegations against Finland, the Philippines, and the Czech Republic, among others. Other TRIPS cases during the first five years targeted the United States, Canada, the EU, and Japan, as well as other nations. For a detailed review of the operation of the TRIPS Agreement in its first five years, see Roberts and McCoy, "TRIPS Around the World," pp. 46–51.

66. An analysis of the various ways developing countries can "maximize the opportunities available under the TRIPS Agreement to tailor intellectual property laws to their domestic circumstances" (p. 125) is Okediji, "Perspectives on Globalization," pp. 117–183.

67. One of the most noteworthy efforts at international cooperation inspired by TRIPS has been the creation of an Association of Southeast Asian Nations (ASEAN) regional patent office to coordinate application and granting of patents between WIPO and other private and public organizations throughout the world on behalf of the ten member nations of ASEAN (Brunei

Darussalam, Cambodia, Indonesia, Laos, Malaysia, Myanmar, Philippines, Singapore, Thailand, and Vietnam). See Nguyen, "A Unitary ASEAN Patent Law," pp. 453–486.

68. "TRIPS under Scrutiny."

69 "Be Prepared." This was also the conclusion of leaders and speakers at meetings of the Asia Pacific Economic Summit 2000, held in Melbourne, Australia, earlier in September; see "Opportunities Abound for Post-WTO China." For an analysis of China's timetable for joining the WTO, see Pomfret, "China's Entry into WTO Unlikely This Year," p. E1.

70. Levy, "Implementing TRIPS," p. 795.

71. The quote is from the CEO of MIH, a South African–headquartered company that provides services for more than fifty developing countries. See Stofberg, "Working Together to Bridge the Digital Divide," p. 11.

5

Content, Privacy, and International Law

A s indicated in Chapters 1–4, elements of both the technical and commercial aspects of the Internet have advanced dramatically over the past few years to the agenda-setting and negotiations stages of regime formation, and international adoption of widely used protocols and standards has resulted in operationalization of the embryonic regime that exists at present. Included in regime architecture thus far have been the establishment of principles and norms for adopting technical protocols and standards, the adoption of rules and procedures of governance for domain names and the root server, and all of those items listed in the summary of soft law, treaty, and private authority arrangements for commercial relations summarized at the end of Chapter 4. Soft law and private authority relationships have also been in evidence in the attempts by international and regional organizations (primarily the EU, WIPO, and the WTO) to encourage both privatization and the role of private investment in burgeoning worldwide Internet-related infrastructural development.

When one goes beyond the technical and commercial components of these early years of the Internet's evolution, however, one encounters a number of elements that are not yet fully within the scope of even rudimentary international regime arrangements. Most of these still rather inchoate aspects of Internet development are closely associated with the concerns of international public law, international private law (often referred to by legal scholars as "international conflict of laws"), and the legal systems of nation-states. This chapter focuses on three of the most significant of these areas, involving questions of *jurisdiction* in cyberspace, issues related to varying national legal arrangements designed to *regulate Internet content*, and concerns for the protection of *privacy* when using computer networks. Although these three issue areas by no means exhaust all of the law-related subjects that might eventually be encompassed in a global Internet regime, they do touch on much of the legal literature on Internet development that has appeared since 1990. Discussion of these three areas is intended to promote understanding of the nature of the difficulties involved in creating regime principles and norms for Internet activity where embedded traditions in both national and international legal systems already exist.

▪ INTERNATIONAL LAW AND CYBERSPACE JURISDICTIONAL ISSUES

Perhaps the major issue areas impacted by the invention and global use of the Internet are those involving international legal jurisdiction in civil and criminal matters, as well as in business law (particularly intellectual property matters). Because materials on the Internet can be composed or uploaded anywhere in the world and sent and downloaded anywhere else, an almost infinite number of legal questions and cases can be imagined when trying to determine which nation's law applies in any particular case when laws are allegedly violated. Particularly in its early years, a number of people involved in the creation of the Internet or among its most enthusiastic users argued that the decentralized, heterogeneous, and diverse nature of Internet architecture would make it impossible for sovereign nation-states to either use existing law to govern Internet activity or enact enforceable new law. It has also frequently been argued that legal controls over the Internet by sovereign states are either undesirable or illegitimate.[1]

Within the last few years, however, a massive body of new law has grown up within nation-states, designed to take account of variables presented by the Internet and related technologies. In addition, existing laws have often been amended or reinterpreted by the courts to deal with issues raised by the increasing intrusion of cyberspace into personal and corporate matters.[2] At the international level some attempts have been made to develop cross-border procedures, regional cooperative mechanisms, international arbitration programs, and several other soft law arrangements related to questions of jurisdiction, some of which are detailed later in this chapter. For the most part, however, world leaders are still substantially convinced that legal authority over Internet activities can be dealt with most effectively by gradually adapting the current legal systems of the individual nation-states as new problems and challenges arise.[3]

In the United States, case law and statutes relating to jurisdiction in cyberspace have begun to accumulate at both the state and federal levels, although the U.S. Supreme Court has not yet agreed to rule on matters of jurisdiction in cyberspace.[4] The threshold test used by most U.S. courts to decide jurisdiction is whether a defendant has purposefully availed a forum's laws, on the basis of which Internet cases can be grouped into three categories:

1. "Purposeful availment" can most readily be established when "a defendant clearly does business over the Internet" with clients from a particular jurisdiction, usually by entering into contracts that require the "knowing and repeated transmission of computer files over the Internet [into that same jurisdiction]."[5]
2. A somewhat less clear area for jurisdiction involves interactive websites where a user can exchange information with the host computer but there is no contract.
3. The third category comprises passive websites, where a defendant has simply posted information on the Web that is accessible to users in foreign jurisdictions.

As Hoegle and Boam have pointed out, U.S. courts have often asserted jurisdiction for activity in the first category but only occasionally for the second and rarely for the third.

A major exception to this pattern for determining jurisdiction in U.S. courts occurred when Minnesota became the first U.S. state government to seek jurisdiction over materials placed on the Internet anywhere outside its territorial boundaries. This action was initiated by Minnesota attorney general Hubert Humphrey III, who issued a memorandum in July 1995 stating that "persons outside of Minnesota who transmit information via the Internet knowing that information will be disseminated in Minnesota are subject to jurisdiction in Minnesota courts for violations of state criminal and civil laws."[6] This memorandum, if enforced, would subject almost everything placed on the Internet—anywhere in the world—to Minnesota law, since those who "transmit information via the Internet" do so knowing that such information might well "be disseminated in Minnesota." If other U.S. states and other nations took such an approach to legal control of Internet content, the potential liabilities to large corporations with attachable assets would be unbearable and e-commerce might become mired in legal entanglements. Thus far, however, the Minnesota law has not been applied to international cases, and most U.S. state governments have taken the position of the Florida attorney general in his formal opinion on the Minnesota memorandum—that "the resolution of these matters must be addressed at the national, if not international, level."[7]

Most legal scholars and analysts agree, as a practical matter, that laws like those contained in the Minnesota memorandum (often referred to as "long-arm jurisdiction"), whether promulgated by U.S. state governments or the governments of nation-states, are unenforceable and inconsistent with international law.[8] This should be the case especially in the United States, where the Supreme Court has always interpreted congressional enactments in accordance with international law and has been consistent in holding state legislatures to the same standard. Most provisions of U.S. foreign relations laws—enacted by the House of Representatives and the Senate—are designed to reserve international subjects for federal lawmakers and administrators, with treaties superior to state law as the "supreme law of the land." In addition, considerations of the international law principle of *comity* (i.e., the respect courts accord one another and the laws of other sovereign nations) would undoubtedly come to the fore in U.S. relationships with other countries if Minnesota ever attempted to assert its jurisdiction over the Internet internationally. To quote from Darrel Menthe's conclusions in this regard,

> Minnesota's approach has several problems. First, Minnesota has ignored the presumption against extraterritoriality in application of U.S. laws. It seems that the Minnesota Attorney General was under the impression that, because the mode of analysis for conflicts of law is the same for conflicts between U.S. states as for conflicts between a U.S. state and a foreign country, the results will always be the same. The sovereignty of individual American states, however, is not as easily offended (or defended) as the sovereignty of nation-states. In other words, courts will accord France's interest in its sovereignty greater weight than Delaware's.[9]

Most U.S. states, the U.S. federal government, and other nation-states use *subjective territoriality* as the basis for determining jurisdiction in international legal cases. Under this principle, an activity that takes place within a given state is subject to the jurisdiction of that state. In cases involving the Internet, courts have also occasionally invoked the principle of *objective territoriality,* also known as *effects jurisdiction,* which is intended for use when an illegal action takes place outside the territory of a given state but the primary effect of that activity is within the state (the classic example is that of a gunman in Canada who shoots an American across the border, with the shot being fired in Canada and the death taking place in the United States). In such a case the United States would have jurisdiction to prescribe under the principle of objective territoriality.[10] Objective territoriality, however, although obviously applicable to the Internet in some specific circumstances, is not, in Menthe's words, "a blanket to be thrown over cyberspace, but is appropriate only in unusual circumstances where (as in the hypothetical example of the Canadian shooting an American) the state asserting jurisdiction on the basis of this principle is somehow the target state, uniquely or particularly affected by an action intended to cause such an effect."[11]

A third commonly used basis for international jurisdiction is *nationality,* where a state asserts the right to enact a law binding on all of its citizens regardless of where they might be residing. Under the law of the Netherlands, for example, a Dutch national "is liable to prosecution in Holland for an offence committed abroad, which is punishable under Netherlands law and which is also punishable under the law of the country where the offence was committed."[12] The idea that nationality should serve as the principle for jurisdiction to prescribe in all international cases involving the Internet has been championed by a number of legal scholars on the basis that there is no sovereignty in cyberspace and therefore no basis for territorial jurisdiction. In this respect, the argument goes, cyberspace is similar to Antarctica, outer space, and the high seas—the three areas where jurisdiction to prescribe has already been established according to the principle of nationality. Menthe describes the following scenario as an example of a system where nationality would serve as the basis for international jurisdiction in cyberspace:

> A webpage, commissioned by a U.S. citizen, is uploaded from Moldova by a Moldovan citizen. If the webpage contains advertising considered fraudulent under U.S. law, that U.S. citizen could be subject to prosecution by U.S. authorities. Additionally, the Moldovan could be subject to the laws of Moldova that regulate uploading. Moreover, a U.S. citizen in Moldova is not immune from U.S. law

simply because he uploads from Moldova (into cyberspace) rather
than from the United States. What the United States cannot do is prescribe a law for a webpage created and uploaded by a Moldovan who
lacks any reasonable connection to an American national . . . merely
because the webpage is "downloadable" in the United States.[13]

Among the many difficulties involved in instituting an international
regime establishing nationality as the principle for jurisdiction in cyberspace is the lack of anything tangible that one might easily register as
the mark of nationality. In the case of Antarctica, scientific personnel
and observers working there are subject to jurisdiction based solely on
their nationality following provisions of the Antarctic Treaty of 1961.
The Basic Treaty on Outer Space (1967), patterned after the regime for
Antarctica, asserts that outer space, including the moon, is not subject
to claims of sovereignty by any one country but instead lays out rules
for carrying on activities authorized by individual states in accordance
with treaty provisions.[14] Menthe argues that a system establishing jurisdiction in cyberspace, based on nationality, might be brought into being
if anyone uploading an Internet file or a web page were required to
mark it with his or her nationality before it could be sent (others have
suggested this might be done automatically by the ISP). In that case,
Menthe suggests, "we may not know 'where' a web page is, but we
[would] know who is responsible for it. The nationality of items in
cyberspace could be determined by the nationality of the person or entity who put them there, or perhaps by the one who controls them."[15]

Menthe's proposal to use nationality as the basis for creating a
more predictable and internationally uniform system of law for the
Internet would encounter considerable opposition from a wide range of
organizations and groups concerned with questions of content regulation and preservation of privacy of communications in cyberspace.
Even more strenuous objection would be raised to a requirement that
the nationality of anyone sending a message over the Internet routinely
be included in the message. Instead of adopting such sweeping proposals, which would fundamentally alter the basis on which jurisdiction to
prescribe has been adopted by most countries, what has been happening
increasingly is the development of cross-border legal cooperation networks among a limited number of nation-states that interact frequently,
which see the need for greater jurisdictional predictability and unifor-
mity in cyberspace but prefer a more gradualist approach to change. For
example, members of the European Community, the three member-
states of NAFTA (Mexico, Canada, and the United States), and mem-

bers of the WTO in their discussion of the GATS agreement are all pursuing expansion of cross-border legal practices and cooperation, with a segment of such activities focusing on the need for adaptation to problems of jurisdiction presented by cyberspace.[16]

A particularly interesting example of cross-border regional cooperation among legal practitioners is found in the Middle East, where the various nations have developed three distinctive types of legal systems, each with a different level of dependence on traditional Muslim law (Sharia): (1) Lebanon, Syria, and Egypt generally follow Western law; (2) Saudi Arabia, Oman, and Yemen have codified their laws drawing primarily from the Sharia; (3) Iraq, Jordan, and Libya have commercial laws that are essentially westernized but have retained Islamic law in the drawing up of contracts and in matters such as the prohibition of interest-bearing loans.[17] In this case, legal scholars from all Muslim-majority nations in the Middle East are trying to facilitate the development of modern commercial transactions by developing a cross-border framework, based on the French law of obligations, "capable of comprehending *Sharia* precepts alongside western commercial practices otherwise invalid under Islamic law, thereby appeasing both the business and the religious interests in the region."[18] The role of Internet-related issues constitutes a significant part of these discussions.

The American Bar Association (ABA) and other professional associations—in Asia, Africa, Latin America, the Middle East, and Central and Eastern Europe—have been cooperating in a number of ways to coordinate national and international law-related initiatives designed to promote electronic commerce, online financial services, and other Internet-related commercial developments. A major project of the ABA's Committee on Financial Services Deregulation and Consolidation has been an analysis of current global trends in the financial services industry, including recommendations for modernizing the world's legal frameworks to maximize the industry's development in the twenty-first century.[19] Growing out of this work is an ambitious "jurisdiction project" organized by the ABA's Subcommittee on International Transactions—which involves leading judges, lawyers, and legal scholars from around the world—designed to analyze jurisdictional problems that impact global electronic commerce. The project, directed by Professor Margaret Stewart of the Chicago-Kent Law School, released its first major findings at the ABA's 2000 annual meetings in New York (July 6–12) and London (July 15–20).

The ABA's Committee on Cyberspace Law has tried to shape laws of electronic commerce worldwide by publishing a Model Web Development Agreement, pressuring the U.S. Congress to include global issues in the development of the Uniform Electronic Transactions Act, and providing technical assistance on Internet-related issues to practitioners and government officials in developing countries. One of the most active ABA projects is the Central and East European Law Initiative (CEELI), being carried out with funding from the U.S. Agency for International Development (USAID). This project, which has funding into 2001, brings U.S. judges, lawyers, and other law professionals together with their CEE counterparts in an effort to identify ways they might work together to help build the legal infrastructures of the former USSR and former Warsaw Pact nations. Internet-related legal issues and jurisdictional matters form a central part of all of these ABA projects.

As in other areas, some of the most contentious jurisdictional issues that have arisen thus far have resulted from differing European and U.S. perspectives and practices. In 1998, for example, a Danish computer user was charged with posting racial slurs on the Internet via a U.S.-based ISP, and Danish authorities originally planned to request an injunction against that speech in the United States. That attempt was dropped when it was realized that such an injunction would violate the U.S. constitution, so the Danish police alternatively charged the user with posting the comments on a Danish Usenet group accessed through the U.S.-based ISP. Unlike a finding that would have been made by a U.S. court on this issue, the location in Denmark of the server for the Usenet group was sufficient for the Danes to assert jurisdiction.

Two other cases where European and U.S. interpretations differ have been the subject of considerable discussion among international lawyers. In the first of these, in 1997 the District Court of Munich asserted its jurisdiction and convicted the local manager of a U.S.-based CompuServe ISP for violations of German antipornography laws, handing down a two-year suspended sentence and a fine of more than $56,000. The decision was widely viewed with alarm because it extended liability to ISPs rather than Internet users. Indeed, the prosecutor in the case has appealed the conviction, and a London-based ISP (Psinet) physically moved its web servers out of Germany in July 1998 for fear of violating Bavarian law.[20] In the second case, in November 2000 a French court ruled that Yahoo! Inc. had to assume responsibility to find ways to prevent Internet users in France from viewing Nazi material on its U.S. website, thereby setting a highly controversial precedent that Internet companies must comply with local laws in any countries from which their websites are accessible.[21]

Even in cases where the courts in one nation might choose to assert jurisdiction over a foreign national based on an offensive use of the Internet in another country, it remains questionable whether such a stance could result in prosecution in many cases, since the country of the offending foreigner will usually object. The extent to which a country might be willing to enforce such a ruling is even more problematic, and in any case, pursuing enforcement in cases resulting from these rulings would be extremely expensive and time-consuming. For these reasons *contractual arbitration* is becoming a preferred method for resolving cyberspace disputes.

One of the model contractual arbitration dispute resolution programs is the CPA WebTrust created jointly by two private organizations—the American Institute of Certified Public Accountants (AICPA) and the Chartered Institute of Certified Accountants (CICA) of Canada. The CPA WebTrust program has established a set of principles and criteria websites must adhere to if they are to receive the WebTrust Seal, which companies can then display on the websites themselves. Applicants for a WebTrust Seal must submit to an audit, conducted by a trained certified public accountant, that explores three aspects of the website: (1) the degree to which the company running the website discloses its business and information privacy practices and executes transactions in accordance with its disclosures, (2) ability of the company to assure customers that their transactions will be completed and billed as agreed, and (3) controls the company has in place to assure that customer information obtained as a result of electronic commerce is protected from uses not related to the business transaction.[22] The WebTrust program includes a system for user recourse and dispute resolution, which is mandatory if a user is dissatisfied with the site's resolution of a complaint. This allows users from all over the world, regardless of nationality, to have their disputes heard by experienced legal professionals in an affordable and safe forum. In the Bill of Rights associated with the arbitration procedure, each party is guaranteed, among other things, "a fundamentally fair process, affordable costs, discovery, impartial decision-makers, and timely decisions." Parties who might not be able to take part in the process for financial reasons can apply for full or partial waiver of the fee, thus allowing all parties potential opportunities for meaningful participation.[23]

■ THE HAGUE CONFERENCE
CONVENTION ON JURISDICTION

At the intergovernmental level, an important project with considerable potential impact on international Internet regime norms is the attempt by the Hague Conference on Private International Law (usually called the "Hague Conference") to develop a new Convention on Jurisdiction and the Recognition/Enforcement of Judgments in Civil and Commercial Matters. The Hague Conference is an intergovernmental organization, composed of forty-seven nations, that meets every four years in diplomatic plenary sessions "to work for the progressive unification of the rules of private international law."[24] The idea of developing international *treaty-level agreement* on matters concerning jurisdiction and recognition/enforcement of judgments originated in the U.S. State Department in the early 1990s, reflecting business and governmental concerns (in the United States and elsewhere) that international law does not provide sufficient guidelines and enforcement mechanisms for enforcing and collecting on civil and commercial judgments that go against companies and individuals outside the United States, Europe, and a few other countries.

Although U.S. courts have become the preferred venue for hearing private international law cases from around the world (essentially because U.S. courts recognize and enforce judgments on a global basis whereas courts in other countries ordinarily do not), U.S. citizens and corporations do not always receive the same considerations from abroad that foreigners expect in U.S. courts. Most legal scholars expect this gap between the United States and other nations to widen in the future. As Edward C.Y. Lau, a member of the U.S. delegation to the Hague Conference, has pointed out, the proliferation of commercial and other international relations—particularly since the spread of the Internet—has resulted in an entirely different world legal environment than existed previously:

> The climate that exists today is very different than in the past, when we were dealing with countries like Germany, Japan and Hong Kong. Most of those countries have companies here [in the United States], so jurisdiction was not a problem. Now we are looking at other countries in the picture, and a lot of them simply do not recognize foreign judgments. Such countries include China, Russia and nations in eastern Europe. The issues of recognition and enforcement will become even more significant in the future as formerly Communist countries like

Russia seek to produce products for world-wide consumption, and as U.S. companies continue to look for cheaper foreign labor.[25]

The U.S. decision to approach the Hague Conference to develop a multilateral treaty was arrived at precisely because the Hague Conference organization includes the countries Lau mentioned and has had extensive experience with international jurisdiction and enforcement mechanisms.[26]

Development of the Convention on Jurisdiction project is being led by Catherine Kessedjian, deputy secretary-general of the Hague Conference, who has coedited a book on the general subject.[27] As part of their activities, in September 1999 project leaders jointly convened (with the University of Geneva) a three-day roundtable meeting "Questions of Private International Law Raised by Electronic Commerce and the Internet," attended by more than a hundred representatives of business, government, and international organizations from twenty-six countries.[28] Many of the roundtable recommendations were included in the Preliminary Draft of the Convention on Jurisdiction, adopted by the Special Commission on October 30, 1999, and will eventually be taken up in a plenary session of the Hague Convention once the draft version has been reviewed and discussed by the member nations of the Hague Conference.

The Draft Convention on Jurisdiction has forty-one articles and an annex that includes three proposals. It is designed to provide "a framework for national courts to use in rulings where there are international civil disputes by establishing jurisdiction guidelines and providing judgment enforcement assurances." In general, the draft is rather conservative, essentially setting down as "convention" practices the world legal community might consensually endorse while at the same time trying to avoid controversial issues. The approach to the document follows the first recommendation of the September 1999 Geneva roundtable—that "[so] far as possible, instead of the creation of new norms for electronic commerce and internet operations, existing principles, rules and procedures can and should be applied." Nonetheless, a number of leading legal scholars and practitioners have argued that the Convention on Jurisdiction, if successful, could have a positive transforming effect on international trade (and especially e-commerce) similar to that of the 1958 New York Convention on the Recognition and Enforcement of Foreign Arbitral Awards, which vastly facilitated enforcement of awards in more than 120 nation-states (that convention, for example, eventually led to a practice wherein most international contracts routinely have a binding arbitration clause).

Perhaps the key trade-off negotiated in discussions of the Convention on Jurisdiction has to do with the kind of judgment enforcement benefits the United States might gain by giving up some degree of jurisdiction. For example, the United States might have to concede the concept of punitive damages, since the legal systems of most other countries do not award damages for such things as loss of quality of life or medical expenses. On matters of jurisdiction, other countries have expressed substantial concern with respect to several aspects of U.S. law, including long-arm jurisdiction; punitive, multiple, and what are often considered excessive damages in tort and product liability cases; and other areas. If the United States were able to gain enforceable assurances of compensatory damages in exchange for concessions in some of these jurisdictional areas, most U.S. business and government leaders would consider that a major step forward. Lau has been quoted as saying, for example, that "compensatory damages is, in our view, really the main course."[29]

Because the Convention on Jurisdiction, once approved, would have the status of a treaty, it would have to be ratified by the U.S. Senate before it could take effect in the United States, and passage is expected to be difficult. With that in mind and to assure that the convention meets the needs of the U.S. legal community, the State Department has put together a study group within the secretary of state's Advisory Committee on Private International Law, with representatives from leading U.S. legal professional organizations. These include the ABA Litigation Section, the Association of Trial Lawyers of America, the National Association of Attorneys General, the American Insurance Association, the American Law Institute, the National Conference of Commissioners on Uniform State Laws, the American Corporate Counsel Association, the American Branch of the International Law Association, representatives of the federal and state court systems, and representatives of the practicing bar.

In terms of international regime theory, one would have to argue that the discussion of legal jurisdiction regarding the Internet is not yet at the agenda-setting stage. There is much activity in this area, and many ideas are being cast about and pursued to varying degrees, but nothing resembling a consensus has yet developed that might form the agenda for global negotiation of a set of generally accepted principles, norms, rules, and procedures. The nearest thing to such an agenda has been the work of the Hague Conference, but that work, as indicated earlier, is still at least a year or two away from agenda setting in international regime terms. A further complicating factor is that negotiated orders are much more difficult to bring about in international society than in domestic society, particularly in an area as complex as international jurisdiction regarding Internet-related matters in an atmosphere where no international regime presently exists for jurisdiction in many other areas as well.

One of two alternatives to a negotiated order in international regime theory is an imposed order, usually imposed by a hegemonic international power. As Oran Young has pointed out, however, an imposed order is almost certainly impossible in present-day international life despite relative U.S. hegemony.[30] This leaves the third of the three possibilities for regime creation Young has identified in his work—formation of a spontaneous order, where expectations eventually converge among a large number of actors in a very complex issue area without a single conscious design and without explicit negotiations until perhaps the very end of the process.[31] Based on this theory, the extensive and often divergent activity powerful private and public organizations are directing toward the establishment of a jurisdictional framework for civil and commercial law might conceivably result in the creation of a spontaneous order for jurisdictional aspects of the international Internet regime. At this point, however, such a denouement appears at best far in the future. It seems more likely that questions related to international legal jurisdiction over Internet-related activities will continue to be worked out by lawyers and judges functioning in national courts while using a variety of innovative private authority and soft law arrangements (e.g., dispute resolution procedures, commercial arbitration, and cross-border cooperative arrangements) to continue to build a body of national and international case law.

▪ **PROPOSALS FOR INTERNET PRIVACY AND CONTENT REGULATION LEGAL FRAMEWORKS**

Two other areas where national and international case law is being accumulated in the absence of clear regime principles and norms involve a variety of matters related to regulation of Internet content and protection of personal privacy in Internet use. This is so because the Internet presents unparalleled opportunities to collect, aggregate, and disseminate information about a person or to develop a profile on a person that might be used by governments, businesses, employers, one's personal enemies, or other organizations and people in society who previously lacked access to such a potentially invasive device. It is also a consequence of the Internet's ability to penetrate homes and living spaces in a much more substantial private manner than any communications media known previously, as indicated dramatically by two common problems (among others) that have arisen in all nations in the past few years. First, throughout the world Internet family users have been alarmed that Internet access has made it possible for pornographic and other literature antithetical to the values of many families to easily enter the home in ways that have presented severe problems for parental and educational guidance; this has given rise to a wide variety of proposed solutions to shield children from such literature, which in turn has led to actions (by governments and private authorities) designed to control Internet content and access. Second, a number of computer viruses have been spread throughout the world, often in just a few hours, destroying computer files worth billions of dollars and causing incalculable harm to tens of millions of Internet users; these and other forms of cyberattacks/cyberterrorism have prompted responses from authorities that have also raised alarms—from citizens and human rights activitists—about the potential for government organizations to invade privacy, seek illegitimate control of Internet code, and otherwise abuse their authority when confronting cybercrime or cyberterrorism.

In general, privacy issues have been taken up at the international level by two significant segments of society with different concerns: (1) consumer privacy on the Internet has been a major focus of private business worldwide, particularly since studies and surveys have consistently concluded that the absence of confidentiality in the use of data for commercial purposes is perhaps the major factor retarding the development of e-commerce; and (2) the impact of the Internet on human rights and personal freedoms has been the focus of civil liberties organizations, which perceive that personal privacy seems increasingly threatened in almost all nations by the introduction and spread of the Internet's capabilities into the hands of government officials, police, and intelligence networks.

Whether in the hands of businesses or governments, network architecture by its very nature facilitates invasion of privacy in three ways:

(1) the user's Internet Protocol (IP) address may be mapped each time the user logs on, so that any organization or individual with access to the user's site visits could develop a profile of the user; (2) small files called "cookies" can be sent directly to and stored on the user's computer the first time a given site is visited, enabling the site operator to collect and store information on the cookies during subsequent visits to the same site (the cookies are stored on the user's hard drive and are usually readable only by the site that sent them); (3) site operators may collect, store, and trade information gathered from online users, either without their permission or with their tacit permission, sometimes gained in devious or questionable ways. A landmark 1999 study of the law of cyberspace by the Harvard Law Review, focusing primarily on the United States, concluded that "despite longstanding scholarly concern for personal privacy, there is no clear legal liability for the collection of personal information [over the Internet]. The current entitlement to personal information benefits the collector and burdens the individual user, thus granting the collector full title to whatever information she can collect and leaving the individual from whom the information is taken with no recourse."[32]

Various approaches toward Internet content regulation and privacy matters by governments are prominent in every society where the Internet has been introduced, and all national legal systems are struggling to come to terms with them. In the United States, for example, more than a dozen bills designed to protect various aspects of Internet privacy were pending before the U.S. Congress in mid-2000, yet a seasoned congressional veteran was reported as saying "there are a lot of ideas floating around, but I don't think there's broad support for any of them."[33] A special forty-member advisory committee of the U.S. Federal Trade Commission (FTC) issued its long-awaited report on Internet privacy in May 2000, including an extensive survey of how information might be gathered and attempts made to protect Internet privacy in the United States. The FTC report found that 90 percent of websites in the United States display privacy policies (a significant jump from previous years), but only 20 percent of sites fully comply with the "fair privacy practices" devised by the FTC. On the basis of its report, the FTC recommended that government regulation be introduced for the first time, a significant departure from the Clinton administration's previous support for business, personal, and web operator self-regulation where Internet privacy matters are concerned.[34] The FTC report immediately provoked controversy and opposition in the U.S. Congress, where support is essential if the recommendations are to become law.

An even greater Internet privacy controversy was provoked in Europe in May 2000 when the government of the United Kingdom announced it was building a $39 million "Internet surveillance center" facility under the direction of the M15 headquarters of British intelligence in London (dubbed the "Internet Spy Center" by the British press), which makes it possible for the government to track any website in the U.K. Scheduled to be fully operational before the end of 2001, the center (officially called the Government Technical Assistance Centre [GTAC]) requires local ISPs to hardwire links directly to it, thus enabling government "security operators" to download Internet and e-mail traffic, monitor mobile phone networks, and decode encrypted messages. Legal authority for GTAC activities is provided by Britain's Regulation of Investigatory Powers (RIP) Bill, passed by Parliament in August 2000, which allows police and security services to legally demand, and require ISPs and Internet users to reveal, passwords and privacy encryption codes subject to two-year prison terms for failure to do so.[35] All of these measures, the Tony Blair government argues, are necessary to counter cyberterrorism and related activities.

The British government's dramatic action came in response to concerns about the security of the Internet, prompted by a series of potentially crippling viruses and cyberterrorism/cyberwar attacks that had resulted in losses of several billion dollars to computer users and companies in the late 1990s and the turn of the millennium. Such cyberattacks, the government argued, might have been avoided or countered more effectively had British intelligence had the benefit of the new surveillance center.[36] British police have also been concerned that demonstrators have been able to use the Internet with increasing effect to organize massive and highly destructive demonstrations in London, such as the May Day 2000 demonstration of anarchists and environmentalists that counted among its considerable damage the near destruction of a McDonald's restaurant and other shops, the spraying of graffiti all over buildings and monuments in downtown London, and the defacing of statues (including one of Sir Winston Churchill that was defaced with a hammer and sickle daubed in scarlet paint). Senior British police officers have attributed both the size and increasing destructiveness of demonstrations like May Day 2000 to the ability of demonstrators to outmaneuver the British police with the use of Internet technology. One senior officer was quoted as saying, "We knew that messages were being exchanged ahead of the demonstrations. The same thing happened last year when my officers actually saw group leaders in the streets with laptops, e-mailing each other, and directing groups of demonstrators to particular places."[37]

Critics of GTAC and RIP argue that they are threats to global privacy rights and cyberliberties, "not just to U.K. citizens, but to citizens in other countries communicating with U.K. citizens by e-mail."[38] Although the British home office has said GTAC will only act on data seized under a search warrant, civil liberties scholars and human rights activists argue that the activities of the center, which will operate on a twenty-four-hour surveillance basis, will vastly increase the potential for invasion of privacy by the government via the Internet. In the words of Michael Geist, a University of Ottawa professor specializing in Internet law,

> The concern is once the structure is in place, obviously the potential for abuse exists. If you say you're targeting Internet terrorists and criminals, that's a good thing. But, on the other hand, it's a pretty broad net and getting caught along with the criminals can be a lot of legitimate speech and a lot of other activity that simply isn't the government's business. . . . The reality is that all the traffic will be running through a government agency. . . . It's one thing to knock on an Internet provider's door, warrant in hand, and demand information, it's quite another to say, "we're going to have access to all that data and we're going to restrict our use to court approval."[39]

Aside from government attempts to monitor online communications, a number of other privacy issues revolve around attempts to censor or block Internet access to certain types of activities, such as reading or viewing pornography or online gambling. One of the first attempts to control Internet pornography was the Communications Decency Act (CDA) in the United States, which was passed by the U.S. Congress in 1996 and struck down by the Supreme Court in a 7-2 decision in 1997 under First Amendment considerations.[40] In countries where First Amendment concerns are less stringent, a number of attempts have been made to censor or block Internet materials relating to pornography and many other items. Some of these attempts are discussed in the companion volume to this one, but one of the most prominent international cases is the Australian law that took effect on January

1, 2000, forcing Australian ISPs to remove objectionable pornographic material from Australian sites.[41] The original draft of the legislation required Australian ISPs to block access to pornographic material on overseas sites as well, but those sections of the legislation were deleted when they met with fierce condemnation by industry and consumer groups. During the first three months following enactment of the legislation, reports indicated that the new law was having little effect on pornography sites in Australia, but it continued to stir up controversy both at home and abroad.[42]

■ PROTECTING PRIVACY WITH ENCRYPTION TECHNOLOGY AND CODE

Because of what they see as an inability thus far of national governments and their conventional law-making procedures to deal satisfactorily with the complex legal issues raised by the Internet, a number of legal analysts and human rights activists have argued for various versions of self-regulating rule-making regimes depending substantially on the development of the new technology itself, perhaps in association with soft law and private authority arrangements, with a lesser emphasis on traditional legislation and judicial authority. One version of this alternative would be a self-regulatory regime articulated and enforced by system operators and users, with the system operator drawing up rules, or "pacts," that would be contracted with those people who choose the rules of that particular system operator over another. System operators would then enforce the rules agreed to for each particular system, using the threat of banishment from the system as their primary tool of enforcement. An Australian theorist, Bernadette Jew, has gone so far as to predict that "it is likely that we will see the emergence of multiple groups of network systems forming their own confederations, each with its own rules or 'constitutional' principles. Content or conduct acceptable in one 'area' of the Internet may be banned in another. It is then up to individuals to choose which laws or 'rules' they are willing to conform to when they choose to access particular areas of cyberspace."[43]

A second suggestion for technology-based self-regulation on the Internet, especially in areas where the right to privacy is involved, is based on the belief that individual users of the Internet should have the right to "encrypt their communication and information without restriction."[44] This has become the watchword of the Global Internet Liberty Campaign (GILC), a project supported by a number of nongovernmental civil liberties and human rights organizations worldwide, which was established in June 1996 at an international conference in Paris. The original purpose of the GILC was to develop a resolution addressed to the Organization for Economic Cooperation and Development (OECD), which has since incorporated at least some of the GILC recommendations into its privacy guidelines (discussed later). Since 1996, however, the GILC project has continued, offering training in the use of cryptographic methods to human rights organizers, journalists, and political activists on a global basis. In addition, the Electronic Privacy Information Center (EPIC), on behalf of the GILC project, has monitored and provided a comprehensive review of policies related to cryptography in virtually every national and territorial jurisdiction in the world.[45]

Encryption is a mathematical process involving the use of formulas (or algorithms) that make it possible to scramble and encode messages in such a way that, ideally, a given encrypted (scrambled) communication can be read (decrypted or unscrambled) only by the person or persons for whom it was intended. The extent to which privacy is assured by using cryptography varies with the quality and reliability of the technology used, but a large variety of modern computer encryption software has made it possible to protect computer files and messages against interception to a very high degree. Prior to the advent of the computer age, encryption technology was deployed almost exclusively to protect the confidentiality of military, intelligence, and diplomatic communications. During the past few decades, however, manufacturers have competed with one another to produce the most up-to-date encryption and authentication software in an effort to keep up with the burgeoning use of Internet-related applications (e.g., electronic mail, electronic fund transfers, exchange of medical records, to name only a few).

The GILC project is based on the assumption that privacy will be best protected in those countries where governments allow their citizens to import encryption software, install it on their computers, and use it to protect the privacy of their Internet activities. When its first survey was conducted in 1996, EPIC found that most countries did not have regulations on the use of cryptography and that cryptography could be freely used, manufactured, and sold without restriction in most parts of the world.[46] Among those countries where rigorous domestic controls over use of cryptography have since been established are Belarus, China,

Israel, Pakistan, Russia, and Singapore. A number of other countries—including most prominently India and South Korea—are considering the adoption of new controls.

In the past the United States has imposed strict export controls on encryption source code, based on policy arguments that this will deter the use of encryption software by criminals, terrorists, and others threatening U.S. national security who wish to conceal their identity. In September 1999, however, the U.S. Court of Appeals for the 9th Circuit, in *Bernstein v. U.S. Department of Justice,* struck down such export controls as an impermissible "prior restraint" on speech protected by the First Amendment. The decision has been widely hailed as a landmark ruling by Americans involved in electronic commerce and by activists in civil liberties and human rights organizations.[47] The business community has long argued that it requires encryption software on products exported from the United States if such exports are to be competitive with e-commerce products exported by other nations. Those who engage in e-commerce also view encryption software favorably because it potentially provides considerable privacy with regard to personal information and signatures exchanged during transactions. In response to pressure from U.S. business leaders, in January 2000 the U.S. government relaxed export regulations of many encryption products by eliminating some export rules, enlarging the scope of export licensing exceptions, allowing any U.S. company to export any encryption item to its foreign subsidiaries without prior review, and creating new licensing exceptions for certain types of encryption such as source code.[48] In July 2000 the Department of Commerce granted permission to export strong encryption (128-bit) technology to any customer within the fifteen EU members, as well as to select European and Pacific Rim countries.[49]

A second major GILC concern with U.S. policy on encryption is the insistence by U.S. military, police, and intelligence communities that some form of key management system be established that would allow government access, under certain circumstances, to the encryption keys that make it possible to decrypt computer code. The U.S. government has proposed at various times different versions of both voluntary and mandatory key escrow systems. In some cases corporations would be allowed to hold their own keys if they agreed to abide by law enforcement rules; in other cases key recovery services might be set up by third-party private entities. Although the U.S. Congress has introduced but failed to enact legislation on key escrow policy, international intelligence and police networks from a number of countries that have working relationships with each other continue to explore ways key management systems might be made more acceptable to civil rights organizations, which universally oppose their introduction as part of a worldwide Internet regime. The GILC has made it clear that it views "the development of restrictive national and international regimes on the use of cryptography . . . as a political and civil rights issue." From the GILC's perspective, "The combined and formidable resources of American and other law enforcement and intelligence agencies, as well as international structures like Interpol and the G-8, could be successful in forcing the world to adopt an international encryption key management infrastructure. Our major goal must be to prevent such an occurrence."[50]

■ OECD PRIVACY AND ENCRYPTION GUIDELINES

At the intergovernmental level, the major attempt to develop an international framework for privacy and encryption guidelines for the Internet has been the work of the OECD, which has put together a series of study groups and committees of experts that has produced guideline documents in three areas directly related to cyberspace privacy concerns.[51]

First, *"Privacy Guidelines" in the Electronic Environment: Focus on the Internet,* published in 1997, is an attempt to update the recommendation of the OECD Council, *Guidelines on the Protection of Privacy and Transborder Flows of Personal Data (Privacy Guidelines),* dated September 23, 1980, which forms the basis for many existing national privacy laws and codes. The 1980 document presents what its authors call "technologically neutral principles" designed to provide "general guidance concerning the collection and management of personal information." The 1997 document "reaffirm[s] that the 1980 Privacy Guidelines are applicable with regard to any technology used for collecting and processing data." Taken together, the 1980 and 1997 privacy guidelines documents are intended to constitute consensus recommendations that contain several sets of principles to guide governments, businesses, and others when handling personal data at the national or international level. These include:

1. Collection Principle—There should be limits to the collection of personal data and any such data should be obtained by lawful and fair means and, where appropriate, with the knowledge or consent of the data subject.
2. Data Quality Principle—Personal data should be relevant to the purposes for which they are to be used, and, to the extent necessary for those purposes, should be accurate, complete, and kept up-to-date.
3. Purpose Specification Principle—The purposes for which personal data are collected should be specified not later than at the time of data collection and the subsequent use limited to the fulfilment of those purposes or such others as are not incompatible with those purposes and as are specified on each occasion of change of purpose.
4. Use Limitation Principle—Personal data should not be disclosed, made available, or otherwise used for purposes other than those specified in accordance with [the Purpose Specification Principle] except: (a) with the consent of the data subject; or (b) by the authority of law.
5. Security Safeguards Principle—Personal data should be protected by reasonable security safeguards against such risks as loss or unauthorized access, destruction, use, modification, or disclosure of data.
6. Openness Principle—There should be a general policy of openness about developments, practices, and policies with respect to personal data. Means should be readily available of establishing the existence and nature of personal data, and the main purposes of their use, as well as the identity and usual residence of the data controller.
7. Individual Participation Principle—An individual should have the right: (a) to obtain from a data controller, or otherwise, confirmation of whether or not the data controller has data relating to him; (b) to have communicated to him, data relating to him within a reasonable time; at a charge, if any, that is not excessive; in a reasonable manner; and in a form that is readily intelligible to him; (c) to be given reasons if a request made under subparagraphs (a) and (b) is denied, and to be able to challenge such denial; and (d) to challenge data relating to him and, if the challenge is successful to have the data erased, rectified, completed, or amended.

8. Accountability Principle—A data controller should be accountable for complying with measures that give effect to the principles stated above.

In addition, the OECD privacy guidelines lay out detailed recommendations for domestic processing and re-export of personal data internationally, based on principles of "uninterrupted and secure free flow of data and legitimate restrictions"; recommendations for establishing legal, administrative, and other procedures or institutions for the protection of privacy and individual liberties in respect of personal data; and recommendations for information exchange, mutual assistance, and other forms of cooperation between nations designed to protect privacy and civil liberties.

The second major OECD guidelines document is entitled *Guidelines for Cryptography Policy* and was approved by the OECD Council on December 19, 1997. The document is intended to strike a balance among the interests of the three major constituencies concerned with cryptography: (1) *commercial firms* that wish to foster confidence in information and communication infrastructures, networks, and systems and in the manner in which they are used; (2) *public safety, law enforcement, and national security organizations* that wish to use cryptography to help them fight crime and uncover threats to national and international security; and (3) *civil liberties and human rights organizations* with interests in protecting personal privacy rights and data security. Principles recommended in the cryptography guidelines include the user's right to choose any cryptographic method, subject to applicable law; protection of individuals' fundamental right to privacy, including secrecy of communications and protection of personal data, in the implementation and use of cryptographic methods; and avoidance by governments of cryptographic policies that present "unjustified obstacles to trade."

The third major OECD guidelines document is a draft *Guidelines for Consumer Protection in the Context of Electronic Commerce*, which was presented to the organization's Third Annual E-Commerce International Forum in Paris in October 1999 and is expected to be approved by the twenty-nine OECD member nations in 2002. This document was developed over a two-year period surrounding the OECD E-Commerce Summit held in Ottawa, Canada, in October 1998, which was attended by more than 300 representatives from forty governments and by hundreds of others from industry, public interest and consumer groups, labor unions, and other organizations.[52] These guidelines set out recommendations for businesses and governments on most issues raised by online commerce, including advertising, marketing, sales, disputes, privacy, and education.

Although the OECD work on privacy guidelines is a frequently quoted measure or standard by which to evaluate or compare the rules and practices of governments and businesses with respect to privacy matters on the Internet, it has had only a limited influence on Internet behavior patterns. A 1999 study by the Center for Democracy and Technology, for example, found that less than 10 percent of websites respected the OECD privacy guidelines regarding the rights of people to expect that any personal data they submit over the Internet will not be used without their consent, that they will have an opportunity to correct any errors, and that they can assume the data will be protected from abuse.[53] Frustration with a lack of implementation of OECD guidelines in Europe was expressed by Jim Murray, head of the Bureau Européen des Unions de Consommateurs (BEUC), when the draft e-commerce consumer guidelines were published in late 1999; Murray reflected at that point that "when the [OECD guidelines] become inconvenient, they disappear."[54] Frustration with a lack of implementation of privacy guidelines was also expressed by U.S. privacy advocates and lawmakers in mid-2000 when the Clinton administration extended by eight months a deadline for the U.S. financial industry to comply with privacy laws Congress had enacted the previous year. The 1999 legislation had mandated that federal agencies were to publish new regulations requiring financial companies to develop privacy policies in line with OECD guidelines by November 12, 2000, but that deadline has been set back to July 1, 2001.[55]

▪ CONCLUSIONS

If one looks to regime theory for guidance with regard to the three major topics considered in this chapter—international jurisdictional questions, control of Internet content, and privacy rights—it quickly becomes apparent that these issue areas are being dealt with for Internet-related matters in much the same manner as has historically been the case for other international regimes. For example, in the world's four most significant transportation and communications regimes established and functioning prior to the Internet (shipping, air transport, telecommunications, and postal services), the development of principles and norms for determining the jurisdiction of various courts over disputes occurring among regime actors was closely related to the degree of robustness exhibited by the regimes as they have evolved and been maintained over time.[56] Questions concerning rights to privacy, however—although they have always been issues for airlines, shipping agents, telecommunications operators, and postal services—have not generally been considered appropriate agenda items in regime negotiations except insofar as they affect commerce. Instead, those privacy issues of greatest interest to human rights advocates have generally been left to be resolved outside the context of international regime principles and norms in almost all international regimes, which is one reason they have been so prominent on the agendas of international and domestic courts and related forums.[57]

Human and privacy rights advocates have argued that their concerns are most effectively addressed not by international regimes in which states are the principal actors but instead, particularly in the international sphere, by the development of an "international civil society" in which "individuals and institutions which are independent of the state and state boundaries" are able to influence governments and other organizations across a spectrum much broader than a given international regime.[58] In this context, international nongovernmental organizations (INGOs), regional public and private human rights organizations, and human rights education play central roles.[59] For these organizations the invention of the Internet is often viewed as particularly important for the development of human rights education in the 21st century—as a medium for communication, an educational tool, and an online library for human rights documentation—but not for its potential interest as a discrete international regime. In the words of Stephen Hansen, "[The Internet] is a medium well-suited for instant communication, alerting the rest of the world to what is happening here and now, and sometimes eliciting an almost immediate response."[60]

One way to understand the salience of jurisdictional questions as compared with concerns about content regulation and privacy in international regime formation is by focusing on the nature of the membership of the key actors in both cases. Where questions of jurisdiction are involved, the significant actors in international regimes are states, and the problematic in international jurisdictional disputes is whether one state or another is going to have the right to legislate, adjudicate, or enforce the laws with regard to a particular legal matter. Mark Zacher and Brent Sutton have found that international states have a fundamental interest in resolving jurisdictional conflicts and developing strong international norms for clarifying jurisdictional rights, primarily because "a lack of clear jurisdictional rights creates high uncertainty of costs, high transaction costs, and impediments to the flow of goods and services."[61] In all four of the international transportation and communications regimes Zacher and Sutton have analyzed in detail, states were willing to negotiate and make concessions with regard to international jurisdictional matters when such negotiations and concessions were clearly in their economic and commercial interests, narrowly conceived. For example, in all four of the transportation and communications regimes mentioned earlier, an "open access norm for international spaces" and other potential constraints on state actions have been accepted when states have considered the adoption of such international norms to be a clear advantage in economic and commercial terms (e.g., when such actions have helped reduce impediments to the international flow of goods and services, promoted orderly commerce and security, or contributed to the growth of national economies and the welfare of citizens).

Where questions of content regulation and privacy matters are concerned, however, the individual actors in institutional arrangements are almost always nonstate actors, and protection of personal privacy and civil rights is usually thought to require enforcement capabilities beyond those commonly associated with international regime rules and procedures. In China, for example, human rights advocates have tried unsuccessfully to link government performance on human rights matters (e.g., government censorship of materials on the Internet or government attempts to routinely monitor e-mail) to the commercial or technical performance aspects of international Internet regime formation. In support of such human rights advocates, in May 2000 the U.S. House of Representatives insisted on the creation of a twenty-three-member commission to monitor Chinese policies concerning freedom of religion, labor rights, and political expression; to keep lists of victims of government abuses; and to develop legislation to respond to abuses as part of the U.S. agreement to grant China permanent normal trading status within the WTO.[62] Such attempts have not been factors in international regime formation because they have been interpreted by the targeted countries—whether China, nations of the Middle East, or elsewhere— as infringements on their sovereignty, a stance consistent with previous such stances by other states when negotiating regime norms for international shipping, air transport, telecommunications, and postal regimes. As Zacher and Sutton have pointed out in their studies of the four international regimes in these other issue areas, states have been able over the years to negotiate principles of international civil society, such as open access and norms, "to allow transit through their sovereign domains" but only "as long as foreign parties do not threaten the self-defined conceptions of 'peace, good order, and security' of the individual sovereign nations that are part of the regime."[63]

In an effort to gain a clearer understanding of these complex relationships, Oran Young has suggested that "what is needed to make progress analytically is a clear separation between regimes, on the one hand, and both international society and global civil society, on the other."[64] In this formulation the relationship between international regimes (which are concerned at their core with organizational and jurisdictional matters) and global civil society (in which questions of personal human and civil rights are central) could be said to parallel the state-society distinction commonly made in domestic political and social systems. Young is quick to point out that his attempt to distinguish between two "pure types of regimes"—*international regimes* (whose members are states) and *transnational regimes* (whose members are nonstate actors and "whose operations center on issues arising in international society")—does not mean regimes and society are unrelated. On the contrary, Young argues, the distinction should make it possible to open a new research agenda focusing precisely on the links between international regimes and international civil society. In Young's words, "It makes no more sense to try to grasp the identity of many nonstate actors without understanding their involvement in global civil society than it does to think of states without paying attention to their connection to international society."

■ **NOTES**

1. For an analysis of the Internet's impact on questions of sovereignty, see Perritt, "The Internet as a Threat to Sovereignty?" pp. 423–440. See also Wriston, "Bits, Bytes, and Diplomacy," pp. 172–183.

2. For example, the Internet Alliance and the National Conference of State Legislatures predicted, on the basis of legislative proposals already identified, that more than 2,000 Internet-related bills would be introduced into the U.S. state legislatures in the year 2000. See Clausing, "States to Consider Flurry of Internet Bills."

3. Substantial agreement also exists among lawyers, judges, and legal scholars that existing law, with considerable adaptation, will be able to provide a framework for development of cyberlaw into the future. At the conclusion of a major international symposium, The Legal Implications for the Internet, for example, Jonathan Bick summarized the consensus conclusion that "while the Internet does represent an evolutionary convergence of technologies . . . it is not a revolutionary change. . . . Legal issues are adequately addressed by existing legal theories if applied correctly. . . . Most legal precepts can be adopted without much difficulty to deal with the novel challenges posed by the Internet." Bick, "Symposium Article," p. 66. See also the conclusions of the 1999 Hague Conference discussed later in this chapter.

4. In the Supreme Court's first opinion about the Internet, *Reno v. ACLU,* 117 S. Ct. 2329, 2334–35 (1997), the Court encouraged those who would like to see cyberspace legally defined as outside national boundaries by including this observation in a case that did not involve jurisdiction: "Taken together, these tools constitute a unique medium—known to its users as 'cyberspace'—located in no particular geographical location but available to anyone, anywhere in the world, with access to the Internet." In 1998 the Supreme Court specifically turned down pleas, "amid a flood of computer-related *certiorari* petitions," to review a case involving jurisdiction over cases implicating foreign proceedings. See "Supreme Court Rejects Three Computer-Related Intellectual Property Cases," p. 16.

5. Quoted from case law in Hoegle and Boam, "Nations Uneasily Carve Out Internet Jurisdiction," pp. 1–7. Other quotations in this paragraph are taken from this same source unless otherwise noted.

6. *Memorandum of Minnesota Attorney General (July 18, 1995),* available at www.state.mn.us/ebranch/ag, quoted in Menthe, "Jurisdiction in Cyberspace," p. 75.

7. *Florida Attorney General, Formal Opinion: AG0 95-70 (October 18, 1995),* quoted in ibid., p. 76.

8. Pasquale and Gemeiner, "Non-Resident Web Sites," pp. 5–8. Pasquale and Gemeiner are professional litigators; they argue that "trying to apply existing laws concerning long-arm jurisdiction to the fast-developing world of the Internet is somewhat like trying to board a moving bus" (p. 5).

9. Menthe, "Jurisdiction in Cyberspace," p. 76.

10. *Jurisdiction to prescribe* is distinguished in the Foreign Relations Law of the United States (1987) from jurisdiction to enforce and jurisdiction to adjudicate. Jurisdiction to prescribe is "the right of a state to make its law applicable to the activities, relations, the status of persons, or the interests of persons in things." Ibid., p. 72.

11. Ibid., p. 79.

12. Ibid., p. 73. As Menthe points out, this Dutch law is similar to that of many other civil law countries.

13. Ibid., p. 90.

14. A discussion of outer space in the context of international regime the-

ory appears in Tan, "Towards a New Regime for the Protection of Outer Space," pp. 145–193.

15. Menthe, "Jurisdiction in Cyberspace," p. 89.

16. See Goldsmith, "Globalization of Laws," pp. 139 ff.; Kossick, "Litigation in the United States and Mexico," pp. 23–65; and Burr, "Will the General Agreement on Trade in Services Result in International Standards for Lawyers," pp. 667–697. Burr points out (p. 671) that the ABA was opposed to inclusion of legal services in the GATS agreement because the ABA had been pursuing bilateral negotiations with the Japanese, and ABA leaders felt the multilateral nature of the GATS process might give the Japanese "a way out of their commitment to open Japan's legal system to U.S. lawyers."

17. Shaaban, "Commercial Transactions," pp. 157 ff.

18. Ibid., p. 162. See also McCary, "Bridging Ethical Borders," pp. 289–339. McCary points out (p. 337) that whereas "emphasis on commercial principles may help to overcome some cultural issues . . . it cannot be relied on to bypass them all."

19. Some relevant ABA activities are outlined in Cheek, "The 21st Century," p. C5. Relevant ABA publications, including *The Law on Interactive Media* and *Developing Corporate E-Mail and Internet Policies,* as well as descriptions of projects and committee work, are available on the ABA's website at www.abanet.org/buslaw/cyber/initiatives.

20. These two cases are outlined in detail in Hoegle and Boam, "Nations Uneasily Carve Out Internet Jurisdiction," pp. 1–7.

21. Pringle, "Some Worry," p. B2.

22. The WebTrust program is described in detail in Brown and Porter, "E-Commerce Arbitration," pp. 32–34.

23. Ibid. The quotation in this paragraph is from this source.

24. An excellent collection of background materials on the Hague Conference is available on its website at www.hcch.net/e/infosheet.html. The First Session of the Hague Conference was convened in 1893 by the Netherlands government on the initiative of T.M.C. Asser, who received the Nobel Peace Prize in 1911. The Seventh Session in 1951 resulted in a *Statute* (entered into force in 1955) that made the conference a permanent intergovernmental organization. The principal work of the conference consists of negotiating and drafting multilateral treaties, or conventions, in the different fields of private international law, which are first approved in the plenary sessions (held every four years) and must then be ratified by the forty-seven member nations that make up the organization for them to become international law.

25. Quoted in Neff, "Treaty Aims to Ease Actions," p. 2.

26. In the first public discussion of the proposed Convention on Jurisdiction by any State Department official, Peter H. Pfund (the special adviser for private international law) told a 1998 symposium at the Brooklyn Law School: "The State Department decided upon a multilateral effort under the auspices of the Hague Conference . . . for many reasons. The Hague Conference has a membership that includes the United States, Canada and

Mexico, and all Member States of the European Union, plus several Latin American countries, China, Japan, Australia, Israel, Morocco, Egypt, and several countries of Eastern Europe. The organization has successfully prepared many sound legal conventions. It has experience with judicial assistance conventions on service of process abroad, taking of evidence abroad, legalization of documents for use abroad, and a 1971 convention dealing with recognition/enforcement of judgments." Pfund, "The Project of the Hague Conference," pp. 11–12.

27. Boele-Woelki and Kessedjian, *Internet*.

28. The program synopsis and a press release announcing the conclusions of the roundtable are available at www.hcch.net/e/workprog/genve3le.html. Quotations in this and the following paragraph are from this source.

29. Quoted in Neff, "Treaty Aims to Ease Actions," p. 14.

30. Young, "Regime Dynamics," p. 103.

31. Ibid., pp. 98 ff.

32. "Developments in the Law," p. 1645.

33. Pressman, "Net Privacy," p. 2.

34. Schwartz, "Republicans Oppose Online Privacy Plans," p. A8

35. Powell, "RIP: Death of Privacy." Detailed analysis of the bill is provided in Campbell, "Online," p. 2.

36. The new center and Britain's new Internet privacy policies associated with its creation are outlined in MacLeod, "UK Moving to Open All (e-)Mail," pp. 1ff.

37. Ibid., p. 9.

38. The quote is from Sara Andrews of the Electronic Privacy Information Center in Washington, D.C., quoted in Landon, "'Big Brother Is Finally Here,'" p. A9.

39. Quoted in ibid.

40. "Developments in the Law," pp. 1581–1582.

41. The legislation is contained in the Broadcasting Services Amendment (Online Services) Bill 1999, which was passed in June 1999. See Murphy, "Australia Passes Law on Limiting Internet."

42. Between January 1 and March 31, 2000, the Australian Broadcasting Authority received 124 complaints under the new law, but less than half were upheld. Of those upheld, the authority ordered ISPs to "pull down 31 individual pages and referred the details of 45 pages hosted outside Australia to Internet filtering companies." At least 17 of the banned Australian pages moved overseas. Quotation from Anthony, "Online Censorship Laws Catch 35 Sites," p. 3. See also "Aussie Censors Crack Down on 27 Websites," p. 22.

43. Jew, "Australia," p. 3.

44. Quoted in Madsen et al., "Cryptography and Liberty," p. 477.

45. EPIC was established in 1994 and is a project of the Fund for Constitutional Government, working in association with Privacy International, a human rights group based in London. Further information can be obtained

from the EPIC website at www.epic.org, or from Hansen, *AAAS Directory,* especially pp. 19, 45, 61.

46. The GILC project designates countries as green (signifying that the country has expressed support for the OECD guidelines on cryptography, which generally favor unhindered legal use of cryptography, or has no cryptography controls), yellow (for countries that have proposed new cryptography controls or shown a willingness to treat cryptographic-enabled software as an item subject to troubling import arrangements), and red (identifying countries with sweeping controls on cryptography). For the latest GILC monitoring information, see its website at www.gilc.com.

47. McClure, "First Amendment Freedoms," pp. 465–488.

48. See Crocker, "Courts Split over Encryption as Protected Speech," p. B14, and Grossman, "Unscrambling the Rules on Encryption," pp. A1 ff.

49. Hulme, "Export Rules Eased for Encryption Tools," pp. 40–42. See also Johnston, "Government Loosens Up on Encryption Policies," pp. 16–20.

50. Quoted in Madsen et al., "Cryptography and Liberty," p. 483

51. These documents are available on the OECD website, at www.oecd.org, from which verbatim descriptions of and quotations from the OECD documents described in the following paragraphs are directly taken.

52. The summit conference was entitled "A Borderless World: Realizing the Potential of Global Electronic Commerce." For a summary of its work, see Banisar, "OECD Finishes E-Commerce Consumer Guidelines," pp. 7–9.

53. Quoted in Friedman, "Foreign Affairs: Little Brother," Section 4, page 17. The Center for Democracy and Technology is a 501(c)(3) organization supported by contributions from foundations and more than three dozen major American companies. More information on its projects is available at www.cdt.org.

54. Quoted in Banisar, "OECD Finishes E-Commerce Consumer Guidelines," p. 8. The BEUC describes itself as "the consumers' voice in the European Union." It is based in Brussels and represents independent national consumer organizations from twenty European countries. For more information, see its website at www.beuc.org.

55. For details, see Day, "Privacy-Law Deadline to Be Put Off," p. E3.

56. These four regimes are analyzed in detail in Zacher with Sutton, *Governing Global Networks.*

57. For a discussion of why, among the many institutional forms available, legal institutions are preferred for the settlement of disputes in some instances but not in others, see Kahler, "The Causes and Consequences of Legalization," pp. 661–684.

58. Kaldor, "Transnational Civil Society," p. 210.

59. See, for example, Andreopoulos and Claude, *Human Rights Education for the Twenty-First Century.*

60. Hansen, *Getting Online for Human Rights,* p. 1.

61. Zacher with Sutton, *Governing Global Networks,* pp. 30–31.

62. Some members of the House wanted to require that China meet certain standards on human rights to retain normal trading relations, but that kind of linkage violates the WTO rule that members must grant one WTO trading partner the same normal trading status granted all others without imposing particular conditions on any one member. For an analysis of the House of Representatives action, see Chandler, "For China, Vote Has Trade-Offs." See also Franda, "China and India Online," chap. 2–3.

63. Zacher with Sutton, *Governing Global Networks,* p. 31.

64. Young, *Governance in World Affairs,* p. 10. The other quotations in this paragraph are also from this source.

6

International Regimes
and Internet Security

I n the literature on international regimes, the possibilities for building
international cooperation in areas related to security are viewed as
more remote than for other aspects of regime formation. This is so
because of the so-called security dilemma that results from the reality
that policies designed to increase the security of one actor automatically, often in unintended ways, decrease the security of others.[1] The difficulties involved in reaching agreement on regime principles and norms
in areas of Internet security are complicated by the existence of so
many different kinds of security threats—to individuals, firms, and
nation-states—presented by the versatility and range of Internet technology. As Lawrence Greenberg has phrased the problem, "The very
openness that contributes to the ubiquity, utility, and power of networked systems may make those systems vulnerable to intrusions or
other attacks that seek to ruin, manipulate, or steal the data that travels
through them, or cause damage to other systems that depend on them or
that they control. As society increasingly depends on such systems, the
potential damages resulting from such intrusions soar."[2]

This chapter examines some of the major proposals put forth by
organizations and individuals seeking to build international cooperation
in areas involving Internet security in an effort to better understand why
regime formation in these matters has not proceeded much beyond the
very early agenda-setting stage. An attempt to sort out the various
aspects of Internet security is summarized in Table 6.1, which differen-
tiates between (1) threats to security from crime, terrorism or "infowar,"
and government violation of human rights and (2) the effects of

Table 6.1 Cybersecurity Threats and Their Effects

	Affects Individual	Affects Firms	Affects Nation-States
Threats to security from crime	Fraud (e.g., misrepresenting products or services being sold), identity theft, stalking/harassment on the Internet or using information illegally obtained from the Internet, Computer viruses, and the like	Fraud, theft of trade secrets and other proprietary information, piracy and counterfeiting; denial of service or other attacks on websites, spreading computer viruses, and the like	Fraud (e.g., fraudulent claims for benefits made possible with information gleaned from the Internet), computer viruses, use of encryption technologies by criminals to prevent detection and arrest
Threats to security from terrorism/ infowar	(may have same effects as crime)	(may have same effects as crime)	Infiltration of secure computers by hackers to obtain information/control, denial of service and other attacks on websites, spread of computer viruses, use of encryption technologies by terrorists to prevent detection and arrest
Threats to security from government violation of human rights	Threats to or violation of privacy rights by government organizations like Echelon or other unsanctioned government access to private communication	Economic or industrial espionage practiced by one country against the firms of another country, use of government networks to damage or destroy reputations of firms or their leadership	Traditional espionage, infiltration of secure computers by hackers to obtain information/control, denial of service and other attacks on websites, computer viruses

Internet-related security threats on individuals, firms, and nation-states. The matrix in Table 6.1 is not intended to be exhaustive of all relevant security-related variables stemming from cyberthreats and their effects but simply to provide major illustrative examples of the kinds of threats of concern to those seeking to build cooperative international Internet security organizations and arrangements to control them.[3]

▪ THREATS TO INTERNET SECURITY
FROM CRIME, TERRORISM, AND INFOWAR

Cybercrime at the commercial level now includes, among much else, forgery and counterfeiting, transmission of threats, harassing communications, child pornography, fraud, theft of trade secrets, and interception of communications. In the area of Internet credit card fraud alone, during a single week in May 2000, four major Internet credit card crimes were reported from different parts of the world in an environment where most cybercrime goes unreported because companies doing business over the Internet do not want the negative publicity about lack of website security (and possible lawsuits) public exposure entails. During that week British police arrested two eighteen-year-old boys charged with stealing more than 26,000 credit card numbers by breaking into a commercial Internet site; a hacker based in Argentina attempted to blackmail an online music store in Spain, threatening to post the credit card details of thousands of customers stolen from the firm's website unless the store paid ransom; Russia's Interior Ministry charged two hackers with making illegal purchases worth 18 million rubles ($640,000) using stolen credit cards; and Belgrade teenagers were reported to be using the city's Internet cafés to order books, clothes, and CDs from U.S. websites on a massive scale, paying their bills with credit card numbers stolen from the Web (the practice is facilitated in Serbia because the Yugoslav Republic does not have cooperative relationships with Interpol and other international law enforcement agencies).[4]

In addition to its effects on firms and companies, cybercrime can also impact national security or sometimes have overlapping impacts on the security of both firms and nation-states (see Table 6.1). This is particularly so for crimes committed by some hackers who are ideologically convinced that either or both big business and big government are illegitimate. Computer hacking as a form of cybercrime dates back to the late 1970s and early 1980s, when some people who became proficient in computer skills decided to use them to pursue illegal acts. One of the earliest high-profile computer hackers was Kevin Mitnick, born in 1964, who began his criminal career in the late 1970s by breaking into high school records to alter the grades of friends, then graduated to a prankster break-in of the North American Air Defense computer systems in Colorado and eventually to break-ins at Digital Equipment

Corporation (where he stole software) and MCI (where he stole long-distance telephone codes).[5] Another early celebrated case involved three hackers from Germany who broke into the Lawrence Berkeley computers in California in 1986 and obtained sensitive information related to munitions, weapons systems, and technical data and sold it to the KGB.[6] In the mid-1990s a group of "cyberactivists" launched a movement known as the Electronic Disturbance Theater, originally to draw attention to the war being waged against the Zapatistas and others in Mexico but later to promote "hactivism" and a "flood net device" that would jam computer networks by overwhelming them with vast numbers of requests—multiplying at geometrical rates—as a means of practicing civil disobedience and direct action on the Internet for a variety of other causes.[7]

Of even greater concern than cybercrime—particularly to intelligence and military leaders—are acts of cyberterrorism, especially what have come to be known as acts of potentially "catastrophic terrorism" (e.g., shutting down energy or water supplies for extended periods by infiltrating computer systems) and possibilities for espionage and cyberwarfare. In 1995 the U.S. Government Accounting Office (GAO) reported more than 250,000 "suspected attacks" on U.S. Defense Department computers, with approximately two-thirds resulting in computer network entry, although the Pentagon claims there were "only" 500 attempts that year.[8] In 1996 computers at NASA's Goddard Space Flight Center detected a computer program called a "sniffer" that had apparently been there for some time and had permitted the perpetrator to download large amounts of complex telemetry information transmitted from satellites.[9] U.S. military leaders conducted a classified "infowar game" exercise in summer 1997, under the code name "Eligible Receiver," in which U.S. military personnel purposely tried to penetrate presumably secure networks using the public Internet. The conclusion drawn from the exercise was that almost all of the military's 2.1 million computers, 10,000 local area networks, and 100 long-distance computer networks could be penetrated fairly easily, leading the Joint Security Commission to call U.S. vulnerability to information warfare (IW) "the major security challenge of this decade and possibly the next century."[10] In interviews with the *Washington Post* in 1998, some U.S. intelligence officials openly discussed vulnerabilities to disruption of computer operations at major U.S. military commands around the world.[11] An internal FBI report in May 1999 detailed

Chinese efforts to attack U.S. government information systems, including the White House network, via the internet.[12]

Many of the most serious known threats to Internet security have been undertaken by thrill-seeking computer experts, often teenagers, experimenting with their networking skills. The first virus to affect computers on a global basis (called "brain"), for example, appeared in 1986 and was believed to have been created by two brothers in Pakistan who viewed the activity simply as a challenge.[13] The least consequential of such crimes has been the defacing of web pages of government and corporate websites around the world; more serious intrusions from a societal perspective have resulted from attacks on entire electronic infrastructures, delivery of malicious coding, and theft or destruction of large amounts of data by organized underground hacker or "cracker" computing groups.

In December 2000 U.S. assistant secretary of defense for command, control, communications, and intelligence, Arthur L. Money, said publicly that the "seminal event" that awakened the Pentagon to the magnitude of its security problems was a February 1998 concerted hacker offensive by two California youths, working under the direction of an Israeli with the code name "analyzer," who claimed to have penetrated 400 U.S. government computers.[14] Although government officials maintained at the time that no sensitive information had been compromised or lost, Deputy Defense Secretary John J. Hamre told Congress in 1999 that a known vulnerability in a commercial software used by the Pentagon had made possible "widespread systematic" penetration into the Pentagon's Solaris operating system by the "analyzer" attackers in February 1998 in a concerted pattern that could conceivably have been "a coordinated attack on the defense information infrastructure."[15] Pentagon officials have become increasingly concerned that commercial computer code—which is often written in Israel, India, Ireland, and other countries—will appear to have "trapdoors" deliberately left by software writers to allow intrusions into secure computers or "backdoors" initially designed to help system administrators that are subsequently discovered by hackers and used to harass secure systems.[16]

Numerous threats and speculation about cyberwar being launched against the United States have included a warning by Russian ultranationalist Vladimir Zhirinovsky in May 2000 that "we will bring the entire West to its knees with our Russian computer specialists" and a strategy for "unrestricted war" proposed by two Chinese colonels in a book published in 1999.[17] The book by Colonels Qiao Liang and Wang Xiangsui, both sons of Chinese military officers, describes unrestricted war as a war that "surpasses all boundaries and restrictions" and therefore will include use of cyberterrorism, computer virus propagation, and disruptive penetration of strategic computer websites as part of modern military strategy. When interviewed about the book, Colonel Qiao told John Pomfret of the *Washington Post,* "I am not a terrorist and have always opposed terrorism, but war is not a foot race; it's more like a soccer game. If it was a foot race, China would never be able to catch up to the United States. But it's a soccer game and the goal is to win. It doesn't matter how you kick the ball into the net."[18]

▪ ATTEMPTS AT GLOBAL COMMERCIAL SECURITY PROTECTION FOR INTERNET TRANSACTIONS

International attempts to develop secure systems for e-commerce and e-business have been led by the U.S. government, the EU, several other governments and international organizations around the world, and private industry leaders, but thus far no consensus has been reached at the global level about how this aspect of the Internet's operations might be molded into an international regime. In its 1997 framework report, the U.S. Department of Commerce suggested negotiation of a "global uniform commercial code" similar to one that presently exists among U.S. states, which would facilitate formation and enforcement of international e-commerce contracts and develop legal protocols for protecting privacy and personal security for Internet users throughout the world. The U.S. goal on Internet security issues, as spelled out in the report, is to "encourage private sector groups to develop and adopt . . . effective codes of conduct, industry developed rules, and technological solutions."[19]

Although the security-relevant sections of the framework report have not resulted in significant international action, they have received enthusiastic backing from leaders of private industry who would like to see governments everywhere delegate responsibility for e-commerce and e-business security systems to self-regulating business networks, software and hardware manufacturers, and Internet users. For example, the Online Privacy Alliance (OPA), a coalition of more than 100 international companies and associations dedicated to promoting consumer confidence online, has established a set of guidelines to assist businesses with privacy and security policies along lines envisaged in the framework report, including recommendations for privacy policy website postings and "seal programs" like BBBOnLine or TRUSTe.[20] Similarly, the Computer Systems Policy Project (CSPP) is an organization of CEOs from major U.S.-based multinationals (Cisco, Compaq, Dell Computer, Hewlett-Packard, Intel, and others) that has tried to promote particular Internet security measures in accordance with the approach of the framework report.[21]

One of the reasons the U.S. Commerce Department has not been able to assiduously pursue the framework Internet security recommendations is the lack of agreement about them within the United States. The Commerce Department, for example, has run into conflicts with other parts of the government, most notably the U.S. Justice Department and the Federal Bureau of Investigation (FBI), both of which have been reluctant to leave security measures primarily in the domain of the private sector. Rather than divest themselves of responsibility for Internet-related security matters, in recent years both government agencies have substantially expanded their capabilities and procedures to prosecute computer crime. The Justice Department's Computer Crimes and Intellectual Property Section, headed by Assistant U.S. Attorney Christopher Painter, has grown from only five lawyers when it was established in 1996 to more than twenty lawyers in Washington, D.C., alone, plus several hundred computer and telecommunications crime coordinators spread out over ninety-three U.S. attorney's offices located in many different parts of the United States. Justice and the FBI have offered to cooperate with the private sector in efforts to both investigate and prevent Internet crime, but companies are concerned that such cooperation (which in the United States would be transparent under the Freedom of Information Act) might lead to charges that business is colluding with U.S. police and intelligence agencies. Business is also wary that cooperation with law enforcement might enhance the possibility of unwanted publicity when company computers are being subject to serious intrusions.[22]

From the perspective of business organizations, network security needs have two related dimensions: (1) protecting the flow of information internal to specific businesses and corporations and (2) securing flows of information between producers and consumers.[23] Perhaps the most extensive intracorporation security network in the world is General Electric, which has arranged for all of its worldwide business units to purchase its internal nonproduction and maintenance, repair, and operations security materials via the Internet for a total of $5 billion![24] Although few companies are able to invest as much in network security as General Electric, all companies entering the world of networked commerce (e.g., electronic access banking, use of smart cards, stored value devices, digital credit systems, and the like) are budgeting increasingly large amounts for security protocols and equipment. These include both software and hardware (modem pools, compact discs, leased lines, secure servers, and access control mechanisms, to name only a small number of devices needed) as well as the expense of computer security and network consultants.

The different approaches of the FBI and the Department of Justice on the one hand and the Department of Commerce and private industry on the other was clearly evident in February 2000, when a series of "denial of service" attacks—perpetrated by computer hackers—bombarded the Internet servers of several companies (including Yahoo! and E*Trade Group, Inc.) with false requests for information, causing several major websites to be unavailable to other users for many hours. Former federal prosecutor Scott Charney argued at the time that the Justice Department was being forced to deal with this twenty-first-century computer crime using twentieth-century telephone trace laws that pre-dated the computer. Charney insisted that to cope with future denial of service attacks, "we need to amend these laws." In sharp contrast, the principal engineer at Qualcomm Corporation in San Diego, Philip Karn, suggested that the threat of denial of service attacks could best be dealt with by rushing the development of software that could locate, trace, and block future such attacks. "When the only tool you have is a hammer," Karn said of the Justice Department's efforts, "the whole world starts to look like a nail."[25]

■ EUROPE, THE G-8, AND
INTERNET SECURITY COOPERATION

The position of the FBI and Justice Department was echoed by European leaders in response to the "I love you" virus when the French interior minister, Jean Pierre Chevenement, announced in May 2000 that the French government was setting up a new office specifically designed to fight crime linked to information and communication technologies. The Council of Europe went even further in April 2000 when it put together a draft treaty proposing "uniform international law enforcement standards in cyberspace," including the requirement that all signatories to the treaty be required to retain "all messages and content sent via the Internet for a period of three months."[26] The proposal to require all countries to retain all e-mail messages and other Internet content for three months was criticized by Austin D. Hill, president of Zero-Knowledge Systems, Inc., as "Orwellian" in its reach and by David Aucsmith of Intel as impossible to implement for lack of enough storage space to hold everything that goes on the Internet for such a substantial period of time.

A significant attempt to place Internet security concerns on the international regime agenda for discussion among nations occurred in May 2000, when 300 representatives from the Group of 8 (G-8) met in Paris for a three-day conference, A Dialogue Between the Public and Private Sectors on Security and Confidence in Cyberspace.[27] The conference included senior government officials, law enforcement agents, information technology leaders from both hardware and software manufacturers, and heads of consumer, Internet user, and electronic commerce/e-business associations from all G-8 nations. A fillip was given to the conference discussion when the "I love you" virus (one of the most vicious in the short history of world electronic networking up to that point), initiated in the Philippines, struck millions of computers across the world a few days before the conference opened. But the conference ended with no announcements and no decisions other than a resolve to continue such meetings in other G-8 forums.[28] Most of those who attended the conference concluded that the meeting was useful because it started a dialogue among the major relevant international organizations concerned with the international aspects of cybercrime. A detailed analysis of the meeting, however, indicated that at least five different perspectives were presented, making it impossible to develop anything resembling a consensus. These perspectives have been described by Peter Ford:

1. Law enforcement officers from around the world want the Web to be as transparent as possible because "police want to be able to find out who did what and when on the Internet."[29]
2. At the other end of the spectrum were human rights advocates and civil liberties lawyers advocating total anonymity on the Web, usually through the development of "uncrackable cryptography."
3. ISPs at the meeting took the position that the sheer volume of

Internet traffic would make it "physically impossible for them to retain traffic logs and other data that governments want them to keep."

4. Leaders of legal and intelligence organizations in the various countries were concerned that attempts to develop a single strategy or set of strategies for combating cybercrime at the international level would invariably lead to conflicts with the laws of particular nations.

5. Industry executives were concerned that government attempts to provide security on the Internet would stifle e-commerce and e-business and considerably slow the growth of the Internet, particularly in some of the less wealthy nations dependent on international IT investment.

▪ THREATS OF GOVERNMENT OVERREACH IN INTERNET SECURITY MATTERS

The absence of an international consensus on issues involving cybercrime and the commercial aspects of the Internet spills over into other security-related aspects of Internet development, with differences among various groups and perspectives becoming even more striking and intense when the possibilities of catastrophic terrorism and cyberwarfare are interjected into the discussion. As indicated in Table 6.1, a major category of concern about Internet security—for individuals, firms, and governments—results from perceived threats stemming from possible government overreach or overreaction when combating cybercrime, terrorism, or infowar. Human rights activists commonly view overreaction by governments in Internet security matters as one of the major threats (if not *the* major threat) to the protection of human rights in the twenty-first century.[30]

Concern among U.S. leaders about government overreach in combating catastrophic terrorism was reflected at a White House conference in April 2000 when Secretary of Commerce William Daley suggested that the Internet era marked "the first time in American history the federal government alone cannot protect our infrastructure."[31] "We cannot hire a police force big enough to protect all of industry's key information assets," Daley said. "Nor would you want us to." Daley was trying to use his dramatic statement to demonstrate the appropriateness of advanced encryption devices and industry self-regulation as key variables for coming to terms with cybercrime and cyberterrorism, but many human rights organizations point out that such statements often have the effect of pushing government officials to look for more extreme law enforcement measures to deal with what they see as unprecedented problems that could easily get out of control.[32]

Because so many international cyberthreats have been directed against the United States and U.S.-based companies, both private industry and the U.S. government have vastly expanded their efforts to build Internet security systems, to a much greater degree than in any other part of the world. Perhaps most U.S. companies now have some form of firewall that isolates their internal private network from external public networks, allowing their own intranet network administrators to circumscribe user access for each IP service. In the early years of the Internet such firewall systems were universally large and expensive, but some more recently invented systems—such as Internet Devices' Fort Knox Policy Router, Radguard's cIPro-FW, Sonic Systems' Interpol, and Technologic's Interceptor—can now be purchased off the shelf for as little as a few thousand dollars.[33] To physically protect the computer routers, servers, and other hardware necessary for network functioning, the world's largest business organizations are increasingly building extremely secure, high-tech physical facilities designed to thwart car bombs and survive earthquakes or other disasters. A California company, Equinix, Inc., is building thirty such facilities, called Internet Business Exchange centers at sites throughout the world. These facilities look like nondescript warehouses from the outside but are "sheathed" by construction materials using an ultramodern substance called Kevlar to ward off potential artillery attack, fitted throughout with bulletproof glass and biometric hand-geometry scanners to identify unapproved intruders, and provided with temperature-regulated cages for individual equipment and generators to ensure uninterrupted electric supply in the event of a power grid meltdown or earthquake disaster.[34]

Within the U.S. government, civilian responsibility for coordinating the counterterrorism activities of the various government departments was transferred from the State Department to the National Security Council (NSC) on May 22, 1998, under Presidential Decision Directive (PDD) No. 62. This directive established the office of National Coordinator for Security, Infrastructure Protection, and Counter-Terrorism within the NSC, with Richard Clarke named the first national coordinator. That same day President Clinton promulgated PDD No. 63, which defines critical infrastructures as "those physical and cyber-based systems that are so vital that their incapacity or destruction would have a traumatic or debilitating impact on the United States."[35] The new national coordinator was given responsibility "to assign roles to 18 federal departments and agencies, including the FBI, CIA [Central Intelligence Agency], and the Pentagon, and to coordinate the law enforcement efforts of state and local governments."[36] In addition, the national coordinator's office was given authority to supervise budgetary requests for those eighteen government agencies with regard to counterterrorism and to allocate tasks among them.

The growth of U.S. capabilities to counter cybercrime, cyberterrorism, and infowar has been watched warily not only by human rights activists but also by intelligence, police, and military organizations in other countries, particularly since legislative and administrative acts in the late 1990s allow the U.S. intelligence community to collect information abroad about non-U.S. persons in support of U.S. law enforcement or counterintelligence investigations merely at the request of a U.S. law enforcement agency.[37] Evidence of vastly enhanced U.S. funding for countering cyberterrorism includes the allocation within PDD No. 62 of more than $500 million in additional funds for counterterrorism, which came on top of vastly stepped-up appropriations over the past few years for the FBI-led National Infrastructure Protection Center (created in 1997) and the Critical Infrastructure Assurance Office in the Department of Commerce (also 1997). In January 2000 U.S. attorney general Janet Reno announced an allocation of $2 billion to fight cybercrime and the establishment of a new Internet "crime squad" within the Attorney General's office.[38]

And yet, despite the rapid growth in U.S. counterterrorism capabilities in recent years, many security experts argue that the United States still has insufficient capability to assure maximum effectiveness in preventing catastrophic terrorism or to deal with cyberwarfare. Some U.S. leaders in the security field have therefore suggested the creation of yet another overarching federal agency—a National Terrorism Intelligence Center (NTIC)—which would have as its specific purpose the collection and analysis of information that would give the U.S. government the best possible advance warning of suspected catastrophic terrorist acts.[39] The authors outlined the structure of the proposed center as follows:

The center would be run by an operating committee chaired by the director of central intelligence and including the director of the FBI, the deputy secretary of defense, the deputy attorney general, the deputy secretary of state, and the deputy national security adviser. The National Foreign Intelligence Program . . . would cover the center's budget while the National Security Council would take up unresolved disputes. The director of the center would come alternately from the FBI and the CIA, and all intelligence organizations would provide a specified number of professionals exempt from agency personnel ceilings. . . . This combination is consistent with public trust and respect for civil liberties: the center would have no powers of arrest and prosecution and would maintain a certain distance from the traditional defense and intelligence agencies. The center would also be subject to oversight from existing institutions, like the federal judiciary, the President's Foreign Intelligence Advisory Board, and the select intelligence committees of Congress.[40]

A key segment of the 1998 NTIC proposal was the recommendation that a National Information Assurance Institute (NIAI) be set up within the private, nonprofit sector to work with the new NTIC, functioning "as an industry laboratory for cyber protection through a public-private partnership."[41] The proposal's authors conceived of NIAI as a consortium of private companies, universities, and existing nonprofit laboratories, governed by a board of directors drawn from the private sector and academia. The authors of the NTIC proposal explained the need for a NIAI-like organization as follows:

Private-sector cooperation is vital but has proven elusive in the fight against cyberterrorism. The President's Commission on Critical Infrastructure Protection stressed that the private sector is reluctant to work with the government on this issue because of the high cost, unclear risk, and the prospect of heavy-handed government action. On the other hand, although the FBI has created a National Infrastructure Protection Center that can help identify weaknesses, it is too overburdened with other operational duties to work successfully with industry or harness the significant resources and expertise in the Pentagon on the cyberproblem.[42]

Concerns that the United States is currently unprepared to deal with cyberterrorism and IW are widely shared by military leaders, who are particularly critical of what they see as a disunited "information operations command structure." An article on the subject by the deputy staff judge advocate in the U.S. Air Force Office of Special Investigations, Lieutenant Colonel Richard W. Aldrich, described the reasoning behind the military's disquiet:

> [Despite PDD 62 and 63] the result is still an uncertain command structure, with the FBI seemingly thrust into the position of being our nation's first line of defense to IW attacks. Still largely undefined is how and when the baton gets passed between local law enforcement agencies, the FBI, the military and the federal judiciary. Without very clearly defined roles and early involvement of the military, the United States could be hit hard and wide before the defenders even have a chance to protect critical assets or otherwise respond. Perhaps most catastrophic would be a highly structured attack disguised as a series of seemingly unrelated unstructured attacks. This would serve to weaken and distract a disjointed command structure. If followed up with a wide-reaching structured attack that hits certain critical points in the infrastructure, the United States could be seriously paralyzed.[43]

▪ INTERNET SECURITY AND GOVERNMENT-TO-GOVERNMENT RELATIONS

In addition to concerns about Internet-related security threats to individual human rights, the enhancement of government capabilities to penetrate Internet websites and networking operations is perceived as an increasing threat to state security at global government-to-government levels. European concern with U.S. technology-driven expansion of counterterrorism and cyberwar capabilities began to peak in January 1998 with the release of a report commissioned by the European Parliament entitled "An Appraisal of Technologies of Political Control," which asserted that "within Europe, all e-mail, telephone, and fax communications are routinely intercepted by the United States National Security Agency (NSA), transferring all target information from the European mainland . . . to Fort Meade in Maryland."[44] The core of this eavesdropping operation, according to the report, was a system code-named "Echelon," which the report suggested has been operating out of NSA since the 1970s under the direction of the U.S./U.K. intelligence alliance, also known as UKUSA, which includes Australia, Canada, and New Zealand (the establishment of Echelon in 1948 is usually traced to close Allied intelligence cooperation growing out of World War II). A subsequent 112-page report to the EU in spring 1999 concluded that the rapid proliferation of surveillance technologies presents "a serious threat to the civil liberties in Europe" with "awesome implications."[45] These reports have stimulated a spate of newspaper and journal articles about Echelon, as well as government and legislative investigations on both sides of the Atlantic.

A Canadian study that tried to piece together reliable public knowledge of the Echelon project described it as a series of electronic intercept stations and deep-space satellites designed to capture "all satellite, microwave, cellular and fibre-optic communications traffic" throughout the world.[46] Each of the states in the UKUSA alliance has primary responsibility for different regions of the world (e.g., Canada for drugs and criminal activities in Central and South America; Britain for Europe, Africa, and Russia west of the Urals; Australia for Indochina, Indonesia, and southern China; New Zealand for the western Pacific; and the United States for most of Latin America, Asia, the Middle East, Asiatic Russia, and northern China). Security experts stress that Echelon is only one of many new tools of intelligence communities around the world, with other major nations attempting to develop similar capabilities. Most of the funding for the Echelon project has apparently come from NSA, which has a global staff of 38,000 and a budget estimated at more than $3.6 billion (more than the totals for the FBI and CIA combined).

Civil liberties and privacy advocates from around the world have targeted Echelon as the focus for investigations of Internet-related human rights abuses and in some cases possible violations of international law. A French lawyer, Jean-Pierre Millet, for example, has launched a class-action lawsuit against the governments of the United States and Great Britain, accusing British and U.S. political leaders of using knowledge gained from the Echelon project to obtain and pass along information that enabled U.S. and British companies to secure a $6 billion contract that otherwise would have gone to France's airbus industry.[47] Parliamentarians in Italy, Germany, and Denmark have demanded public investigations of charges that Echelon violated privacy laws and rights in those nations. Websites devoted to monitoring Echelon's activities have sprung up in several countries, including the United States, where the associate director of the American Civil Liberties Union, Barry Steinhardt, described Echelon as "a black box, and we really don't know what is inside it. . . . We don't know who is being targeted, what they are being targeted for or what is being done with the information."[48]

Government-to-government concerns about Internet security in

Asia and Eurasia, the Middle East, and Central/Eastern Europe, particularly in the context of cyberterrorism and cyberwar, are detailed in the companion volume to this one. Despite the overwhelming evidence in that volume and elsewhere that the governments of nation-states are increasingly preoccupied with various attempts to control international computer networking in the name of state and national security, many members of the computer engineering and business-technical communities suggest that the nature of Internet technology and the increasing globalization of the world will eventually combine to produce a "network security collective image" that will internationalize the security interests of states and even paralyze state autonomy and power. In Ronald Deibert's words:

> As more states mold their policies according to liberal-capitalist principles and in the direction of so-called "knowledge economies" (partially as a product of the structural pressures of transnational capital) the constituencies resisting or contradicting the network security collective image wither in importance and influence. . . . Certainly states have not disappeared, nor should we expect them to. However, they are in the process of being turned "inside-out"—locked-in and interpenetrated by an electronic web of their own spinning.[49]

Deibert argues that as dominant security concerns shift to focus on the advantages to be gained from global computer networking, the exercise of world power will increasingly be manifested in a new "space-of-flows" rather than the old Westphalian "control-of-territory," with "regulation, direction, and restriction of the tempo and access to circuits of information" becoming the key components in amassing significant political power. Deibert describes the result of this interaction as a "new medieval world order" in which "transnational private security regimes could . . . very well represent a new political species arising on the world political landscape," suggesting "a dispersal of authority to a much wider domain of non-state and private actors, oriented around new frames of space-time references beyond territoriality."[50]

■ PROPOSALS FOR A UNIFORM INTERNATIONAL LEGAL FRAMEWORK OR TREATY

Perspectives like Deibert's, which envisage the facilitation of some form of "international civil society" through computer networking, are

often echoed by nongovernmental organizations, leaders of less powerful foreign governments, and legal scholars who fear the burgeoning
networking capabilities commanded by more powerful governments—
especially by U.S. intelligence, criminal justice, and military organizations—are veering out of control. This fear has been heightened in the
last few decades by the expanding reach of U.S. extraterritorial jurisdiction in several other areas. As Bruce Zagaris has pointed out, "For a
wide variety of crimes the United States now stations its own law
enforcement agents abroad, conducts wiretaps and undercover stings,
and arrests foreigners for conduct (such as export control or Internet
gambling) that is criminalized only in the United States."[51] In this
atmosphere, the increasingly dominant U.S. role in Internet-related
jurisdictional, privacy, and security matters has often been viewed with
alarm, even by long-standing U.S. allies.[52] Particularly when coupled
with other facets of the globalization process taking place over the last
few decades, the unique nature of the Internet and the U.S. relationship
to it have led a number of leaders in the world's legal and judicial communities to search for ways to move beyond sovereignty and create
increasingly more significant and meaningful international Internet-
related global legal institutions.

One of the clearest statements of the position described here was
outlined by the chief justice of the Supreme Court of Canada, Beverley
McLachlin, in a speech delivered to the Faculty of Law at Hong Kong
University in June 1999:

> The increasing globalization of crime . . . presents the world with two
> options. The first is to respond to the new problems, if we respond at
> all, in an *ad hoc,* uncoordinated way. Relying on a crisis-driven sys-
> tem of responses will lead to increasing lawlessness, victimization and
> terror throughout the world. The second option is to extend the power
> of the law to deal with the emerging problems of international crime.
> It is here argued that the world must urgently pursue this second
> option if we are to avoid becoming a global society endlessly destabi-
> lized by international outlaws. This in turn means moving the criminal
> law beyond the boundaries of sovereign states and onto the world
> stage. The rule of law must become international.[53]

Justice McLachlin's specific proposal for moving Internet-related
criminal law "beyond the boundaries of sovereign states" is based on a
1992 article by Steve Shackelford, suggesting that an "international
statute" be adopted by an international convention creating three uni-

versal types of computer offenses: (1) intentional and (knowing) unauthorized access to computer networks, (2) unauthorized access with further criminal intent, and (3) intentional unauthorized modification.
Shackelford suggested that offenses involving fraud or theft might
remain under the sovereignty of nation-states, but those could be dealt
with by an international regime, in some circumstances, under the second type of offense covered by the statute. In Shackelford's proposal,
enforcement would be carried out at the national level but *without* the
requirement that the alleged offense be committed within the jurisdiction, as is generally the case for the nation-based law of most countries
today. Instead, all that would be required for a state to prosecute a case
of cybercrime would be a "sufficient link" to the prosecuting jurisdiction (for example, a person who downloads a criminal message outside
a given nation-state might be prosecuted within that nation-state if the
message was conveyed to a computer located in that nation-state).
There would be no need to show that the intended criminal offense or
fraud actually took place within the state.[54]

Alternative proposals for transnational legal frameworks to address
multinational computer-related crime appeared in the *American
Criminal Law Review* in mid-1999 and the journal *Studies in Conflict
and Terrorism* in mid-2000.[55] The first of these proposals called for an
international convention or treaty that would standardize domestic
statutes from around the world and facilitate cooperative enforcement
efforts. The second advocated negotiation of international "clusters of
rules or conventions" to form an "international regime for information
assurance." Included in these proposals are ideas for (1) more consistent
international law with regard to extradition of criminals, (2) enhanced
international cooperation in the retention of witnesses and evidence, (3)
recognition and enforcement of criminal judgments issued by the courts
of particular nations, and (4) cooperation among national law enforcement and prosecutorial organizations.[56]

A third proposal for an international legal regime relating to security aspects of cyberspace revolves around the creation of a new international criminal court. One of the most detailed of such proposals was
put forth by Howard L. Steele in 1997. Steele summarized the arguments for such an arrangement as follows:

> There are numerous advantages with having an international criminal
> court which would hear matters regarding cyber-crime. First and fore-
> most, the international criminal court would provide a neutral alterna-

tive forum when a nation is reluctant to extradite a criminal. Second, where the cyber-criminal has committed an activity which lends itself to concurrent jurisdiction between two or more separate nations, a single international court's consolidation of the action in one forum would be much more efficient than the tangled morass of determining who gets the criminal first. Third, the international criminal court could also facilitate the concept of mutual assistance in the discovery of evidence located in other nations in cases where the countries involved do not have extradition treaties. Lastly, a structural vehicle would be provided for enforcement of international criminal claims without having to rely on unilaterally imposed enforcement mechanisms such as imposition of sanctions or even military attack.[57]

A fourth proposal for an international legal framework to promote Internet security grew out of a two-year study by the American Bar Association that was reported to the association membership in June 2000. Based on ideas originally developed by the EU, the study recommended the establishment of a Global Online Standards Commission that would attempt to find ways to regulate on a global basis Internet transactions and communications related to consumer protection, privacy, intellectual property, banking, securities, taxes, and gaming.[58] Although the study has not yet been accepted by the ABA and does not yet represent association policy, the ABA has asked industry leaders to offer formal comments on the report and does plan to pursue the idea further.

Proposals for building an international legal framework, treaty or criminal court arrangement, or both for effecting cooperation in areas related to Internet security have generally not been enthusiastically received by governments, the courts, the legal profession, the business community, or law enforcement agencies in most parts of the world. Much of this reluctance can be traced to the security dilemma, mentioned at the beginning of this chapter and observable throughout history, which has the effect of pressuring both large international firms and nation-states to focus on and guard their own security systems, thereby inadvertently making others feel less secure and resulting in a vicious circle or spiral of security-insecurity to which there is no permanent and lasting solution.[59] Because of a basic distrust of the security preparedness of organizations and nation-states other than one's own, particularly across sovereign boundaries, leaders will often pay lip service to the need for international security cooperation and try to gain what they can from international cooperation while continuing to prepare their own security plans based on positions of self-reliance domestically and among their allies. The secretary-general of Interpol, Raymond Kendall, articulated this approach forcefully in May 2000, when he told an Internet Defense Summit meeting of security officials from more than a hundred countries that to be effective, cooperative efforts to fight computer crime had to focus on specific crimes and bring together government, business, and legal organizations with specific short-run interests in solving the crime. With regard to proposals for longer-range international cooperation, Kendall simply commented, "It takes a long time to get legislation adopted nationally. It takes an even longer time to get international conventions adopted which can help deal with these problems and be used as a legal basis."[60]

■ CONCLUSIONS

In a classic article relating concepts of international security to the literature on international regimes, Robert Jervis has argued that the best example of a security regime is the Concert of Europe that prevailed full-blown from 1815 to 1823 and lasted in "attenuated form" until the Crimean War in the 1850s. Jervis suggests four reasons why historically there have been few cases where security regimes have come into existence, why security regimes have not lasted very long, and why security-related issues in the context of international regimes differ substantially from such issues in nonsecurity areas.[61]

1. Security issues often involve greater competitiveness than do those related to economics and other nonsecurity aspects of human behavior.
2. Protection of one's interests in nonsecurity areas is usually costly, but it does not necessarily harm or menace others, as is often the case where security is involved.
3. The stakes are higher in security areas, since security is usually the most highly valued goal, is a prerequisite for so many things, and is unforgiving (e.g., the costs of living up to the rules of a security regime are extremely high if other actors are not living up to the rules; even temporarily falling behind others can produce permanent harm).
4. Detecting what others are doing and measuring one's own security are much more difficult than gaining such intelligence in

other (e.g., economic or environmental) fields; this creates much higher degrees of uncertainty and distrust in security-related areas.

All four of the factors Jervis has identified have been prominent in discussions of Internet security in many different contexts in all parts of the world. Nations as well as business firms have quickly realized both the significance and the vulnerability of the Internet in the security area and have therefore attempted to create each for itself the most secure and inaccessible networks for data storage/retrieval and other transactions they can afford, often with some form of Internet firewall attempted to separate themselves and Internet communication with other countries or firms. Although firewalls have not always been effective, the numerous attempts to build them have produced or exacerbated distrust among various organizations and states where use of the Internet is concerned, resulting in a number of highly competitive struggles to better secure one's own Internet files and, in some cases, to penetrate the files of others.

One case among many that could be cited is that of India, where the government has generally been reluctant to introduce Internet-related technology on a widespread basis but has made substantial commitments to domestic high-technology manufacturing that has to do with national interests, security, and defense (India's 2000 military budget was the highest in history). In such matters as parallel computing, nuclear, and satellite technology, for example, there has been a commitment within India to develop local industries capable of producing world-class products. With regard to the Internet, the Indian defense establishment has set up its own secure intranet for communicating internally about military matters and has begun to explore the dynamics that might be involved in future infowars. Of particular concern to Indian strategic thinkers are reports that China is among a handful of states that have undertaken "extraordinary" steps to develop an Internet warfare capability.[62]

Indian military and security personnel became particularly concerned with the role of the Internet in state security in June 1999 when a group of international hackers calling themselves "MilwOrm" broke into the website of the Bhabha Atomic Research Center in Gujarat through a series of Telnet connections that enabled them to travel to India in cyberspace through servers in the United States belonging to the NASA Jet Propulsion Laboratory, the U.S. Navy, and the U.S.

Army.[63] In October 1998 Indian Defense Ministry officials reported that suspected Pakistani intelligence operatives had hijacked the Indian Army's only Internet site designed to present the Indian point of view on Kashmir as part of a cyberwar launched in advance of Indo-Pakistani border talks. Indian defense officials blamed the break-in on problems resulting from the absence of a satisfactory Internet policy at the ministry level and called for greater coordination between civilian and defense agencies on Internet matters. When a group of rebels in northeastern India—belonging to the banned United Liberation Front of Assam—opened an effective website in September 1999 attacking Indian military activities, the Indian Army opened its own website in Assam to counter what it called "a cyberwar launched by militants." A year earlier, a report of the Indian Navy had suggested that coordination between Indian military and intelligence agencies was "regrettably ineffective" and called for a series of measures to improve IT capabilities and link them to other intelligence activities.[64] Key recommendations of the report included (1) developing a national strategy to enhance "survivability" of information networks against what was termed "hard and soft kill measures," and (2) "building . . . a legal system that standardizes, safeguards and promotes the application of IT."[65]

As in the case of India and other nations, with few exceptions China (like the United States and major international corporations) has been unwilling to share significant information about Internet security measures with other nations and organizations or to engage in negotiations that would impose restraints on behavior in the belief that others would reciprocate with restraint.[66] This is consistent with the consensual political science understanding of the role of security matters in international regime analysis in other issue areas. As Jervis concluded in another context, security regimes (or one might argue in this case the security dimensions of an international regime for the Internet) are "difficult to achieve, because the fear [each actor has] that the other is violating or will violate the common understanding is a potent incentive for each state to strike out on its own even if it would prefer the regime to prosper."[67]

▪ NOTES

1. One of the earliest essays on the security dilemma is Herz, "Idealist Internationalism and the Security Dilemma," pp. 157–180; see also Jervis, "Security Regimes," pp. 173–194.

2. Greenberg, "Danger.com," p. 301.

3. I am grateful to one of the reviewers of the book manuscript for Lynne Rienner Publishers for suggesting this table.

4. See Bransten, "G-8 Countries Tackle Cybercrime."

5. After he was convicted of these crimes and given probationary punishment as a minor and a one-year prison sentence as an adult in the early 1990s, Mitnick was released but was later (1995) rearrested and convicted of charges that, among other things, he had used computer networks to disconnect his probation officer's phone, alter his judge's credit record, and erase records of his previous arrests and convictions. See Moschovitis et al., *History of the Internet*, p. 140.

6. The case was investigated by Cliff Stoll, an administrator at Berkeley, when federal law enforcement authorities were reluctant to become involved. Stoll has written a book on the case entitled *The Cuckoo's Egg: Inside the World of Computer Espionage*. For legal analyses of this and many other cases of international cybercrime, see Goldston and Shave, "International Dimensions of Crimes in Cyberspace," pp. 1924–71.

7. A conference on Hacktivism: A Mapping of Extraparliamentarian Direct Action Net Politics was organized by cyberactivist Stefan Wray at Drake University in November 1999. See http://lafreepress.callme.net/ecd.html and www.nyu.edu/projects/wray/wwwhack.html.

8. The varying interpretations are analyzed in Maier, "Is U.S. Ready for Cyberwarfare?" p. 18. Maier also quotes a Justice Department official who said five of seven identified intruders to the Pentagon's mainframes in 1999 were foreigners.

9. Sources for this and other information in this paragraph are detailed in Terry, "Responding to Attacks on Critical Computer Infrastructure," pp. 170–190. Colonel Terry is a former legal counsel to the chairman of the U.S. Joint Chiefs of Staff.

10. See Jackson, "DOD Set to Fight Hackers," p. 8; see also Drogin, "U.S. Scurries to Erect Cyber-Defenses."

11. Reported in Graham, "U.S. Studies New Threat," p. A1.

12. In addition to discussion in Colonel Terry's article, Chinese efforts to penetrate the White House, State Department, and other government computer systems are discussed in Gertz, "Chinese Hackers Raid U.S. Computers," pp. C1 ff.

13. Grier, "Global Computer Virus."

14. Pincus, "Hacker Hits on Pentagon Computers," pp. A8–9. For the original Pentagon accounts of the threat, see Madsen, "Teens a Threat, Pentagon Says."

15. Quoted in Pincus, "Hacker Hits on Pentagon Computers," p. A9.

16. Ibid., pp. A8–9. The Pentagon was able to accurately count for the first time attacks on its more than 10,000 computer systems and 1.5 million computers after it installed elaborate monitoring devices in December 1998. In 1999, 22,144 attempts to probe, scan, hack into, infect with viruses, or disable

computers were detected, with about 3 percent (more than 600) of these incidents causing temporary shutdowns or other damage.

17. Zhirinovsky's statement appears in Anidjar, "Cyber Threat Is Constant Worry for United States." The book by Wang and Qiao has a title that translates *Unrestricted Warfare* and is analyzed in detail in Pomfret, "China Ponders New Rules of 'Unrestricted War,'" p. A25.

18. Quoted in Pomfret, p. A25.

19. *A Framework for Global Electronic Commerce,* p. 15.

20. For more information, see the OPA website at www.privacyalliance. org. The OPA is particularly opposed to new legislation aimed at providing Internet security, arguing that new laws will only get in the way of industry efforts and technology, which already provide consumers with significant protections.

21. The essence of the CSPP approach to Internet security is contained in the first two sentences of its *Proposed Security Principles,* available at www.cspp.org: "Users have the right, responsibility, and need to determine the type and strength of protection required. The absence of a centralized security system [for the Internet] requires individuals and companies to bear the primary responsibility for their own security."

22. See Hamilton, "Redesigning the Internet," p. B1.

23. A discussion of business security networks, on which this paragraph is based, is Deibert, "Circuits of Power."

24. *The Emerging Digital Economy,* available online at http://www. ecommerce.gov/emerging.htm, cited in ibid.

25. The exchange between Charney and Karn is traced in Rovella, "Justice Department Prepares for a Cyberwar," p. 5. The Justice Department came in for considerable criticism in March 1999, when a presidential commission called the Working Group on Unlawful Conduct on the Internet suggested that U.S. law enforcement needed substantially enhanced funding to deal with Internet-related criminal behavior and referred to anonymity on the Internet as a "thorny issue." The *New York Times* immediately quoted an American Civil Liberties Union (ACLU) press release to the effect that "the report treats the anonymity of Internet users as a 'thorny issue,' rather than a constitutional right. An end to Internet anonymity would chill free expression in cyberspace and strip away one of the key structural privacy protections enjoyed by Internet users." See "Republicans, ACLU Decry Cybercrime Report."

26. Quoted in Dahlburg, "G-8 Seeks Unity on Policing Internet," p. C3. Information in the remainder of this paragraph is from the same source.

27. The Group of 8 was originally the Group of 6 (the United States, Britain, Canada, France, Germany, and Italy) when it held its first summit in France in 1975 to coordinate policies on issues crucial to Europe and the United States. The group was shortly expanded to include Japan and, in the late 1990s, Russia. The first discussion of international organized crime was held at the 1995 summit of the then Group of Seven, held in Halifax, Canada. Since

that summit senior officials from the Internal Affairs and Justice Ministries of the group have met three times each year to discuss countermeasures to arms smuggling, computer crime, and other offenses. For a report on the Internet security-related conclusions from the July 2000 G-8 Summit, held in Okinawa, Japan, see Chapter 7. See Hajnal, *The G7/G8 System,* especially pp. 1–45. A summary of the Internet security aspects of the agenda for the Okinawa summit appears in "G-8 Officials to Discuss International Organized Crime."

28. For various assessments of the results of the G-8 meeting, see Fisher, "Cybercrime Summit Crashes," p. 43.

29. All quotations in this list of conference positions are from Ford, "New Cooperation in Taming the Wild Web," pp. 1, 7.

30. See, for example, Gunkel, "The Empire Strikes Back," pp. 83–84.

31. "U.S. Treasury Chief Warns of Cyber Threats," p. 2.

32. A thoughtful discussion of the issue appears in Ermann, Williams, and Shauf, *Computers, Ethics, and Society;* see especially pp. 240–270.

33. For an analysis of the various firewall systems available in 1998, see Schultz, "The Ultimate Computer Protection," pp. 28–33.

34. "Net Hardware at Secure and Secret California Site."

35. The new U.S. structure for counterterrorism is analyzed in Kellman, "Catastrophic Terrorism," pp. 537–562. Critical infrastructure systems generally include electrical power, gas and oil, telecommunications, banking and finance, transportation, vital government operations, emergency services, and water supply systems.

36. Ibid., p. 542.

37. Lewis, "The New Anti-Terrorism, pp. 24–30.

38. "Casting the Net," p. 17.

39. The proposal was outlined in an article in *Foreign Affairs* (cf. Carter, Deutch, and Zelikow, "Catastrophic Terrorisim"), signed by former assistant secretary of defense Ashton Carter, now at Harvard University; former CIA director John Deutch, now at MIT; and former National Security Council staff member Philip Zelikow, now at the University of Virginia.

40. Ibid., pp. 84–85.

41. Ibid., p. 84.

42. Ibid.

43. Aldrich, "How Do You Know You Are at War?" p. 267.

44. The document is analyzed in Richelson, "Desperately Seeking Signals," pp. 47–52, from which quotations in this paragraph are taken.

45. Quoted in Goodspeed, "The New Space Invaders," p. C3.

46. Ibid.

47. This and other concerns with various facets of the Echelon project are discussed in Loeb, "Critics Questioning NSA Reading Habits," pp. A3 ff.

48. Quoted in ibid., p. A3.

49. Deibert, "Circuits of Power." All quotations in this paragraph are from this source.

50. In addition to ibid., from which quotes in this paragraph are taken,

similar ideas are spelled out in Luke, "The Discipline of Security Studies," pp. 315–344.

51. Zagaris, "The Future of Internationalism," p. B3.

52. Adding to the concerns of allies and domestic civil rights groups were revelations in 1999–2000 about an Internet surveillance system managed by the FBI called "Carnivore," which uses specialized software, usually installed at an ISP, to record online traffic. In an effort to put at rest concerns that Carnivore was designed to control Internet content or invade privacy, the FBI appointed a group of five prominent IT specialists, headed by Professor Henry Perritt Jr. of the Chicago-Kent College of Law, and gave them access to Carnivore activities. The group's final report concluded that some of the larger concerns about Carnivore's activities were "overblown" but urged the FBI to make changes in the system to "prevent tampering with electronic evidence and to ensure that only information is collected as authorized by a court order." See Bridis, "Carnivore Review Still Doesn't Ease Privacy Concerns," p. B6.

53. McLachlin, "Criminal Law," pp. 448–449.

54. For the more detailed proposal, see Shackelford, "Computer Related Crime," pp. 479–505.

55. Hatcher, McDannell, and Ostfeld, "Computer Crimes," pp. 397–457, and Valeri, "Securing Internet Society," pp. 129–147.

56. A variation on the 1999 proposal is Grewlich, "A Charter for the Internet," pp. 273–279.

57. Steele, "The Web That Binds Us All," p. 512.

58. The study, "Achieving Legal and Business Order in Cyberspace: A Report on Global Jurisdiction Issues Created by the Internet," is available online at http://www.abanet.org/buslaw/cyber/initiatives/jurisdiction.html. See also Gold, "US Lawyers Riff on EU Plans."

59. In the modern period, John H. Herz developed the security dilemma concept in his "Idealist Internationalism and the Security Dilemma," pp. 157–180. The concept was further developed and related to game theory in Jervis, *Perception and Misperception in International Politics.*

60. Quoted in Niccolai, "Interpol Head Calls on Private Sector," p. 2. For an analysis of INTERPOL's approach to computer crime, see Imhoff and Cutler, "INTERPOL," pp. 10–17.

61. Jervis, "Security Regimes," pp. 174–175.

62. "Extraordinary" was the word used by George Tenet, director of the CIA, in a report to the U.S. Senate; see "A Prelude to InfoWar." See also Gompert, "Right Makes Might," pp. 69 ff.

63. Denning, *Information Warfare and Security,* pp. 229 ff.

64. *Strategic Defence Review: The Maritime Dimensions*, a Naval Vision report prepared under the guidance of Chief Admiral Vishnu Bhagwat, quoted in www.infowar.com, November 17, 1998.

65. "Indian Navy Suggests Creation," p. 1.

66. See Franda, *Launching into Cyberspace.*

67. Jervis, "Security Regimes," p. 174.

Challenges to the
Global Internet Regime

A nascent international regime for the Internet could be said to have come into being during the mid-1990s with the acceptance of TCP/IP protocol as a de facto global standard. This was not an imposed order in any sense because no single or even multiple international authority could dictate or convince innumerable organizations in 190 independent nations that TCP/IP was preferable to other possible choices for a world standard. Nor was the creation of the international regime for the Internet essentially a negotiated order, although considerable negotiation among the supporters of TCP/IP, proprietary protocols and standards, and the X.25 protocols did take place in the 1980s and 1990s. As indicated in Chapter 1, the international regime for the Internet is an excellent example of spontaneous regime creation, driven initially by the widespread acceptance of TCP/IP by network administrators—and eventually by governments and corporations throughout the world—precisely because of the eclectic and flexible nature of the technology. Governments that preferred the X.25 protocols could continue to use them within their sovereign territories and still gain the benefits of worldwide networking by simply connecting their local networks globally through international networks using TCP/IP. In a similar way, companies could use and sell the proprietary network protocols they had developed because those protocols could be used in local networks that could also, like the X.25, be connected globally through international networks using TCP/IP.

Indeed, the almost amoebalike spread of TCP/IP to all corners of the earth in the 1980s and 1990s made it possible—almost mandatory—

for network administrators and Internet users to accept the two international regime principles and the two regime norms that alone would enable them to become part of the first truly worldwide computer network. As detailed in Chapter 1, the two principles that initiated the technical aspects of the international regime are (1) that authority for operationalizing the Internet be decentralized internationally, and (2) that the process for developing international technical standards be inclusive rather than proprietary or government directed. The two norms for the physical functioning of the Internet internationally are (1) that operation of the global Internet be designed to handle diversity at all network levels, and (2) that the Internet be characterized by interoperability and heterogeneity both within and among networks.

Although principles and norms for the technical aspects of the international regime grew fairly spontaneously, the development of regime principles and norms for the management and governance aspects of the regime has been much more labored. The U.S. government, which retains authority for the "heart of the Internet" (i.e., the root server and the various domain servers that interact with it), has passed this authority among various U.S. agencies—from the Defense Department to the National Science Foundation and now to the Department of Commerce—and has experimented with a number of different ways the private sector might become involved in and even lead Internet development and growth on a global scale. As detailed in Chapter 2, this has produced firm negotiating positions around the following proposed principles and norms:

1. The *principle* that the private sector should take the lead in the development of Internet governance and management and the concomitant *norm* that governments should avoid placing undue restrictions on the Internet while facilitating its development by enforcing a predictable, minimalist, consistent, and simple legal environment
2. The *principle* of openness in the organization of the Internet's governance and management functions, with the concomitant *norms* that some form of at-large membership, functional and geographic representation of international stakeholders and users, and international participation in decisionmaking be built into the structure of the Internet's governing and management mechanisms

Although substantial consensus exists among nations and organizations involved with the Internet about these principles and norms for management and governance, the precise rules and procedures by which they might be operationalized have not yet gained widespread acceptance. Much of the reason for this has been the rather tentative beginnings of ICANN, the key organization around which governance and management functions of the Internet will presumably be built. Under the terms of agreements negotiated in 1999–2000, detailed in Chapter 2, ICANN appears to have at least a four-year period (and possibly as long as eight years) in which to prove itself in a role that could potentially be one of the most creative in the history of international relations institution building or, alternatively, might represent only a transitory attempt to create a form of cyberspace democracy in a nongovernmental organization.

In the late 1990s and the early twenty-first century, basic regime principles and norms for the operationalization of the commercial aspects of the Internet gained widespread acceptance among major world actors and interests. The two working principles in this area are (1) that the private sector will play a lead role in the development of electronic commerce on a global basis, and (2) that regulatory and other government activities should avoid undue restrictions on Internet commercial activities while facilitating the development of international electronic commerce by the private sector. The two working regime norms that have been widely accepted are (1) that diverse sets of national rules and procedures governing Internet commerce will be accommodated at the international level by soft law arrangements designed to promote global cooperation and expand commercial activities, and (2) that regional and international organizations (e.g., WIPO, OECD, WTO) will play key roles in facilitating the growth of the regime for the commercial aspects of the Internet on a global basis.

Principles and norms in the commercial arena have resulted from a number of compromises hammered out during a series of negotiations over the past few years, as outlined in Chapter 3. Negotiations have already produced several creative soft law arrangements, such as the safe harbor mechanism for reconciling different data privacy practices and various new forms of online arbitration for settling commercial disputes, which are likely to become enduring features of the international regime for the Internet for many years into the future. Negotiations on commercial aspects of regime formation have also led directly to the creation of new, internationally powerful private-sector organizations, such as the GBDe, which have demonstrated their ability to exercise private authority in matters central to Internet regime concerns. The roles of large private IT corporations, as well as regional and global organizations—especially the EU, WIPO, and WTO—have been instrumental, as discussed in Chapter 4, in gaining acceptance beyond Europe and the United States (even in the developing world) for the regime principles and norms relating to international commercial aspects of the Internet outlined earlier.

Identification of emergent international regime principles and norms for operationalizing the Internet does not mean a robust regime has emerged full-blown since the mid-1990s. Chapters 5 and 6 make clear that in a number of areas related to international legal and security matters it has been impossible even to develop a workable agenda for negotiating rudimentary international frameworks. From the perspective of the international regime literature in political science this is not unusual, since a number of complex legal issues involving individuals (such as those relating to jurisdiction and privacy) are often left outside the boundaries of international regime architecture, considered more appropriately matters for national courts and international law. Security issues are almost always excluded from international regime building because of the pervasive and ubiquitous nature of the so-called security dilemma, as discussed in Chapter 6.

■ **REGIME BUILDING AND THE LDCs**

Since almost all of the initial inventions that made international computer networking possible were products of the United States and Europe, it is not surprising that those two parts of the world have been in the forefront of the Internet's formation and growth. Only a relatively small portion of the rest of the world has been catching up quickly and has started to play a role in Internet-related matters, ranging from the manufacturing of computers and the development of software to acceptance of or challenge to the regime's commercial, legal, and governance frameworks. The Information Society Index (ISI) for 2000, assembled by IDC and the *World Times*, identified 55 countries (accounting for 97 percent of global gross national product and 99 percent of IT expenditures) as among those with the basic infrastructures needed to take advantage of the information age. This leaves 131 independent states without such infrastructures early in the twenty-first century.[1]

Among the 55 leading countries in the ISI index, 16 (the United States, Canada, Australia, the Scandinavian countries, Japan, Singapore, Hong Kong, and 6 other countries of Western Europe) were the top 16 countries in both the 1999 and 2000 annual IDC/*World Times* studies, identified as the countries "in a strong position to take full advantage of the Information Revolution because of advanced information, computer, Internet and social infrastructures."[2] A second tier of 13 countries (New Zealand, Taiwan, South Korea, Israel, the United Arab Emirates, the Czech Republic, Hungary, and 6 other countries of Western Europe) were identified in the index as having "much of the necessary infrastructure in place." A third tier of 18 countries (primarily from Central and Eastern Europe, Latin America, and Southeast Asia but including South Africa, Saudi Arabia, Mexico, and Turkey) were described in the index as "moving forward in spurts" but being held back somewhat by shifts in priorities as a result of domestic "economic, social and political pressures." The last 7 of the 55 countries on the ISI2000 list (Jordan, Egypt, China, Indonesia, Peru, India, and Pakistan) were analyzed as "moving ahead, but inconsistently, often because of limited financial resources in relation to their vast populations."

The positions of the many countries and various regions of the world relative to the global Internet regime are taken up in the companion volume to this one.[3] For purposes of the present discussion, however, it is important to note two significant aspects of the so-called digital divide between the better-off and worse-off IT nations that are most likely to impact Internet regime dynamics into the future. The first of these is the sheer inability of the world's poorest nations to become involved in anything but a peripheral way in the building of international protocols, frameworks, norms, rules, and procedures because of their lack of infrastructure and resources. An attempt to better understand the interaction between advanced IT societies and the poorest regions of the world in this regard constitutes a significant portion of the companion volume.

The second aspect of the digital divide is the attempt by many LDCs to somehow wall themselves off from the rest of the computer networking world or at least from those parts of that world they see as threatening or undesirable. As mentioned early in this book, the PRC has been perhaps the key world actor in this respect, in part because its attempts to create an Internet firewall on a national scale have been so persistent but also because of the sheer size of its population, the exuberant enthusiasm of its leadership in promoting Internet growth, and the massive investments it has attracted—from all over the world and primarily from the private sector—in Internet-related information technology ventures.

China is representative of many countries because it has based some of its internal computer networks on the X.25 protocol, thus providing a larger role for government in network administration and more possibilities for government control of the Internet than would be the case if either TCP/IP or proprietary protocols were adopted as the national standard. But China is also an excellent example of a country that has gained from international regime principles and norms that permit the PRC to have its own X.25 protocols while being fully interoperable with the large array of other types of networks worldwide. Chinese attempts to develop Internet firewalls or to otherwise seal itself off from some parts of the global Internet, although not entirely successful, have thus far been within the bounds of existing international regime principles and norms and in this respect are not unlike similar efforts attempted in many other nations.

Particularly striking has been the way the Chinese communist government has enthusiastically accepted international regime rules and procedures for privatizing the governance and management aspects of the global Internet and for developing a predictable, minimalist, consistent, and simple legal environment at the international level. As Chapter 2 makes clear, this position of PRC leaders is understandable because such an approach to governance and management provides significant opportunities for Chinese input into world Internet governance structures, particularly with the election of a leading Chinese Internet entrepreneur to the ICANN board of governors in 1999. It is also not surprising that China has accepted regime arrangements that assign lead roles for the evolution of commercial aspects of the regime to the private sector at the international level, to a variety of soft law arrangements, and to regional and international organizations like WIPO, WTO, and OECD. If only to continue to attract the massive amounts of Internet-related foreign investment coming into China each year since the mid-1980s, it will be essential for China to continue to find ways to accommodate the international regime frameworks that make such arrangements possible.

The one area where China has refused thus far to be accommodating toward proposed international regime principles and norms has to do with internal government regulation and control, where the leadership in Beijing has made it clear that it is not going to subscribe fully to the EU-U.S. conception, traced in Chapter 4, that regulatory and other government activities should avoid undue restrictions on Internet commercial activities while facilitating the development of international electronic commerce by the private sector. Indeed, a major test of China's compatibility with the international regime for the Internet will revolve around conflicting aspirations relating, on the one hand, to the compelling need of the PRC's leadership to exercise significant government control over the Internet domestically and, on the other hand, to the unquestioned preference among leading regime actors that China exhibit greater openness. This matter extends beyond Internet-related issues to many other aspects of China's relationship with the rest of the world as well.

China may be the test case among many challenges to the global Internet regime, in part because of its conspicuous position as the largest and most powerful of the LDCs refusing to accept proposed regime norms for free flow of communications and free flow of electronic commerce but also for its rather aggressive posture in seeking to capture and monopolize a separate Internet governance structure for all Chinese-language communication.[4] In China's case, these positions flow from PRC leaders' insistence that "open political competition and freedom of speech are incompatible with [Chinese] Communist Party [CCP] control of the reform process."[5] Based on this perception, the CCP often publicizes its position that free flow of communications and electronic commerce would be destabilizing for China. At the same time, when speaking at diplomatic functions or trying to move closer to a Western position in diplomatic negotiations, Chinese officials have frequently tried to depict their Internet policies as moving toward the goal of openness—but defined more ambiguously than is usually the case in the West—with the requirement that movement toward openness "must be done in stages."[6]

▪ WARNINGS OF INTERNET BALKANIZATION

Although the degree of domestic control China's central authorities exercise over Internet access can be viewed as fairly consistent with the principles and norms of the global regime, the PRC's determination to gain a worldwide monopoly over the key governing mechanisms of all Internet service in the Chinese language would, if realized, almost certainly result in a severe break with regime norms. Beijing's position on the issue is that registration of domain names in Chinese, and authority over the root servers that control those domain names, should not be in the hands of NSI/VeriSign or other ICANN registrars. Within the PRC Internet community, registration of domain names in the Chinese language by companies and organizations outside the mainland is often viewed as an effort to recolonize China in cyberspace, a sentiment often accompanied by assertions that the Chinese language "belongs to Chinese" and "should not be run by a foreign company." Leading Chinese IT authorities have been quoted in the state-run press, arguing that foreign registration of domain names violates PRC sovereignty, will result in "a rush of foreign exchange outflow," creates "potential threats to state security," and is "humiliating."[7]

Since Chinese is spoken by more than twice as many people as English, with the vast majority of the world's Chinese-language speakers living within China's boundaries, one might assume that the PRC's China National Network Information Center (CNNIC) would have the advantage over other organizations in the competition to become the authority for establishing a Chinese-language domain name world framework. ICANN has designated CNNIC as the management organization to oversee the "cn" country domain in English, and CNNIC is the government organization China's leadership has assigned to set standards for Chinese-language domain names for all of the mainland. But many Chinese speakers outside the PRC are either reluctant or simply refuse to register domain names with CNNIC because of its official connections to the communist government in Beijing, which not only requires and stores substantial personal information about those applying for domain names and addresses but adds or eliminates domain names in a manner often considered arbitrary or ideological.

Competition to become the international authority for registering and supervising Internet domain names in Chinese has come from a number of organizations outside China, most notably from i-DNS in Singapore.[8] During the last several years at least a dozen Chinese and non-Chinese private firms—in addition to i-DNS and CNNIC—have been registering literally hundreds of thousands of domain names in Chinese, despite people's relative inability to use such domain names with any regularity until a framework can be developed to facilitate their routing on local and international networks.[9] A number of technical problems sorting out Chinese-language domain name administration stem from the differences among various forms of written Chinese, including simplified (used in mainland China) and traditional (used in Taiwan) characters. But engineers and linguists argue that technical differences can be resolved fairly quickly if a willingness to cooperate exists among all major parties with interests in Chinese-language domain name management. In the absence of successful negotiation, in the words of a leading PRC computer expert, "the registration of Chinese domain names is meaningless and domain names are invalid until such a framework emerges."[10]

A major complicating factor in the worldwide use of Chinese on the Internet emerged in November 2000, when NSI/VeriSign—in its capacity as the leading registrar of domain names authorized by ICANN—began accepting domain names in Chinese, Korean, and Japanese characters for the first time. Chinese authorities immediately struck back, with CNNIC announcing a rival—and incompatible—system for registering Chinese-language names, prompting widespread concern among Chinese-language Internet users.[11] Pindar Wong, the first Chinese person elected to the ICANN board, a former vice chairman of ICANN, and a leading figure in Hong Kong Internet circles, warned that the conflict between Beijing's leadership and ICANN on this issue risked "balkanization of the Internet." Trying to pull both sides back from a protracted conflict, Wong asked everyone to remember that "global connectivity is the most precious aspect of the Internet. Anything that might jeopardize that needs to be considered very carefully."[12]

Those who oppose world capitulation to Beijing in its attempts to establish the standards for and run the global domain name system for the Chinese language base their apprehension in part on the threats to free speech and privacy evident in the domain name system CNNIC has devised. Free of cost, the system requires that users download special software that routes all requests to a central "dictionary" located on computers in Beijing. With complete authority over this dictionary, those controlling the system in Beijing can, in effect, decide who in the system is and who is not able to use the Internet in Chinese. To quote a *Wall Street Journal* article, "China's system is a home-grown method of handling Chinese-language domain names completely separate from those currently in use—a change as fundamental as if China decided to use a globally incompatible system of telephone numbers."[13] In the words of Matthew McGarvey, senior Internet analyst for IDC research in Beijing, "It's a classic case of [the Chinese] trying to develop the

Internet the way it suits them rather than what suits the rest of the world."[14]

■ CONCLUSIONS

Recognizing that international regimes are rather fragile—especially in their formative stages and even more particularly when they are highly decentralized—a number of Internet users and scholars have warned that various aspects of the emergent regime architecture might be threatened in a variety of ways.[15] Some focus on the possibility of balkanization along geographical or linguistic lines, such as those inherent in China's aspirations to create firewalls and linguistically isolated networks. Most others envisage challenges stemming from the expansion of Internet traffic:

> [The incredible growth is creating] a dysfunctional [and] dangerous mess, a mishmash of government, corporate and public networks straining the simple limits of what [the Internet] was originally designed to do. This billion-tentacled beast, incubated 30 years ago to ensure defense communications, now hauls billions of missives, billions of dollars in transactions, two-way video, music files, auctions, phone calls and more. The content zooms and clatters over an array of archaic and futuristic gear, from aging copper phone lines to light-bending optical switches. The demand rises so fast that some big data haulers increase their capacity tenfold every year—a millionfold increase in six years, with no end in sight.[16]

A leader of the Internet's original design team, Vinton Cerf, has said, "It's terrifying when you think about scaling and reliability. . . . The Internet Protocol (IP) that governs most data now runs over everything—including you if you don't get out of the way."[17] Another of the Internet's founders, Robert Metcalfe (inventor of Ethernet), has recently been predicting an impending "gigalapse"—a blackout spanning a billion person-hours—leading him and others to look for ways to completely restructure global computer networking architecture. Suggestions for restructuring sometimes call for highly rational, centrally planned versions similar to an airline system's hub-and-spoke model, with big users near big-content Internet backbones and as many direct routes as possible for smaller users on the periphery. But highly organized, systematic, and centralized global computer network architectures along highly rational lines like those of the airline route model are routinely rejected by computer scientists and engineers. No matter how much more efficient and capacious than the existing architecture, such models have come to be viewed as threatening by network leaders who have learned to live with and highly value what Quentin Hardy has called "the chaotic nature of the beast, with the guiding philosophy being—'hey, nobody owns this thing.'"[18]

As indicated in earlier chapters, a third founding father of the Internet, Tim Berners-Lee (the lead inventor of the World Wide Web), has dedicated his own work and his organization at MIT (W3C) to the search for ways to increase the capacity of the Internet and the Web but without surrendering the highly decentralized and flexible characteristics of the existing regime. In addition to the many new protocols and standards Berners-Lee has helped operationalize through the W3C, he has recently suggested creating a new domain name system that would give everyone in the world the same domain name for their entire lifetime.[19] But Berners-Lee quickly cautions that attempts to change the domain name structure of the Internet should be implemented only in the most prudent manner: "Any centre point is a weak point, so [the Internet's domain name system] has to be managed very carefully. . . . You don't often move the crown jewels—you want to very carefully reconsider any changes at that level, which will affect the integrity of the whole Internet."[20]

In the final analysis, the extent to which the embryonic international regime outlined in these pages endures and becomes more robust will depend on the willingness of both leaders and citizens of all involved nations to continue to maintain workable rules and procedures in accordance with regime principles and norms. Even at this early stage of regime formation, it is clear that the legitimacy or robustness of the Internet as an international enterprise cannot be derived by individual nations waiving national sovereignty, as might be the case in a more highly centralized regime, or for that matter by the waiving of personal interests. The Internet became operational on a worldwide basis very rapidly in the 1990s because the vast majority of world governments found it compatible with sovereignty and because most organizations and individuals who use it found it a positive communication device to achieve organizational or personal aspirations. No matter how decentralized and chaotic it may appear at times, the international regime for the Internet has evolved essentially from these two factors.

■ NOTES

1. The U.S. State Department listed 190 independent states in the world in mid-2000 (see www.state.gov/www/regions/independent_states.html), of which 174 are detailed in the statistical tables (pp. 51–56) of the UNDP *Human Development Report 1999* for Internet hosts, personal computers, and other aspects of information technology that contribute to the ISI Index. Subtracting the 55 countries listed in the ISI2000 count from UNDP's 1999 list would leave 119 countries without IT infrastructures, but the list does not include 12 additional countries not on the ISI list that are significantly lacking in IT infrastructures as well (Afghanistan, Bosnia, Kiribati, Liberia, Marshall Islands, Micronesia, Nauru, North Korea, Palau, Somalia, Tonga, and Tuvalu). The UNDP was unable to obtain reliable data on these countries for its 1999 report. In addition, four countries (Andorra, the Holy See, Liechtenstein, and San Marino) not on the UNDP list had IT infrastructures comparable to some of those on the ISI list but were too small to be included in the ISI2000 count.

2. Quoted from *ISI2000 Information Society Index,* pp. 1–2. The index is based on twenty-three indicators clustered under four categories: computer infrastructure, Internet infrastructure, information infrastructure (telecommunications, television, radio, fax, and the like), and social infrastructure (education, newspaper readership, press freedom, civil liberties). For more information, contact wwelch@worldtimes.com or mtoolan@idc.com. The six other countries of Western Europe were the U.K., Germany, the Netherlands, Switzerland, Belgium, and Austria.

3. See Franda, *Launching into Cyberspace.*

4. Franda, "China and India Online."

5. Mueller and Tan, *China in the Information Age,* p. 12.

6. Quoted, for example, in O'Neill, "Beijing Commits on Easing Net Laws."

7. See, for example, reports in the PRC press in "And They're Off!" and "Give Me Back My Name!"

8. A company called i-DNS.net International Inc. (Palo Alto, California) was spun off from the Development Unit of National University of Singapore (NUS) in October 1999. A software package developed at NUS, called internationalized domain name system (iDNS) enables i-DNS.net International to convert Internet naming, which uses the ASCII character set to display letters of the Western alphabet, to and from Unicode, a system that makes it possible to represent the complex characters used in many of the world's other languages, including Chinese. On the origins of i-DNS.net see "Short Circuits," *tele.com,* 5:23 (November 27, 2000), pp. 42–43. See also Martin Fackler, "Dispute Over Chinese Web Sites Threatens to Split Internet," *Associated Press,* December 20, 2000.

9. See, for example, "China Introduces Chinese Character Web Site Domain Names"; "BusinessChina Offers Deal on Name Registration";

Greenberg, "Domain Registrars Scramble to Dominate in China"; and "China Channel, CNNIC Disagree."

10. Quoted in "Who Will Manage Chinese Domain Names?" p. 3.

11. "42,000 Chinese Domain Names Successfully Registered." A seven-page outline of CNNIC's domain name system appears in "Complete CNNIC Rules" (portions of the rules are also available on the website Sina.com).

12. Quoted in Manuel and Chang, "Will Language Wars Balkanize the Web," p. C22.

13. Ibid.

14. Ibid.

15. On the fragility of international regimes, see Cook, *The Rise and Fall of Regimes.*

16. Hardy, "Weaving the Perfect Net," p. 140.

17. Quoted in ibid.

18. Ibid., p. 141.

19. The idea, which Berners-Lee suggests could be based on the British method of creating license plates for vehicles, is outlined in Harvey, "The Web's Watchful Parent," pp. 17–18.

20. Ibid., p. 18.

Acronyms

ABA	American Bar Association
ABT	Agreement on Basic Telecommunications (of the WTO)
AICPA	American Institute of Certified Public Accountants
APNIC	Asia Pacific Network Information Center
ARIN	American Registry for Internet Numbers
ARPA	Advanced Research Projects Agency (of the DOD)
ARPANET	the original computer network of ARPA
ASEAN	Association of Southeast Asian nations
ASO	Address Supporting Organization (of ICANN)
B2B	business to business
BEUC	Bureau Européen des Unions de Consommateurs
BIRPI	Bureaux for the Protection of Intellectual Property
BWG	Boston Working Group
CCITT	Consultative Committee on International Telegraphy and Telephony (of the ITU)
CCP	Chinese Communist Party
ccTLD	country code Top-Level Domain
CDA	Communications Decency Act (U.S.)
CEE	Central and Eastern Europe
CEELI	Central and East European Law Initiative (of the ABA)
CEO	chief executive officer
CERN	Centre Européen pour la Recherche Nucléaire
CFA	Committee on Fiscal Affairs (of the OECD)
CIA	Central Intelligence Agency
CICA	Chartered Institute of Certified Accountants

CIX	Commercial Internet eXchange
CNNIC	China National Network Information Center
CORE	Council of Registrars
CSNET	Computer Scientists Network
CSPP	Computer Systems Policy Project
DARPA	Defense Advanced Research Projects Agency (of the DOD)
DECNET	Digital Network Architecture (of Digital Equipment Corporation)
DNS	Domain Name System
DNSO	Domain Name Supporting Organization (of ICANN)
DOD	Department of Defense
EC	European Community
EEC	European Economic Community
EPIC	Electronic Privacy Information Center
EU	European Union
FBI	Federal Bureau of Investigation
FDI	foreign direct investment
FTC	Federal Trade Commission
FTP	file transfer protocol
G-7	Group of 7
G-8	Group of 8
GAC	Government Advisory Committee (of ICANN)
GAO	General Accounting Office (U.S.)
GATS	General Agreement on Trade in Services
GATT	General Agreement on Tariffs and Trade
GBDe	Global Business Dialogue on Electronic Commerce
GILC	Global Internet Liberty Campaign
GTAC	Government Technical Assistance Centre (U.K.)
gTLD	generic Top-Level Domain
HML	Hardware Markup Language
HTML	Hyptertext Markup Language
http	hypertext transfer protocol
IAB	Internet Activities/Architecture Board
IAHC	International Ad Hoc Committee
IANA	Internet Assigned Numbers Authority
IATA	International Association of Transport Airlines
IBM	International Business Machines Corporation
IBX	international business exchange
ICANN	Internet Corporation for Assigned Names and Numbers

ICAO	International Civil Aviation Organization
ICCB	Internet Configuration Control Board
IDC	International Data Corporation
iDNS	internationalized domain name system
IESG	International Engineering Study Group (of the IETF)
IETF	Internet Engineering Task Force
IFWP	International Forum on the White Paper
IMF	International Monetary Fund
INGO	international nongovernmental organization
INTA	International Trademark Association
IP	Internet Protocol
IPR	intellectual property right(s)
IPU	International Postal Union
IRTF	Internet Research Task Force
ISI	Information Society Index
ISO	International Organization for Standardization
ISOC	Internet Society
ISP	internet service provider
IT	information technology
ITU	International Telecommunications Union
IW	information warfare
LANs	local area networks
LDC	less developed country
MILNET	an operational Military Network within the DOD
MIT	Massachusetts Institute of Technology
MITS	Model Instrumentation Telemetry Systems
MoU	memorandum of understanding
NAFTA	North American Free Trade Agreement
NASA	National Aeronautics and Space Administration
NCC	Network Coordination Centre (of RIPE)
NIAI	National Information Assurance Institute
NII	National Information Infrastructure
NSA	National Security Agency
NSC	National Security Council (U.S.)
NSF	National Science Foundation (U.S.)
NSI	Network Solutions, Inc.
NTIA	National Telecommunications and Information Administration (of the U.S. Department of Commerce)
NTIC	National Terrorism Intelligence Center (U.S.)
NWG	Network Working Group

OECD	Organization for Economic Cooperation and Development
OEEC	Organization for European Economic Cooperation
OPA	Online Privacy Alliance
ORSC	Open Root Server Confederation
OSI	Open Systems Interconnection (of the ISO)
PC	personal computer
PCT	Patent Cooperation Treaty
PDD	Presidential Decision Directive (U.S.)
PICS	Platform for Internet Content Selection
POC	Policy Oversight Committee (of CORE)
PRC	People's Republic of China
PSO	Protocol Supporting Organization (of ICANN)
PTO	Patent and Trademark Office (U.S.)
PTT	Post, Telephone, and Telegraph Company
RFC	request for comments
RIP	Regulation of Investigatory Powers (U.K.)
RIPE	Reseaux IP Européens (European IP Networks)
SNA	Systems Network Architecture
SO	supporting organization (used by ICANN)
SPA	Software Publishers' Association
TCP	Transmission Control Protocol
TCP/IP	Transmission Control Protocol/Internet Protocol
TLD	Top-Level Domain
TPO	Transport Protocol
TRIPS	Trade-Related Aspects of Intellectual Property Protection
UDRP	Uniform Domain-Name Dispute-Resolution Policy (of WIPO)
UK	United Kingdom
UKUSA	United Kingdom and United States of America
UMTS	Universal Mobile Telecommunications System
UNDP	United Nations Development Program
URL	Universal Resource Locator
USAID	U.S. Agency for International Development
USC	University of Southern California
USC-ISI	University of Southern California's Information Sciences Institute
USSR	Union of Soviet Socialist Republics
VAT	value-added tax
VSAT	very small aperture terminal

W3C	World Wide Web Consortium
WAIS	Wide-Area Information Server
WCT	WIPO Copyright Treaty
WIPO	World Intellectual Property Organization
WPPT	WIPO Performance and Phonograms Treaty
WTO	World Trade Organization
X.25	a set of three protocols developed initially in the 1970s that has become an international standard favored by government telecommunications companies
XHTML	a specification developed by the W3C to make it possible for an XML document to work with the old HTML browsers
XML	Extensible Markup Language

Bibliography

Abbate, Janet. *Inventing the Internet*. Cambridge: MIT Press, 1999.

Abbott, Kenneth W. "Modern International Relations Theory: A Prospectus for International Lawyers." *Yale Journal of International Law,* 14 (1989), pp. 335–411.

Abreu, Elinor. "Poking Holes in Linux." *The Standard,* April 25, 2000.

"Administration Unveils China Enforcement Effort." *Associated Press,* May 3, 2000.

Akin, David. "Internet Adjudicator Gets into Dispute over Name." *National Post* (Ottawa), March 8, 2000, p. C6.

Aldrich, Lt. Colonel Richard W. "How Do You Know You Are at War in the Information Age?" *Houston Journal of International Law,* 22:2 (winter 2000), pp. 223–267.

Alexander, Garth. "Cybersquatters Banned from Holding Web Names to Ransom." *Times* (London), January 9, 2000.

"Algeria Ratifies Patent Treaty." *Middle East Business Intelligence,* 19:5 (March 5, 2000), p. 6.

"And They're Off! Domain Names in Chinese Characters Trigger Stampede." *China Online,* November 9, 2000.

Andreopoulos, George J., and Richard Pierre Claude (eds.). *Human Rights Education for the Twenty-first Century.* Philadelphia: University of Pennsylvania Press, 1997.

Andrews, Edmund L. "Europe Plans to Collect Tax on Some Internet Transactions." *New York Times,* March 2, 2000.

Anidjar, Patrick. "Cyber Threat Is Constant Worry for United States." *Agence France Press,* May 13, 2000.

Anthony, Shaun. "Online Censorship Laws Catch 35 Sites." *West Australian,* April 20, 2000, p. 3.

"Aussie Censors Crack Down on 27 Websites." *Straits Times* (Singapore), March 22, 2000, p. 22.

"Be Prepared: China Not Ready for WTO Membership, Official Says." *China Online*, September 19, 2000.

Berners-Lee, Tim, with Mark Fischetti. *Weaving the Web.* New York: HarperSan Francisco, 1999.

Berners-Lee, Tim, Robert Cailliau, Ari Luotonen, Henrik Frystyk Nielsen, and Arthur Secret. "The World-Wide Web." *Communications of the ACM*, 37:8 (August 1994), pp. 76–82.

Bick, Jonathan D. "Symposium Article: Why Should the Internet Be Any Different?" *Pace Law Review*, 19 (fall 1998), pp. 41–67.

Blackhurst, Richard. "The Capacity of the WTO to Fulfill Its Mandate," in *The WTO as an International Organization*, ed. Anne O. Krueger. Chicago: University of Chicago Press, 1998, pp. 31–58.

Boele-Woelki, Katharina, and Catherine Kessedjian (eds.). *Internet: Which Court Decides? Which Law Applies?* The Hague: Kluwer Law International, 1998.

Borland, John. "AT&T Fights Back with Net2Phone Investment." *New York Times,* March 31, 2000.

———. "Technology Tussle Underlies Wireless Web." *New York Times*, April 19, 2000.

Borrus, Michael, and John Zysman. "Wintelism and the Changing Terms of Global Competition: Prototype of the Future?" *BRIE Working Paper 96B.* Berkeley: University of California Press, 1997.

Bransten, Jeremy. "G–8 Countries Tackle Cybercrime." *Radio Free Europe/Radio Liberty,* May 19, 2000.

Bridis, Ted. "Carnivore Review Still Doesn't Ease Privacy Concerns." *Wall Street Journal,* December 5, 2000.

Brinkley, Joel, with Steve Lohr. "Tangled Path Led to the Government's Decision to Seek a Breakup of Microsoft." *New York Times,* April 30, 2000.

Brown, Curtis, and Kristen Porter. "E-Commerce Arbitration: The Solution for New Legal Issues." *Metropolitan Corporate Counsel,* February 2000, pp. 32–34.

Browning, John. "Africa 1, Hollywood 0." *Wired,* March 1997.

Buchen, Katarzyna A., and Brian T. Belowich. "Global Anti-Cybersquatting." *National Law Journal,* March 13, 2000, p. B7–12.

Burr, Mara M. "Will the General Agreement on Trade in Services Result in International Standards for Lawyers and Access to the World Market?" *Hamline Law Review,* 20 (1997), pp. 667–697.

"BusinessChina Offers Deal on Name Registration." *BusinessChina,* May 30, 2000.

Caher, John. "New Rules for Domain Name Arbitration Produce Results." *New York Law Journal,* March 14, 2000, pp. 1–3.

Campbell, Duncan. "Online: The Spy in Your Server." *The Guardian* (London), August 10, 2000.

Cane, Alan. "Out with the Old, In with the New: Huge and Rapid Growth in

Mobil Phones and the Internet Is Fuelling Transition." *Financial Times* (London), January 29, 1999, p. 3.

Carter, Ashton, John Deutch, and Philip Zelikow. "Catastrophic Terrorism: Imagining the Transforming Event." *Foreign Affairs,* 77:6 (November-December 1998), pp. 80–95.

"Casting the Net." *New Scientist,* 165:2222 (January 22, 2000), p. 17.

"CEO Group Tools to Set E-Biz Rules." *Wall Street Journal,* January 15, 1999.

Chan, Karen. "European Web Use Increased by 7.6% During October." *Wall Street Journal,* Eastern Edition, November 27, 2000, p. A6.

Chandler, Clay. "For China, Vote Has Trade-offs: Beijing Applauds Outcome But Bristles at Rights Provision." *Washington Post,* May 26, 2000.

Chartrand, Sabra. "Federal Agency Rethinks Internet Patents." *New York Times,* March 30, 2000.

Cheek, James H. III. "The Twenty-first Century Will Demand New Laws and Lawyers." *National Law Journal,* 20:49 (August 3, 1998), p. C5.

"China Channel, CNNIC Disagree over Chinese Character International Domain Names." *China Online,* October 10, 2000, translated from *Zhongguo Qingnian Bao* [China Youth Daily], September 30, 2000.

"China Introduces Chinese Character Web Site Domain Names." *Beijing Qingnian Bao* [Beijing Youth Daily], January 20, 2000, translated and analyzed in *China Online,* January 24, 2000.

Clausing, Jeri. "Europe and U.S. Reach Data Privacy Pact." *New York Times,* March 15, 2000.

———. "Internet Board Agrees to Overhaul Election Plan." *New York Times,* March 10, 2000.

———. "New Internet Board Could Shake up Country Domains." *New York Times,* November 27, 1998.

———. "One American Elected to Internet Board." *New York Times,* October 28, 1999.

———. "Private Takeover of Internet Administration to Begin." *New York Times,* November 25, 1998.

———. "States to Consider Flurry of Internet Bills." *New York Times,* January 4, 2000.

Coase, Ronald. *The Firm, the Market, and the Law.* Chicago: University of Chicago Press, 1990.

"Complete CNNIC Rules for Domain-Name Disputes." *China Online,* November 10, 2000.

"The Consensus Machine: The Internet Has Matured to the Point Where People Are Asking: Who Runs It and on Whose Behalf?" *The Economist* (London), June 10, 2000, pp. 73–79.

"Consumers' Rights Companies 'Ignorant' of Tougher Sanctions." *Financial Times* (London), February 8, 2000.

Cook, Terrence E. *The Rise and Fall of Regimes: Toward a Grand Theory of Politics.* New York: Peter Lang, 2000.

Crandall, Robert W., and Leonard Waverman. *Who Pays for Universal Service?* Washington, D.C.: Brookings Institution Press, 2000.

Crane, Susan L. "Domain Name Disputes ICANN's New Policy: What It Covers." *E-Commerce,* 16:9 (January 2000), pp. 1–4.

Crocker, Thomas. "Courts Split over Encryption as Protected Speech." *National Law Journal,* September 20, 1999, p. B14–18.

Cutler, A. Claire, Virginia Haufler, and Tony Porter (eds.). *Private Authority and International Affairs.* Albany: State University of New York (SUNY) Press, 1999.

"Cyber Threat Is Constant Worry for United States." *Agence France Press,* May 13, 2000.

Dahlburg, John-Thor. "G–8 Seeks Unity on Policing Internet." *Los Angeles Times,* May 18, 2000, p. C3.

Dasaneyavaja, Borisuthiboun. "Electronic Business Indicators Suggest Asian E-Business Is Up." *Bangkok Post,* October 27, 1999.

Davies, R.E.G. *Rebels and Reformers of the Airways.* Washington, D.C.: Smithsonian Institution Press, 1987.

Dean, Katie. "UN Proposes Global Email Tax." *Wired News,* July 13, 1999.

deBony, Elizabeth. "EC Takes Countries to Court on Data Privacy." *CNN.com,* January 17, 2000.

———. "European Union to Revamp Telecommunications Legislation." *Infoworld,* 21:48 (November 29, 1999), p. D62.

Deibert, Ronald. "Circuits of Power: Security in the Internet Environment," in *Information, Power, and Globalization,* ed. J. P. Singh and James Rosenau. Albany: SUNY Press, forthcoming.

de Jonquie'res, Guy. "Japan-US Summit: Internet Rules Agreed." *Financial Times* (London), May 15, 1998, p. 6.

———. "World Trade System: Success Brings New Challenges." *Financial Times* (London), November 29, 1999, pp. 1, 7–8. (London), November 16, 1999.

Denning, Dorothy. *Information Warfare and Security.* Reading, Mass.: Addison Wesley Longman, 1999.

"Developments in the Law of Cyberspace." Student authored (anonymous). *Harvard Law Review,* 112:7 (May 1999), pp. 1574–1704.

de Visscher, Fernand. *Le Regime Nouveau des Detroits.* Bruxelles: M. Weissenbruch, 1924.

Dickie, Mure. "Taiwan Set to Break Telecoms Monopoly." *Financial Times* (London), April 15, 1999.

Doan, Amy. "NetPD Wants to Be Web's Police Department." *Forbes,* May 5, 2000.

Dodgson, Charles. "Chinese and Indian Governments Release New Telecom Policy." *Exchange Telecommunications Newsletter,* 11:12 (April 2, 1999), p. 1.

Domain Name Agreements Between the U.S. Department of Commerce, Network Solutions, Inc., and the Internet Corporation for Assigned Names and Numbers. Fact Sheet, September 28, 1999. Washington, D.C.: Department of Commerce, 1999.

Drogin, Bob. "U.S. Scurries to Erect Cyber-Defenses." *Los Angeles Times,* October 31, 1999.

Dunne, Nancy, and Dan Lerner. "Role for Business in Trade Disputes: Governments Will Have a Smaller Part to Play, Predicts US Trade Official." *Financial Times* (London), April 3, 2000, p. 12.

Eaglesham, Jean, and Deborah Hargreaves. "Rules and Red Tape May Weigh Down the Web." *Financial Times* (London), February 1, 2000, p. 13.

Eaglesham, Jean, and John Mason. "US 'Not a Safe Harbour for Data Transfer.'" *Financial Times* (London), November 6, 2000, p. 26.

"E-Commerce Band to Battle Net Regulators." *PC Dealer,* January 20, 1999.

Edgecliffe-Johnson, Andrew. "Corporate Security: Dirty Tricks Brigade Cleans Up Its Act." *Financial Times* (London), March 3, 2000, p. 2.

Electronic Commerce and the Role of the WTO. Geneva: World Trade Organization, 1998.

The Emerging Digital Economy. Washington, D.C.: Department of Commerce, 1998.

Engelman, Andrea B., Heather R. Goldstein, David M. Lange, Chad J. Peterman, and Tamir Young. "Additional Countries Ratify WIPO Internet Treaties," *The Journal of Proprietary Rights,* 12:2 (February 2000), p. 20.

Ermann, M. David, Mary B. Willliams, and Michele S. Shauf. *Computers, Ethics, and Society,* 2d ed. New York: Oxford University Press, 1997.

"EU, U.S. Hammer out Privacy Agreement." *Reuters News Service,* March 15, 2000.

"Fed Panel Urged to Keep Web Tax Free." *New York Times,* December 15, 1999.

Fisher, Matthew. "Cybercrime Summit Crashes: G-8 Mostly Bark, No Byte." *Toronto Sun* (Ottawa), May 18, 2000, p. 43.

Flax, Ryan A. "NAFTA and the Patent Systems of Its Members: Is There Potential for a Unification of the North American Patent Systems?" *NAFTA: Law and Business Review of the Americas,* 5 (summer 1999), pp. 461–501.

Ford, Peter. "EU's 'Dotcom' Summit Plays Catch-up with US." *Christian Science Monitor,* March 24, 2000.

———. "New Cooperation in Taming the Wild Web." *Christian Science Monitor,* May 18, 2000.

"42,000 Chinese Domain Names Successfully Registered, 758,000 Rejected." *China Online,* November 30, 2000, translated from *Jisuanji Shijie Ribao* [China Computer World], November 29, 2000.

Foster, Will A., Anthony Rutkowski, and Seymour E. Goodman. "Who Governs the Internet?" *Communications of the ACM,* 40:8 (August 1997), pp. 15–20.

A Framework for Global Electronic Commerce. Washington, D.C.: White House Task Force, July 1997.

France, Mike. "Why We Don't Need Patent Reform—Yet." *Business Week,* December 20, 1999.

"France: Protocol-Linkup Plan Would Stymie IBM." *Electronics,* 51:12 (June 8, 1978), pp. 69–70.

Franda, Marcus. "China and India Online: The Politics of Information Technology in the World's Largest Nations." Unpublished manuscript, 2001.

———. *Launching into Cyberspace: Internet Development and Politics in Five World Regions.* Boulder: Lynne Rienner, forthcoming.

"G-8 Officials to Discuss International Organized Crime." *Daily Yomiuri* (Tokyo), February 7, 2000.

Gertz, William. "Chinese Hackers Raid U.S. Computers." *Washington Post,* May 16, 1999, pp. C1, C17.

Gidwitz, Betsy. *The Politics of Air Transport.* Lexington, Mass.: D. C. Heath, 1980.

Gillett, Sharon Eisner, and Mitchell Kapor. "The Self-Governing Internet: Coordination by Design," in *Coordinating the Internet,* ed. Brian Kahin and James H. Keller. Cambridge: MIT Press, 1997, pp. 3–38.

"Give Me Back My Name! Foreign Registration of Chinese-Language Domain Names Causing Concern." *China Online,* October 24, 2000.

"Global Group on E-Commerce Meets to Set Standards." *Japan Economic Newswire,* January 14, 1999.

Gold, Steve. "US Lawyers Riff on EU Global Net Rule Plans." *Newsbytes News Network,* July 11, 2000.

Goldsmith, Peter. "Globalization of Laws—Tearing Down the Walls," in *Global Law in Practice,* ed. J. Ross Harper. Boston: Kluwer Academic Publishers, 1997, pp. 139 ff.

Goldston, David, and Betty-Ellen Shave. "International Dimensions of Crimes in Cyberspace." *Fordham International Law Journal,* 22 (June 1999), pp. 1924–71.

Gompert, David C. "Right Makes Might: Freedom and Power in the Information Age," in *The Changing Role of Information in Warfare,* ed. Zalmay M. Khalilzad and John P. White. Santa Monica: Rand Project Air Force, pp. 45–73.

Goodspeed, Peter. "The New Space Invaders: Spies in the Sky." *National Post* (Ottawa), February 19, 2000.

Goodwin, Irwin. "Washington Briefings." *Physics Today,* 51:10 (October 1998), p. 70.

"Government Opens Overseas Telecommunications Market to Competition." *Canadian Corporate Newswire,* October 1, 1998.

"Government Planning to Tax Transactions on Internet." *Hindu,* July 13, 1998, p. 14.

Graham, Bradley. "U.S. Studies New Threat: Cyber Attack." *Washington Post,* May 24, 1998, p. A1.

Greenberg, Jonah. "Domain Registrars Scramble to Dominate in China." *Digital PRC,* June 2, 2000.

Greenberg, Lawrence. "Danger.com: National Security in a Wired World," in *Economic Strategy and National Security: A Next Generation Approach,* ed. Patrick J. DeSouza. New York: Council on Foreign Relations, 2000, pp. 299–320.

Grewlich, Klaus W. "A Charter for the Internet: Telecommunications Policy." 22:4-5 (1998), pp. 273–279.

Grier, Peter. "Global Computer Virus Highlights the Annoying Side of Internet Age." *Christian Science Monitor,* May 5, 2000.

Grossman, Mark. "Unscrambling the Rules on Encryption." *Broward Daily Business Review,* April 18, 2000.

Grossman, Mark, and Allison K. Hift. "Anti-Cybersquatting Act Leaves Many Questions Unanswered." *Texas Lawyer,* February 7, 2000, pp. 62–67.

Guidelines for Consumer Protection in the Context of Electronic Commerce. Paris: Director of Information, Organisation for Economic Cooperation and Development, 1999.

Guidelines for Cryptography Policy. Paris: Director of Information, Organisation for Economic Cooperation and Development, 1997.

Guidelines on the Protection of Privacy and Transborder Flows of Personal Data. Paris: Director of Information, Organisation for Economic Cooperation and Development, 1981.

Gunkel, David J. "The Empire Strikes Back: The Cultural Politics of the Internet," in *Cyberimperialism: Global Relations in the New Electronic Frontier,* ed. Bosah Ebo. London: Praeger, 2001, pp. 83–92.

Gunn, Angela, and Charles Pappas. "What a Short, Strange Trip It's Been . . . A Brief Net History." *Yahoo! Internet Life,* September 1998, pp. 72–74.

Haas, Ernst B. *When Knowlege Is Power.* Berkeley: University of California Press, 1990.

Hajnal, Peter I. *The G7/G8 System: Evolution, Role, and Documentation.* Aldershot, U.K.: Ashgate, 1999.

Hamilton, David P. "Redesigning the Internet: Can It Be Made Less Vulnerable?" *Wall Street Journal,* February 11, 2000, p. B1.

Hansen, Stephen A. *Getting Online for Human Rights.* Washington, D.C.: American Association for the Advancement of Science, 1999.

———— (ed.). *AAAS Directory of Human Rights Resources on the Internet.* Washington, D.C.: American Association for the Advancement of Science, 1998.

Hardy, Quentin. "Weaving the Perfect Net." *Forbes,* July 3, 2000, pp. 140–141.

Hargreaves, Deborah. "Brussels Acts over Slow Liberalisation of Telecoms Market." *Financial Times* (London), March 30, 2000.

————. "Fast Track for E-Commerce Laws: Brussels Sets End-of-Year Deadline to Help Boost EU Internet Economy." *Financial Times* (London), January 27, 2000, p. 1.

————. "Light Touch on the Web: Europe's Liberalisers Are Gaining the Edge in the Debate over E-Commerce Regulation." *Financial Times* (London), December 7, 1999, p. 25.

Harvey, Fiona. "The Web's Watchful Parent: Interview Tim Berners-Lee." *Financial Times* (London), October 12, 2000, p. 17.

Harwood, John H. II, William T. Lake, and David M. Sohn. "Telecommunications Law: Unscrambling the Signals, Unbundling the Law: Competition in International Telecommunications Services." *Columbia Law Review,* 97 (May 1997), pp. 874–903.

Hasenclever, Andreas, Peter Mayer, and Volker Rittberger. *Theories of International Regimes.* Cambridge: Cambridge University Press, 1997.

Hatcher, Michael, Jay McDannell, and Stacy Ostfeld. "Computer Crimes." *American Criminal Law Review,* 36 (summer 1999), pp. 397–457.

Hedblom, Milda K., and William B. Garrison Jr. "European Information Infrastructure Policy Making in the Context of the Policy Capacity of the European Union and Its Member States: Progress and Obstacles," in *National Information Infrastructure Initiatives,* ed. Brian Kahin and Ernest Wilson. Cambridge: MIT Press, 1997, pp. 490–507.

Herz, John H. "Idealist Internationalism and the Security Dilemma." *World Politics,* 2:2 (January 1950), pp. 157–180.

Hill, Steven. "Election Day on the Internet." *Washington Post,* September 28, 2000.

Hoegle, Robert L., and Christopher P. Boam. "Nations Uneasily Carve out Internet Jurisdiction." *IP Worldwide,* July-August 1999, pp. 1–7.

Hold, Eddie. "Who Pays? Who Cares?" *The Standard,* April 24, 2000.

Holson, Laura M. "Which Direction Now for Digital Music? Recording Labels Are Ready to Move, But the Path Is Uncertain." *New York Times,* November 20, 2000, p. C1.

Hong, Carolyn. "Getting Ready for a Cyber Court." *New Straits Times* (Malaysia), October 22, 2000, p. 28.

Hopper, D. Ian. "Groups Encourage Democracy on the Internet." *Associated Press Newswires,* July 7, 2000.

Hulme, George V. "Export Rules Eased for Encryption Tools." *Information Week,* 796 (July 24, 2000), pp. 40–42.

Human Development Report 1999. New York: Oxford University Press for the United Nations Development Program, 1999.

"ICANN Accredits Eleven New Domain Name Registrars." ICANN press release, October 26, 1999.

Imhoff, John J., and Stephen P. Cutler. "INTERPOL: Extending Law Enforcement's Reach Around the World." *FBI Law Enforcement Bulletin,* 67:12 (December 1998), pp. 10–17.

Implications of the WTO Agreement on Basic Telecommunications. Paris: OECD Working Papers 7:65, 1999.

Improvement of Technical Management of Internet Names and Addresses. Washington, D.C.: Department of Commerce, January 1998.

"Indian Navy Suggests Creation of Defence Intelligence Agency." Press Trust of India News Agency Report, appearing in *BBC Worldwide Monitoring,* October 18, 1998, pp. 1–2.

"Information Technology in the News." *Educause Review,* 35:6 (November-December 2000), pp. 4–5.

"Information Technology Industry Council Hails WIPO Passage." *Information Today,* 15:9 (October 1998), pp. 59–60.

ISI2000 Information Society Index: Info Revolution Reshaping the Globe. Framingham, Mass.: IDC/World Times, 2000.

Jackson, William. "DOD Set to Fight Hackers Both Foreign and Domestic." *Government Computer News,* August 23, 1999, pp. 8–11.

"Japan Planning to Levy Taxes on Internet." *Nihon Keizai Shimbun* (Tokyo), summarized in *The Financial Times* (London), February 22, 2000.

Jarvis, Steve. "ICANN Sets Rules for Resolving Disputes." *Marketing News,* October 23, 2000.

Jayaraman, K. S. "India Set to Allow Patents for Products." *Nature,* 394:6695 (August 20, 1998), pp. 709–714.

Jervis, Robert. *Perception and Misperception in International Politics.* Princeton: Princeton University Press, 1976.

———. "Security Regimes," in *International Regimes,* ed. Stephen Krasner. Ithaca: Cornell University Press, 1983, pp. 173–194.

Jew, Bernadette. "Australia: Cyber Jurisdiction: Emerging Issues and Conflicts of Law When Overseas Courts Challenge Your Web." *Monday Business Briefing,* January 7, 2000, pp. 1–8.

Johnston, Margaret. "Government Loosens Up on Encryption Policies." *InfoWorld,* 22:30 (July 24, 2000), pp. 16–20.

Joseph, Regina. "MP3.com's Questionable IPO." *Forbes,* May 17, 1999.

Kahin, Brian. "The U.S. National Information Infrastructure Initiative: The Market, the Web, and the Virtual Project," in *National Information Infrastructure Initiatives,* ed. Brian Kahin and Ernest Wilson III. Cambridge: MIT Press, 1997, pp. 150–189.

Kahin, Brian, and Ernest Wilson III (eds.). *National Information Infrastructure Initiatives.* Cambridge: MIT Press, 1997.

Kahn, Joseph. "U.S. Loses Dispute on Export Sales." *New York Times,* February 24, 2000, p. 1.

Kellman, Barry. "Catastrophic Terrorism: Thinking Fearfully, Acting Legally." *Michigan Journal of International Law,* 20 (spring 1999), pp. 537–562.

Keohane, Robert O. *After Hegemony: Cooperation and Discord in the World Political Economy.* Princeton: Princeton University Press, 1984.

———. "The Analysis of International Regimes: Towards a European-American Research Programme," in *Regime Theory and International Relations,* ed. Volker Rittberger with the Assistance of Peter Mayer. New York: Oxford University Press, 1993, pp. 23–45.

———. "The Theory of Hegemonic Stability and Changes in International Economic Regimes, 1967–1977," in *Changes in the International System,* ed. Ole R. Holsti, Randolph M. Siverson, and Alexander L. George. Boulder: Westview, 1980, pp. 131–162.

Kim, Sangbae, and Jeffrey Hart. "The Global Political Economy of Wintelism:

A New Mode of Power and Governance in the Global Computer Industry," in *Information, Power, and Globalization,* ed. J. P. Singh and James Rosenau. Albany: SUNY Press, forthcoming.

Kirtley, Jane E. "Is Implementing the EU Data Protection Directive in the United States Irreconcilable with the First Amendment?" *Government Information Quarterly,* 16:2 (1999), pp. 87–91.

Kline, David, and Kevin G. Rivette. "Discovering New Value in Intellectual Property." *Harvard Business Review,* 78:1 (January-February 2000), pp. 54–66.

Kossick, Robert M., Jr. "Litigation in the United States and Mexico: A Comparative Overview." *University of Miami Inter-American Law Review,* 31 (Spring 2000), pp. 23–65.

Krasner, Stephen D. *Sovereignty: Organized Hypocri*sy. Princeton: Princeton University Press, 1999.

——— (ed.). *International Regimes.* Ithaca: Cornell University Press, 1983.

Lai, Stanley. "Substantive Issues of Copyright Protection in a Networked Environment." *Information and Communications Technology Law,* 8:2 (June 1999), pp. 127–140.

Lambro, Donald. "The Plot to Tax the Internet." *Regardie's Power,* 3:1 (January-February 2000), pp. 77–84, 109.

Landon, Lara. "'Big Brother Is Finally Here': British System to Monitor Internet Traffic." *Ottawa Citizen,* May 11, 2000.

LeBlanc, Larry. "Canadian Government Commits to Signing Two WIPO Treaties." *Billboard,* 110:2 (January 10, 1998), pp. 3–4.

——— . "Canadian Government Is Slow to Propose WIPO Legislation." *Billboard,* 111:22 (May 29, 1999), pp. 43–44.

Leive, David M. *International Regulatory Regimes.* Lexington: D. C. Heath, 1976.

Lessig, Lawrence. "A Bad Turn for Net Governance." *Industry Standard,* September 18, 1998.

——— . *Code and Other Laws of Cyberspace.* New York: Basic, 1999.

——— . "Straitjacket on the Internet?" *Washington Post,* October 25, 2000, p. A31.

Levy, Charles S. "Implementing TRIPS—a Test of Political Wills." *Law and Policy in International Business,* 31:3 (spring 2000), pp. 789–795.

Lewis, Flora. "The New Anti-Terrorism." *New York Review of Books,* 46:2 (February 4, 1999), pp. 24–30.

Libicki, Martin, James Schneider, David R. Frelinger, and Anna Slomovic. *Scaffolding the New Web: Standards and Standards Policy for the Digital Economy.* Santa Monica: Rand Science and Technology Policy Institute, prepared for the Office of Science and Technology Policy of the U.S. Government, 2000.

Lim, Wendy. "Government Comfortable with Telecom Policy Refinement." *Business Times* (Malaysia), May 5, 1998.

Loeb, Vernon. "Critics Questioning NSA Reading Habits: Politicians Ask if the

Agency Sweeps in Private Data." *Washington Post,* November 13, 1999.

Lofthus, Kai R. "Dr. Kamil Eltayed Idris: Sudan's Copyright Advocate Repositions WIPO for the New Century." *Billboard,* 112:2 (January 8, 2000), pp. 62–65.

Lohr, Steve. "U.S. and European Union Agree Not to Have Internet Tariffs." *New York Times,* December 15, 1997.

"A Look Inside China's Biggest Tech Firm." *Computerworld* (Hong Kong), September 28, 1999.

Lovelock, Peter. *E-China: Putting Business on the Internet.* New York: Maverick Research and Virtual China, 1999.

Luke, Timothy W. "The Discipline of Security Studies and the Codes of Containment: Learning from Kuwait." *Alternatives,* 16:3 (summer 1991), pp. 315–344.

Macavinta, Courtney. "Analysts: NSI Remains Dominant." *CNET News.Com,* September 29, 1999.

———. "Election Begins for ICANN Board Seats." *CNET News.Com,* October 11, 1999.

MacKie-Mason, Jeffrey K., and Hal R. Varian. "Economic FAQs About the Internet," in *Internet Economics,* ed. Lee W. McKnight and Joseph P. Bailey. Cambridge: MIT Press, 1997, pp. 27–62.

MacLeod, Alexander. "UK Moving to Open All (e)-Mail." *Christian Science Monitor,* May 5, 2000.

Madsen, Wayne. "Teens a Threat, Pentagon Says." *Wired News,* June 2, 1998.

Madsen, Wayne, David L. Sobel, Marc Rotenberg, and David Banisar. "Cryptography and Liberty: An International Survey of Encryption Policy." *John Marshall Journal of Computer and Information Law,* 16:3 (spring 1998), pp. 475–528.

Maier, Timothy W. "Is U.S. Ready for Cyberwarfare?" *Insight on the News,* April 5, 1999.

Malawer, Stuart S. "International Trade and Transactions: 'National Governments Should Defer to the Private Sector and Avoid Undue Restrictions on Electronic Commerce,'" *Legal Times,* February 8, 1999.

Management of Internet Names and Addresses: Statement of Policy. Washington, D.C.: U.S. Department of Commerce, June 10, 1998.

Manuel, Greg, and Leslie Chang. "Will Language Wars Balkanize the Web? Battle over Chinese Sites Portends an Internet of Isolated Domains." *Wall Street Journal,* November 30, 2000, p. C22.

Markoff, John. "The Concept of Copyright Fights for Internet Survival." *New York Times,* May 10, 2000.

Marks, Paul. "US Thinks Again on Net Patents." *New Scientist,* April 8, 2000.

Marsan, Carolyn Duffy. "Domain Group Lacking Strong U.S. Presence." *Network World: An IDG.net Site,* November 2, 1999.

McCary, M. "Bridging Ethical Borders: International Legal Ethics with an

Islamic Perspective." *Texas International Law Journal,* 35 (spring 2000), pp. 289–339.

McClure, David. "First Amendment Freedoms and the Encryption Export Battle: Deciphering the Importance of *Bernstein v. United States Department of Justice.*" *Nebraska Law Review,* 79 (2000), pp. 465–488.

McCrum, William A. "Data Interchange: State of the Art of OSI," in *Open Systems Interconnection: The Communications Technology of the 1990s: Papers from the Pre-Conference Seminar, London, August 12–14, 1987,* ed. Christine H. Smith. Munchen: K. G. Saur, 1988, pp. 24–33.

McElligott, Tim. "A New Magistrate: Network Solutions Adopts New Dispute Policy." *Telephony,* January 10, 2000, pp. 3–5.

McHugh, Josh, and Robert Kahn. "Packet Man." *Forbes,* July 7, 1997, pp. 328–329.

McKnight, Lee W. et al. "Information Security for Internet Commerce," in *Internet Economics,* ed. Lee W. McKnight and Joseph P. Bailey. Cambridge: MIT Press, 1997, pp. 435–452.

McKnight, Lee W., and Joseph P. Bailey (eds.). *Internet Economics.* Cambridge: MIT Press, 1997.

McLachlin, Beverley. "Criminal Law: Toward an International Legal Order." *Hong Kong Law Journal,* 29 (1999), pp. 448–462.

McLure, Steve. "Approval of Japanese Copyright Law Amendments Expected." *Billboard,* 111:12 (March 20, 1999), pp. 79–82.

McMahon, William J. "China Needs Open Internet—Experts." *China Online,* November 8, 1999.

Menthe, Darrel C. "Jurisdiction in Cyberspace: A Theory of International Spaces." *Michigan Telecommunication and Technology Law Review,* 4 (1997–1998), pp. 69–103.

Messmer, Ellen. "U.S., Europe at Impasse over Privacy: Cultural Differences Highlight Deadlock." *Network World Fusion,* December 7, 1998.

Metcalfe, Robert M. *Packet Communication,* a volume in the series "Computer Classics Revisited." San Jose: Peer-to-Peer Commmunications, 1996.

Michels, Robert. *Political Parties.* Originally published in 1912 in Italian, translated into English by Eden and Cedar Paul. New York: Dover, 1959.

"MII Vice Minister: China Will Not Issue Licenses Only to Mobile Communications Provider." *China Online,* March 30, 2000, translated from *Yuemo Caijing Ban* (Financial Monthly Review), June 14, 2000.

Morrison, Scott. "Canadian Telecoms: Fundamental Shake-up to Sector Is Just Beginning." *Financial Times* (London), October 8, 1999, p. 10.

Moschovitis, Christos J.P., Hilary Poole, Tami Schuyler, and Theresa M. Senft. *History of the Internet: A Chronology, 1843 to the Present.* Santa Barbara: ABC-CLIO, 1999.

Mowshowitz, Abbe. "Virtual Feudalism," in *Beyond Calculation: The Next Fifty Years of Computing,* ed. Peter J. Denning and Robert M. Metcalfe. New York: Springer-Verlag, 1997, pp. 213–231.

"MP3.com: Lawsuit Magnet Sued Again." *USA Today,* November 15, 2000.

Mueller, Milton. "ICANN and Internet Governance: Sorting Through the Debris of 'Self-Regulation,'" *Info,* 1:6 (December 1999), pp. 497–520.

Mueller, Milton, and Zixiang Tan. *China in the Information Age.* Washington, D.C.: Center for International and Strategic Studies, 1996.

Mullaney, Timothy J. "Those Web Patents Aren't Advancing the Ball." *Business Week,* April 17, 2000.

Mullineaux, W. Mark, and Mark E. Jakubik. "Keeping Up with Developments in Domain Name Registrations, Litigation." *Legal Intelligencer,* December 14, 1999, pp. 3–7.

Murphy, Jamie. "Australia Passes Law on Limiting Internet." *New York Times,* June 30, 1999.

Nader, Ralph. "A Framework for ICANN and DNS Management: Initial Proposals." Unpublished paper presented to a conference organized by Computer Professionals for Social Responsibility, Alexandria, Virginia, September 25, 1999.

Nakamoto, Michiyo. "EU Challenges Japan over Telecoms Reform." *Financial Times* (London), February 24, 1999, p. 5.

Neff, Elizabeth. "Treaty Aims to Ease Actions Against Foreign Defendants." *Chicago Daily Law Bulletin,* September 20, 1999, pp. 1–3.

"Net Hardware at Secure and Secret California Site." *Reuters,* April 11, 2000.

"Net Losses: Profit Is a Rarity for Beijing's Internet Cos." *China Online,* August 15, 2000, translated from *Zhengquan Shibao* (Securities Times), August 6, 2000.

Nguyen, Christian H. "A Unitary ASEAN Patent Law in the Aftermath of TRIPS." *Pacific Rim Law and Policy Journal,* 8 (March 1999), pp. 453–486.

Niccolai, James. "ICANN Curtails NSI's Influence over Net Policy." *IDG News Service,* August 12, 1999.

———. "Interpol Head Calls on Private Sector to Stop Hackers." *The Standard,* May 10, 2000.

Okediji, Ruth Gana. "Perspectives on Globalization from Developing States: Copyright and Public Welfare in Global Perspective." *Indiana Journal of Global Legal Studies,* 7 (fall 1999), pp. 117–183.

O'Neill, Mark. "Beijing Commits on Easing Net Laws." *South China Morning Post,* September 23, 1999.

Onuf, Nicholas Greenwood. *World of Our Making: Rules and Rule in Social Theory and International Relations.* Columbia: University of South Carolina Press, 1989.

Open Systems Interconnection Protocols. A Memorandum for Secretaries of the Military Departments, the Chairman of the Joint Chiefs of Staff, and Directors of Defense Agencies, by Donald Latham. Washington, D.C.: The Pentagon, July 2, 1987.

"Opportunities Abound for Post-WTO China—But for a Price, Say Speakers at Trade Forum." *China Online,* September 14, 2000.

Oram, Andy. "Groucho Marx and Online Governance: ICANN." *Web Review,* February 21, 2000.

Paine, Jenifer DeWolf. "New Weapons Against Cybersquatters." *Metropolitan Corporate Counsel,* March 2000.

Pasquale, Kenneth, and Robyn Gemeiner. "Non-Resident Web Sites and Long-Arm Jurisdiction." *New York Law Journal,* 223:81 (April 27, 2000), pp. 5–8.

Passmore, L. David. "The Networking Standards Collision." *Datamation,* 31:3 (February 1, 1985), pp. 98–106.

"Patent Nonsense." *The Economist* (London), April 8, 2000.

Pearlstein, Steven. "WTO Negotiators' Reach Far Exceeded Grasp of Complexities." *Washington Post,* December 5, 1999, p. A47.

Penenberg, Adam L. "Habeas Copyrightus." *Forbes,* July 11, 1997.

Perine, Keith. "Congress Seeks Global E-Commerce Tax Ban." *The Standard,* October 26, 1999.

———. "ICANN Carves out a Compromise." *The Standard,* November 8, 1999.

Perritt, Henry H., Jr. "The Internet as a Threat to Sovereignty? Thoughts on the Internet's Role in Strengthening National and Global Governance." *Indiana Journal of Global Legal Studies,* 5 (spring 1998), pp. 423–440.

Pfund, Peter H. "The Project of the Hague Conference on Private International Law to Prepare a Convention on Jurisdiction and the Recognition/Enforcement of Judgments in Civil and Commercial Matters." *Brooklyn Journal of International Law,* 24 (1998), pp. 7–15.

Pincus, Walter. "Hacker Hits on Pentagon Computers Up 10 Percent This Year." *Washington Post,* December 9, 2000, pp. A8–9.

Pisciotta, Aileen A. "International Legal Developments in Review: Business Transactions and Disputes." *International Lawyer,* 33 (summer 1999), pp. 33–65.

Pomfret, John. "China Ponders New Rules of 'Unrestricted War.'" *Washington Post,* August 8, 1999, p. A25.

———. "China's Entry into WTO Unlikely This Year: Beijing Officials Cite Domestic Concerns." *Washington Post,* October 28, 2000, p. E1.

Post, David. "Governing Cyberspace: Where Is James Madison When We Need Him?" *ICANN Watch,* June 6, 1999, pp. 1–6.

Powell, Nigel. "RIP: Death of Privacy on the Internet?" *The Times* (London), January 22, 2001.

"A Prelude to InfoWar." *Reuters,* June 24, 1998.

Pressman, Aaron. "The Changing of ICANN's Guard." *Industry Standard,* November 6, 2000.

———. "Net Privacy: More Options, No Solutions." *The Standard,* May 15, 2000.

———. "A New Leader for ICANN." *Industry Standard,* July 31, 2000.

Preston, Lee, and Duane Windsor (eds.). *The Rules of the Game in the Global*

Economy: Policy Regimes for International Business, 2d ed. Boston: Kluwer Academic Publishers, 1997.

Pringle, David. "Some Worry French Ruling on Yahoo! Will Work to Deter Investments in Europe." *Wall Street Journal,* November 22, 2000.

"Privacy Guidelines" in the Electronic Environment: Focus on the Internet. Paris: Director of Information, Organisation for Economic Cooperation and Development, 1997.

"Protecting IPR in China: Progress and Problems." *East Asian Executive Reports,* 20:11 (November 15, 1998), p. 9.

"Provisional Model of Open-Systems Architecture." *Computer Communications Review,* 8:3 (July 1978), pp. 49–62.

"Qatar: Set to Finalise Laws for Intellectual Property." *Mondaq Business Briefing, Abu-Ghazaleh Intellectual Property (AGIP),* December 24, 1999.

Quarterman, John S., and Josiah C. Hoskins. "Notable Computer Networks." *Communications of the ACM,* 29:10 (October 1986), pp. 932–971.

Raymond, Eric. *The New Hacker's Dictionary,* 3d ed. Cambridge, Mass.: MIT Press, 1996.

"Report: Germany Plans 'Internet Tax.'" *CNN.com,* September 6, 2000.

"Republicans, ACLU Decry Cybercrime Report." *The Standard,* March 10, 2000.

Richelson, Jeffrey. "Desperately Seeking Signals." *Bulletin of the Atomic Scientists,* 56:2 (March-April 2000), pp. 47–52.

Richtel, Matt. "Chairman of Amazon Urges Reduction of Patent Terms." *New York Times,* March 12, 2000, p. C4.

Riordan, Teresa. "Patents Considered Vital to Thrive on the Internet." *New York Times,* December 20, 1999, p. C39.

Roberts, Bill. "The Truth About Patents." *Internet World,* April 15, 2000.

Roberts, Christopher, and Stanford K. McCoy. "TRIPS Around the World: Enforcement Goes Global in 2000." *Legal Times,* April 10, 2000.

Rony, Ellen, and Peter Rony. *The Domain Name Handbook: High Stakes and Strategies in Cyberspace.* Lawrence, Kans.: R&D Books, Miller Freeman, 1999.

Rovella, David E. "Justice Department Prepares for a Cyberwar." *New York Law Journal,* 223:49 (March 14, 2000), pp. 5–7.

"Russia: Internet Tax Would Be 'Europe-Driven.'" *Segodnya* (Moscow), April 17, 2000, translated and published in *BBC Monitoring International Reports,* April 19, 2000.

Ryan, Michael P. *Knowledge Diplomacy: Global Competition and the Politics of Intellectual Property.* Washington, D.C.: Brookings Institution Press, 1998.

Sasamotou, Hiromi. "British Telecom Targets Golden Opportunity in Japan." *Daily Yomiuri* (Tokyo), November 11, 1998, p. 12.

Schatz, Bruce R., and Joseph B. Hardin. "NCSA Mosaic and the World Wide Web: Global Hypermedia Protocols for the Internet." *Science,* 265 (August 12, 1994), pp. 895–901.

Schnockelborg, Robin. "Book Review of *Intellectual Property Rights,* ed. Bibek Debroy (New Delhi: Rajiv Gandhi Institute for Contemporary Studies, 1998)," in *Wisconsin International Law Journal,* 18 (winter 2000), pp. 347–352.

Schultz, Keith. "The Ultimate Computer Protection." *Internetweek,* 722 (July 6, 1998), pp. 28–33.

Schwartz, John. "Republicans Oppose Online Privacy Plans." *Washington Post,* May 21, 2000, p. A8.

Schwarz, Jonathan. "Profound Threat to Revenues." *Financial Times* (London), October 1, 1999, p. 10.

Scott, Phil. *The Pioneers of Flight: A Documentary History.* Princeton: Princeton University Press, 1999.

Shaaban, H. S. "Commercial Transactions in the Middle East: What Law Governs?" *Law and Policy in International Business,* 31:1 (fall, 1999), pp. 157–172.

Shackelford, Steve. "Computer Related Crime: An International Problem in Need of an International Solution." *Texas International Law Journal,* 27 (1992), pp. 479–505.

Shannon, Victoria. "CEOs Lobby for E-Commerce." *International Herald Tribune,* September 14, 1999, p. E3.

Sherwood, Robert M., Vanda Scartezini, and Peter Dirk Siemsen. "Promotion of Inventiveness in Developing Countries Through a More Advanced Patent Administration." *IDEA: The Journal of Law and Technology,* 39 (1999), pp. 473–508.

Slaughter, Anne-Marie, Andrew S. Tulumello, and Stepan Wood. "International Law and International Relations Theory: A New Generation of Interdisciplinary Scholarship." *American Journal of International Law,* 92 (July 1998), pp. 367–392.

Smith, Craig S. "Ambivalence in China on Expanding Net Access." *New York Times,* August 11, 2000, p. C3.

Soete, Luc, and Karin Kamp. "Bit Tax: The Case for Further Research." Maastricht: Maastricht Economic Research Institute on Innovation and Technology Occasional Papers, 1997.

Soltan, Karol, Virginia Haufler, and Eric Uslaner (eds.). *Institutions and Social Order.* Ann Arbor: University of Michigan Press, 1998.

Steel, Howard L., Jr. "The Web That Binds Us All: The Future Legal Environment of the Internet." *Houston Journal of International Law,* 19:2 (winter 1997), pp. 495–518.

Stellin, Susan. "Internet Domain Administrator Holds Its First Election." *New York Times,* October 12, 2000, p. C6.

Stern, Christopher. "MP3.com to Pay Universal $53 Million." *Washington Post,* November 15, 2000, p. E3.

Stofberg, Cobus. "Working Together to Bridge the Digital Divide." *Christian Science Monitor,* September 7, 2000.

Stoll, Cliff. *The Cuckoo's Egg: Inside the World of Computer Espionage.* New York: Pocket Books, 1990.

Strange, Susan. *"Cave! Hic Dragones:* A Critique of Regime Analysis," in *International Regimes,* ed. Stephen D. Krasner. Ithaca: Cornell University Press, 1983, pp. 337–354.

————. *State and Markets.* London: Pinter, 1988.

Straubhaar, Joseph D. "From PTT to Private: Liberalization and Privatization in Eastern Europe and the Third World," in *Telecommunications Politics: Ownership and Control of the Information Highway in Developing Countries,* ed. Bella Mody, Johannes M. Bauer, and Joseph D. Straubhaar. Mahwah, N.J.: Lawrence Erlbaum, 1995, pp. 3–30.

"Supreme Court Rejects Three Computer-Related Intellectual Property Cases." *Intellectual Property Litigation Reporter,* 4:20 (May 27, 1998), p. 16.

Tan, David. "Towards a New Regime for the Protection of Outer Space as the 'Province of All Mankind.'" *Yale Journal of International Law,* 25 (winter 2000), pp. 145–193.

Tan, Zixiang (Alex), William Foster, and Seymour Goodman. "China's State-Coordinated Internet Infrastructure." *Communications of the ACM,* 42:6 (June 1999), pp. 44–52.

Taxation Principles and Electronic Commerce. Paris: OECD Committee on Fiscal Affairs, October 1998.

Taylor, Edward. "Napster Decision Emboldens Europe in Piracy Prevention." *Wall Street Journal,* February 16, 2001, p. A9.

Taylor, Georgina. "Trading in Cyberspace: The Legal Complications of Going Global." *Brand Strategy,* January 21, 2000, pp. 19–20.

Terry, Colonel James P. "Responding to Attacks on Critical Computer Infrastructure: What Targets? What Rules of Engagement?" *Naval Legal Review,* 46 (1999), pp. 170–190.

Timmers, Paul. "Electronic Commerce Policy and the European Commission," in *Cyberidentities: Canadian and European Presence in Cyberspace,* ed. Leen d'Haenens. Ottawa: University of Ottawa Press, 1999, pp. 195–200.

"TRIPS Under Scrutiny at WTO." *The Hindu,* October 18, 2000.

"TRUSTe Unveils European Union Safe Harbor Privacy Seal Program." *PR Newswire,* November 1, 2000.

Tyson, Ann Scott. "Should World Wide Web Be a Tax-Free Zone?" *Christian Science Monitor,* February 28, 2000, p. 3.

Uimonen, Terho. "Internet Privacy Issues Focus of Paris Summit." *IDG.net,* September 16, 1999.

Ungerer, Herbert, and Nicholas Costello. *Telecommunications in Europe: The Challenge for the European Community.* Luxembourg: Office for Official Publications of the European Community, 1988.

"US Continues Lead in New Patents, Germans Narrow Gap." *Deutsche Press-Agentur,* February 25, 2000.

"US, Others Pan Saudi WTO Market Access Offer." *Journal of Commerce,* November 20, 1998, p. 10A.

"U.S. Treasury Chief Warns of Cyber Threats." *Reuters News Agency,* April 18, 2000.

Valeri, Lorenzo. "Securing Internet Society: Toward an International Regime for Information Assurance." *Studies in Conflict and Terrorism,* 23:2 (April-June 2000), pp. 129–147.

Venturelli, Shalini. "Information Liberalization in the European Union," in *National Information Infrastructure Initiatives,* ed. Brian Kahin and Ernest Wilson. Cambridge: MIT Press, 1997, pp. 457–489.

Wagstyl, Stefan. "Survey—Eurozone Economy." *Financial Times* (London), February 25, 2000.

Wang, Georgette. "Regulating Network Communication in Asia: A Different Balancing Act?" *Telecommunication Policy,* 23:3–4 (April-May 1999), pp. 277–287.

Wasserman, Elizabeth. "ICANN Moves into Action." *The Standard,* March 4, 1999.

———. "ICANN to Can NSI Domain-Name Monopoly." *The Standard,* April 21, 1999.

———. "Tax Panel Agrees They Can't Agree." *The Standard,* March 27, 2000.

"Web Threatens Chinese Government." *Associated Press,* March 22, 2000.

Weber, Max. *Economy and Society: An Outline of Interpretive Sociology,* Vol. 2. Berkeley: University of California Press, 1978.

Weise, Elizabeth. "With Dissidents on Board, Net Could See Revolution." *USA Today,* October 31, 2000.

Welch, John L. "Modernizing for the Millennium: The 1999 Amendments to Trademark Law." *Intellectual Property Today,* January 2000.

Wen, H. Joseph, and J. Michael Tarn. "The Impact of the Next-Generation Internet Protocol on E-Commerce Security." *Information Strategy: The Executive's Journal,* 17:2 (winter 2001), pp. 22–28.

"Who Will Manage Chinese Domain Names?" *China Online,* February 9, 2000.

"Will China Tax the Internet?" *Caijing Shibao* [Financial Daily], May 10, 2000, translated in *China Online,* May 11, 2000.

Williams, Frances. "WIPO Applications Reach Record." *Financial Times* (London), February 28, 2000, p. 12.

Williams, Frances, and Neil Buckley. "China/WTO: Europe the Next Stop on Negotiation Trail." *Financial Times* (London), November 18, 1999.

"WIPO Cyber Arbitration Kicks Off to Flying Start . . . Gains Success." *Financial Times* (London), February 23, 2000.

Wolffe, Richard. "US Aid for Africa Telecoms." *Financial Times* (London), June 2, 1999, p. 7.

Wood, Nicholas. "Protecting Intellectual Property on the Internet: Experience and Strategies of Trade Mark Owners in a Time of Chance." *International Review of Law, Computers, and Technology,* 13:1 (March 1999), pp. 21–29.

Wriston, Walter B. "Bits, Bytes, and Diplomacy." *Foreign Affairs,* 76:5 (September-October 1997), pp. 172–183.

The WTO Telecom Agreement: Results and Next Steps. Hearing Before the Subcommittee on Telecommunications, Trade, and Consumer Protection,

Committee on Commerce, U.S. House of Representatives (Serial No. 105-11), March 19, 1997.

WTO 2000: The Next Round. Hearing Before the Subcommittee on Telecommunications, Trade, and Consumer Protection, Committee on Commerce, U.S. House of Representatives (Serial No. 106-71), November 4, 1999.

Yeomans, Matthew. "The Great Fire Wall of China: Government Wants the Net—and Strict Control over All That It Carries." *Industry Standard,* September 17, 1999.

———. "Planet Web: The Language Gap." *The Standard,* January 20, 2000.

Yerkey, Gary G. "U.S., European Union Set to Begin Talks on Industry Safe Harbor Privacy Guidelines." *U.S. Law Week,* 67 (November 17, 1998), pp. 2284–2285.

Young, Oran R. *Creating Regimes: Arctic Accords and International Governance.* Ithaca: Cornell University Press, 1998.

———. *The Effectiveness of Environmental Regimes: Causal Connections and Behavioral Mechanisms.* Cambridge: MIT Press, 1999.

———. *Governance in World Affairs.* Ithaca: Cornell University Press, 1999.

———. *International Cooperation: Building Regimes for Natural Resources and the Environment.* Ithaca: Cornell University Press, 1989.

———. "Regime Dynamics: The Rise and Fall of International Regimes," in *International Regimes,* ed. Stephen Krasner. Ithaca: Cornell University Press, 1983, pp. 93–113.

Yurcik, W., and Zixiang (Alex) Tan. "The Great (Fire)wall of China: Internet Security and Information Policy Issues in PRC." *Proceedings of the 24th Telecommunications Policy Research Conference,* Soloman, Maryland, October 1996.

Zacher, Mark W., with Brent A. Sutton. *Governing Global Networks: International Regimes for Transportation and Communications.* Cambridge: Cambridge University Press, 1996.

Zagaris, Bruce. "The Future of Internationalism: Beyond National Interests." *Washington Post,* April 18, 1999, p. B3.

Zaret, Elliot. "Internet Pioneer Urges Overhaul: TCP/IP Co-Inventor Kahn Sees a New Net Where Content Is Truly King." *MSNBC and Wall Street Journal Business,* November 21, 2000.

Zarocostas, John. "Kyrgyzstan Nears Joining WTO, Agrees to Norms." *Journal of Commerce,* July 21, 1998, p. 3A.

Zegas, Alan L. "Cybercrime's Many Faces." *New Jersey Law Journal,* 160:5 (May 1, 2000), pp. 392–396.

Zimmerman, Michael R. "McCain: Internet Tax 'Pernicious.'" *PC Week,* January 11, 2000.

Zittrain, Jonathan. "ICANN: Between the Public and the Private—Comments Before Congress." *Berkeley Technology Law Journal,* 14 (fall 1999), pp. 1071–1092.

Index

243

About the Book

G overning the Internet explores the many complex issues and challenges that confront governments, technocrats, business-people, and others as they try to create and implement rules for a truly global, interoperable Internet.

Though focusing on those countries that have the most advanced information technology infrastructures, Franda also discusses the development of the Internet in China as a test case for accommodating the majority of the world's citizens in an international regime. His further study of the Internet and the politics of its spread to Africa, Asia, the Middle East, Eurasia, and central and eastern Europe will be published later this year.

Marcus Franda is professor of government and politics at the University of Maryland.